# Tom Fitzmorris's New Orleans Food

# Tom Fitzmorris's New Orleans Food

More than 225 of the City's Best Recipes to Cook at Home

## Tom Fitzmorris

Stewart, Tabori & Chang
New York

Produced for Stewart, Tabori & Chang by
gonzalez defino
New York, New York
www.gonzalezdefino.com
EDITORIAL DIRECTOR Joseph Gonzalez
ART DIRECTOR Perri DeFino
EDITOR Julia Lee
COPYEDITOR Marilyn Knowlton

PRODUCTION MANAGER Jane Searle

Library of Congress Cataloging-in-Publication Data:
Fitzmorris, Tom, 1951-
    Tom Fitzmorris's [*sic*] New Orleans food : more than 225 of the city's best recipes
to cook at home / by Tom Fitzmorris.
        p. cm.
    Includes bibliographical references and index.
    ISBN 1-58479-524-7
    1. Cookery, American—Louisiana style. 2. Cookery—Louisiana—New Orleans.  I. Title: New
Orleans food. II. Title: Tom Fitzmorris's New Orleans food. III. Title: Tom Fitzmorris' New
Orleans food. IV. Title.

TX715.2.L68F584 2006
641.59763—dc22

                              2005030811

The text of this book was composed in Tribute.

Printed and bound in the United States of America
10 9 8 7 6 5 4 3 2 1

HNA
harry n. abrams, inc.
a subsidiary of La Martinière Groupe

115 West 18th Street
New York, NY 10011
www.hnabooks.com

# Contents

On Monday, August 29, 2005, one of the most vital and important capitals of the culinary world came to a complete and abrupt halt. Hurricane Katrina, the most destructive storm in the history of the United States, shut down all of the restaurants in New Orleans and those within a hundred miles in every direction. The population of the entire metropolitan area—about a million and a half people—was told to evacuate.

The storm did unimaginable damage to the Mississippi Gulf Coast, destroying man-made structures right down to roads and slabs. In New Orleans, the damage from the storm's winds was less severe. But the storm came in at the perfect angle to blow a deluge of water from Lake Pontchartrain through breaks in the levees into the city. The levees had always protected the city before, but they'd never faced a storm like this one. Eighty percent of the city was flooded, in some places more than 10 feet deep. Hundreds of people died, and many were displaced.

I'm writing this note three weeks after the storm. About half of the city is still flooded as the world's largest drainage pumping station labors to send the water back to where it came from. Most of the area is still evacuated. No restaurants have reopened, although many of them are making plans, usually for weeks to months from now.

I am still in evacuation myself. I know that my home is okay and that my family is safe. So I'm better off than a substantial percentage of my fellow Orleanians, many of whom are in temporary shelters in cities across America. My worst problem is that my occupation since college—writing and broadcasting about New Orleans restaurants and food—is, at best, compromised.

I can't stand to do nothing. So while waiting to return, I put the finishing touches on this collection of what I think are the best recipes from my three decades of reporting on Creole and Cajun cuisines. Until our city is healthy again, I will donate half (or more, if we really sell a lot of books) of my profits from this edition to the recovery effort. Thank you for helping with that.

I dedicate this book to all the people who love great New Orleans food.

Tastefully yours,

*Tom Fitzmorris.*

September 19, 2005

# Foreword

On the day before we officially opened Emeril's in New Orleans—my first restaurant—we served dinner to a full house of friends. It was our dress rehearsal for the real thing. Tom Fitzmorris was there, with his wife and their one-year-old baby boy.

I first met Tom eight years before that. I was the new chef at Commander's Palace. He was the person you thought of when somebody said "restaurant critic" in New Orleans. Dick and Ella Brennan ran Commander's then and invited him to anything special we had going on. Eventually Dick started having dinners once a month with Tom and our mutual friend Marcelle Bienvenu.

We had a lot of fun with those dinners because nothing we could throw at that table would be considered too far out. Tom especially was game to try anything, and then he would want to know where the idea came from, how we cooked it, and even how much it cost to put the dish together.

I noticed something else about Tom's interest in food. The more something tasted like a New Orleans dish, the better he liked it. I feel that way, too. I say that if we're going to be in New Orleans, we're going to cook with fresh Louisiana ingredients with a Creole and Cajun flavor. We kick it up a notch with the flavors of the world, but if you asked me what kind of food we serve in New Orleans, I'd say we serve New Orleans food.

It didn't surprise me when, in addition to his restaurant reviews, Tom started writing about cooking. Every person who likes to eat sooner or later heads for the kitchen and starts playing around. Now here he is with a cookbook. I love the title. *New Orleans Food* is what he's all about, and he knows it as well as anybody.

Especially in this tender, bruised time in the history of that marvelous city, we need to celebrate the uniqueness of New Orleans cuisine. It makes me smile to know that the first things everybody wanted after the hurricane were red beans and rice, poor boys, and gumbo. It told me that New Orleans is still New Orleans. I'm happy to be there, and I'm happy to see its best reporter on the subject of eating is still at it.

# Introduction

This is a collection of the best dishes that I accumulated during my ridiculously long tenure as a New Orleans restaurant critic. Researching a weekly column for 33 years and a daily three-hour radio food show for 17 years, I've tried, loved, endured, and remembered thousands of dishes. I've learned how to cook the ones I liked best—and here they are.

The cooking part of my career came well after the eating part. Although that was an accident, I would recommend that progression to anyone enthusiastic about food. First, learn how to eat well. That done, learn how to cook. If that moves you, develop the skill to anticipate what might taste good if you experiment a little.

It's certainly been a lot of fun for me.

Many of the dishes herein come from my persistent infatuation with New Orleans restaurants. But these are not restaurant recipes. All of them have passed through my kitchen, usually more than once, before they made it into print. I'm not saying that I know better than the chefs do. Just that restaurant recipes rarely translate well into the home kitchen. So, in every case, I took liberties with the original recipes in order to make the dish taste the way I think it should.

That process is what started me cooking in the first place. I wanted to eat things that restaurants wouldn't or couldn't serve me. I had no formal training, and my equipment was poor. But I did possess what I think is the most important ability a cook can have: I knew how the final product should look and taste. With that, it was only a matter of experimenting until I got it right.

This is the great advantage of being able to cook. It gives you the ability to create dishes exactly to your own taste. I encourage you to do that by using these recipes as a starting point and adjusting them to your own pleasure.

### THE HERITAGE STYLE

My favorite cuisines are those I grew up with: Creole and Cajun. New Orleans food. I admit also to a preference for dishes whose tastes ring familiar notes. Although innovative dishes are fun to write about, few of them persist into the next season. That's because they appeal more to the mind than to the palate. And one of the hallmarks of the New Orleans palate is that it is not easily fooled by public relations.

On the other hand, the young, adventuresome chefs that inspired our restaurants during the last 20 years have added much to our pleasure. We now have a far greater variety and quality of foodstuffs to cook with than we did a decade or more ago. Not only can you buy fresh foie gras and fresh chanterelle mushrooms now, but almost every avid diner knows what they taste like.

This is also true of current cooking methods. While deep-frying is still the default technique in most New Orleans restaurants, chefs and diners have found that many dishes formerly fried are much better grilled, seared, or broiled.

I tell you all this to answer a question so obvious that I've asked it myself: "Do we really need another new version of gumbo, bread pudding, or oysters Rockefeller with all the hundreds of recipes for those dishes already out there?"

Yes, we do. Creole cooking evolves. Gumbo is much thicker and spicier than it was 20 years ago. We cook with ingredients unavailable back when. That's one of the ways in which I've adapted the recipes here. They're written with the latter-day food cornucopia in mind.

And tastes have changed. When I started writing about food, dishes like veal Oscar were everywhere. Now the idea of covering veal (or fish or chicken or soft-shell crabs) with gloppy sauces riddled with crabmeat and crawfish seems excessive.

## What Is New Orleans Food?

Early in my career, I wrote for a now extinct weekly newspaper called *Figaro*. On our masthead was a quotation whose source I don't remember, but I think it rings true: "Localism alone leads to culture."

New Orleans food is, above all other things, distinctly local. It's comparable in that respect to the regional and local cooking styles you find in France and Italy, where if you drive 100 kilometers, you discover that the food has changed noticeably.

New Orleans Creole is the oldest comprehensive regional cuisine in America. It was recognized as a thing apart in the late 1800s, when the earliest Creole cookbooks appeared. It had a French face, a Spanish soul, and African hands. Soon it would get an Italian heart and a Cajun smile. Like other great regional cuisines, it doesn't travel well. I've never had a gumbo outside New Orleans that I thought tasted like gumbo, even though the attempt may have been tasty enough.

Not even a lifelong Orleanian who thinks about food all the time (like me, for instance) can explain exactly what's missing. We just know gumbo when we taste it, and we know when we're not tasting it.

So what does gumbo—or any other Creole or Cajun dish—taste like? The only way I can really explain it is to give you the recipes that I know create what I think of as real Creole or Cajun flavor.

Try to generalize, however, and you don't come up with much. Obviously, we love seafood in South Louisiana. With very good reason: We have plenty of it, and its quality is world-class. We also like big flavors. The kind that you can't miss, as opposed to those you have to sit and think about to know whether or not you're tasting them. Creole cooking's main appeal is not to the mind, but to the flesh. If a lengthy explanation of what it is we should be tasting is needed, there's a good chance the food isn't really Creole or Cajun.

There is a downside to this. Certain New Orleans dishes would not make a healthy steady diet. We cook with oceans of heavy cream, boulders of butter, and herds of smoked pork, among other foods from the "Use Sparingly" part of the food pyramid. That's okay. Just don't eat the richer dishes all the time. Unless you are really ill, you can eat anything once in a while.

Seasoning rarely needs to be added at the table to New Orleans food. It's saltier than the food of most other regions. French chefs who move here tell me that when they return to France for a visit, dishes that they once loved taste bland to them.

That said, the salt levels in most New Orleans dishes have declined in recent memory. Recipes I published 20 years ago often had two or three times as much salt as the amount I think tastes right now. I've lowered the salt content in most of my recipes. You can always add more salt, but once it's in there, you can't get it out.

On the other hand, pepper levels continue to rise. They were always above average, but starting with the baby-boom generation, the appreciation for hot, spicy food has done nothing but grow. All kinds of peppers are used in Creole dishes, often in combination. And pepper sauce, that great South Louisiana invention of which Tabasco is the original, is essential. Those little bottles are on every table and in every kitchen. It not only tastes good, but I'm persuaded that capsaicin—the active ingredient in hot chile pepper—is good for you.

Okay. Let's start illustrating all of these points by adjourning to the kitchen to do some cooking. I hope you have a great New Orleans meal today!

# Amuse-Bouche

Small, delicious nibbles before the dinner really begins set the tone for the entire repast. This is why so many restaurants—especially at the upper levels—send out a pre-appetizer course. The French expression *amuse-bouche*—"entertain the mouth"—is well enough known now that it's been shortened to just "the amuse."

This new first course gives the opportunity to use very expensive ingredients. Almost by definition, an *amuse-bouche* is just a bite or two. So you don't have to use very much of the precious foodstuff.

Not that pre-appetizers must be expensive. As you will see in the recipes that follow, the only requirement is that a bite fill the mouth with a good, savory flavor. My own preference is that pre-appetizers be a little salty and a little rich. Smoked, cured, and acidic flavors are also good.

I'm wary of using sweet or peppery flavors in an *amuse-bouche*. Those tastes are delicious, but they need to be kept subtle. The point is to sharpen your palate, not dull it.

One other food seems inappropriate for a small first course. Cheese is for the end of the meal, not the beginning. I love cheese, but it can be an appetite killer.

Many familiar New Orleans delicacies work well as pre-appetizers. Notable among them are shrimp, oysters (especially when baked on the half shell), crabmeat, and all our Cajun and Creole sausages. Add to that, international classics like smoked salmon, caviar, olives, pâtés, and charcuterie meats, plus refreshing fruits and crisp vegetables, and the variety of flavors stretches endlessly in all directions.

The best pre-appetizer course includes several small dishes, each offering a flavor and color contrast with the others. For example, a great trio would be smoked boudin slices, asparagus with aioli, and shrimp with Creole rémoulade.

All this could be served with cocktails or Champagne or a light white wine. We like to offer our pre-appetizers at the counter in the kitchen because everybody's going to be in there anyway. Then it's an easy matter to start pulling the oysters Bienville out of the oven and shouting, "Okay, here comes the first course! Everybody sit down!"

# Shrimp Rémoulade with Two Sauces

*There are two kinds of rémoulade sauce served around New Orleans, and everybody has a favorite. My preference is the orange-red kind that's utterly unique to our area. White rémoulade sauce, made with mayonnaise, is actually closer to the classic French recipe. It's so good that in recent years I've taken to making both sauces and letting people take their pick. What the sauces have in common is the main active ingredient: Creole mustard—a rough, brown, country-style mustard mixed with a bit of horseradish.*

*The shrimp for shrimp rémoulade should be medium size, about 25–30 count to the pound. If you're making only the red style of rémoulade, a good trick is to underboil the shrimp slightly, then marinate them in the rather acidic sauce. The shrimp will finish cooking in the sauce in much the same way they do in a ceviche marinade.*

*The word "rémoulade," by the way, is an old French dialect word that refers to a kind of radish that hasn't been part of the recipe for centuries.*

**SHRIMP**
Leafy tops from a bunch of celery
5 bay leaves
3 whole cloves
2 cloves garlic, peeled and crushed
1 large lemon, sliced
½ cup salt
3 lb. medium shrimp (25–30 count)

**RED REMOULADE SAUCE**
½ cup chili sauce (bottled) or ketchup,
   plus more to taste
½ cup Creole mustard,
   plus more to taste
1 Tbsp. paprika
½ tsp. salt
2 Tbsp. lemon juice
¼ tsp. Tabasco
½ tsp. minced garlic

1 cup olive oil
3 green onions, green part only,
   finely chopped

**WHITE REMOULADE SAUCE**
1 cup mayonnaise
½ cup Creole mustard
2 Tbsp. lemon juice
½ tsp. Tabasco Garlic Pepper Sauce
1 tsp. Worcestershire sauce
½ tsp. salt
3 green onions, green part only,
   finely chopped

*(continued)*

1. Bring a gallon of water to a boil in a large pot and add all of the shrimp ingredients except the shrimp. Boil the water for 15 minutes, then add the shrimp. Remove the pot from the heat immediately and allow the shrimp to steep for 4 minutes, or until the shell separates easily from the meat.

2. Drain the shrimp in a colander and set aside until cool enough to handle. Peel and devein the shrimp.

3. To make the red rémoulade sauce: Combine all the ingredients except the olive oil and green onions in a bowl. Add the oil a little at a time, stirring constantly, until all oil is absorbed. Taste the sauce and add more chili sauce or Creole mustard if needed. Stir in the green onions.

4. To make the white rémoulade sauce: Combine all the ingredients in a bowl and stir to blend.

5. Place the shrimp on a leaf of lettuce, sliced avocados, sliced tomatoes, or Belgian endive leaves. Drizzle half the shrimp with one sauce, half with the other. The sauces can also be served in pools for dipping. MAKES EIGHT APPETIZER PORTIONS OR SIX ENTREE SALADS.

# Sautéed Crab Claws

*Crab fingers—the claw with the bottom jaw removed and the shell peeled from the meat—are the most economical form of blue crabmeat. They make a wonderful appetizer that can be prepared in a number of ways. This is probably the version that packs the greatest number of calories, but so what? Eat a few as an appetizer and then move on to the tofu if you think the crab will kill you.*

1 stick (8 Tbsp.) butter
1 small head garlic, cloves separated, peeled and chopped
1 lb. blue crab fingers
1 tsp. salt-free Creole seasoning
¼ tsp. salt
¼ cup dry white wine
1 Tbsp. lemon juice
2 green onions, finely chopped
Toasted French bread crescents, for dipping

1. Melt the butter in a large skillet over medium heat. Add the garlic and sauté until fragrant.

2. Add the crab fingers and sprinkle with the Creole seasoning and salt. Shake the skillet to cook the crab fingers evenly.

3. After 2 minutes, mix the wine and lemon juice together, and pour into the skillet. Add the green onions. Shake the skillet to combine the ingredients and simmer for 2 minutes more. The sauce should have a somewhat creamy appearance.

4. Transfer the crab claws and all the sauce to a bowl and serve with toasted French bread crescents for dipping. SERVES FOUR.

# Oysters with Pepper Butter

*This is the oyster version of Buffalo chicken wings—a tremendous improvement on the latter. The idea first hatched at Mr. B's, Ralph and Cindy Brennan's terrific French Quarter bistro. When Ralph opened the casual Red Fish Grill a block away, he took this with him and turned it into that restaurant's signature dish.*

*Use a less-hot hot sauce (in other words, not Tabasco) to make the sauce. When reducing it, make sure the ventilation is good because steaming hot sauce can burn your eyes.*

**SAUCE**

2 oz. Louisiana hot sauce, such as
    Crystal Hot Sauce
1 tsp. lemon juice
2 Tbsp. dry white wine
1 stick (8 Tbsp.) butter, softened

**OYSTERS**

Vegetable oil, for frying
1½ cups flour

2 Tbsp. salt-free Creole seasoning
2 Tbsp. salt
36 fresh, shucked oysters

**TOAST AND GARNISH**

Thirty-six ½-inch-thick slices French
    bread, toasted and buttered
Crumbled crisp bacon, for garnish
½ cup blue cheese dressing, for dipping

1. To make the sauce: Bring the liquid ingredients to a light boil in a small saucepan. Reduce by about a third.

2. Remove the pan from the heat. Whisk in the butter, a tablespoon or so at a time, until you have a creamy-looking orange sauce. Keep warm, but don't keep the pan on a continuous burner or the sauce may separate.

3. To make the oysters: Pour the oil into a Dutch oven to a depth of 2 inches. Heat over medium-high heat until the oil reaches 375 degrees.

4. Combine the flour, Creole seasoning, and salt in a bowl, and mix with a fork. Toss the oysters in the mixture to coat, and shake off the excess flour.

5. Fry the oysters, in batches, until plump and light brown. Drain on paper towels.

6. Put an oyster on each piece of toast, drizzle on the sauce, and garnish with the bacon. Serve the dressing on the side for dipping. MAKES THIRTY-SIX PIECES.

# Caviar on Savory Lost Bread

*The most challenging dinners I cook all year are the ones I serve in the homes of people who buy my services at charity auctions. I'm never quite sure that what I cook will be worth what the people paid for it. For years, until Beluga caviar became endangered, I started these dinners with an appetizer of that rare roe, served over a traditional New Orleans lost bread, but any good caviar will do. Lost bread, or* pain perdu, *is New Orleans–style French toast (see recipe, page 268). This version is made without the sweet elements (sugar and vanilla) and with a little onion in the custard.*

2 eggs
1 cup milk
Pinch of nutmeg
¼ tsp. salt
Pinch of ground white pepper
2 Tbsp. pureed white onion
Small French baguette, cut into ¾-inch-thick slices
Vegetable oil, for frying
¼ cup sour cream
2 Tbsp. finely chopped chives
4 oz. caviar

1. Blend the eggs, milk, nutmeg, salt, pepper, and pureed onion in a wide bowl. Soak the bread rounds until they're wet with the custard mixture all the way through but not falling apart.

2. In a large skillet, heat about ¼ inch of the oil until it shimmers at the surface. Fry the bread, in batches, until they are well browned on both sides, turning once. Drain on paper towels and keep warm.

3. Spread a little sour cream on each bread round. Sprinkle with chives and top with a generous spoonful of caviar. SERVES EIGHT.

# Mushrooms and Foie Gras Under Glass

*This is an old and wonderful appetizer from Antoine's, which has, unfortunately, fallen from the menu. The reason for its demise was that the glass bells under which it was served were expensive and seemed to last through only one or two servings. My version of this incredibly rich and aromatic dish moves it from the era of Antoine's to our own, with its much better and more varied selection of mushrooms and fresh foie gras.*

4 oz. fresh foie gras, sliced into eight ¼-inch-thick pieces
Salt and freshly ground black pepper
1½ sticks (12 Tbsp.) butter
2 cups mushrooms, the more exotic the better, sliced about ¼ inch thick
2½ cups whole milk
¼ cup flour
⅓ cup dry sherry
Eight ½-inch-thick slices French bread, toasted

1. Sprinkle the foie gras slices with a little salt and pepper. Heat a large skillet over medium-high heat and sear the foie gras until lightly browned on both sides. Transfer to a plate and keep warm.

2. Return the skillet to medium-high heat, add 1 stick (8 Tbsp.) of the butter, and bring to a bubble. Add the mushrooms and cook until tender.

3. Meanwhile, make a thin béchamel. Heat the milk until warm but not steaming. In a saucepan, melt the remaining ½ stick (4 Tbsp.) of butter. Sprinkle in the flour and stir the mixture until it turns into a roux, about 2 minutes. Don't let it brown. Lower the heat and gradually whisk in the warm milk, stirring constantly until the sauce thickens.

4. Add the sherry to the mushrooms and bring to a boil until the alcohol has evaporated, about 2 minutes. Lower the heat to a simmer and stir in the béchamel. Add salt and pepper to taste and cook over very low heat, stirring lightly, until the sauce penetrates the mushrooms.

5. Place 2 slices of toast on each of 4 salad plates. Top each toast with a foie gras slice and pour about ½ cup of the mushroom mixture over each serving. SERVES FOUR.

# French-fried Parsley

*The Bitoun brothers—Jacques, Maurice, André, and Simon—ran a number of restaurants in the New Orleans area for many years, separately and together. Their best remembered dish was a complimentary appetizer: a simple basket of fried parsley. Maurice called it French popcorn. It's much better than you can imagine, and intrigues everyone who eats it.*

*There are two tricks to this recipe. First, it works better when the oil has been used previously, especially for fried chicken. Second, use curly-leaf parsley because it holds the batter much better than the flat-leaf variety.*

Vegetable oil, for frying (preferably used before, but clean)
2 bunches of curly-leaf parsley
1½ cups flour
2 Tbsp. salt-free Creole seasoning
1 Tbsp. salt
1 egg
1 cup milk

1. Pour the oil into a Dutch oven to a depth of 2 inches. Heat over medium-high heat until the temperature reaches 350 degrees.

2. Wash the parsley well and shake dry. Trim off the bottom parts of the stems.

3. Combine the flour, Creole seasoning, and salt in a bowl, blending it with a fork. Whisk the egg and the milk together in a second, much larger bowl. Add the dry ingredients to the wet ingredients and whisk to make a thin batter. Add a little water, if necessary, to make the batter runny.

4. Toss the parsley in the batter to coat evenly. Shake off any excess batter.

5. Working in batches, carefully drop the parsley into the hot oil and fry until it just begins to brown, about a minute. Drain on paper towels and serve immediately. SERVES EIGHT.

# Creole-Italian Pot Stickers

*My son, Jude, developed an intense love for Chinese pot stickers at a time in his life when his list of acceptable foods was so short that he was hard to feed. At Trey Yuen, one of our favorite Chinese places, he typically ate three full orders of the things. His record is 32 pot stickers.*

*This passion is easy to understand. Good pot stickers are very good indeed. They're Chinese ravioli, balls of meat with seasonings and vegetables wrapped in a noodle disk. First you steam them (after which they're already pretty good) and then you fry them in a hot pan with a little oil. They're easy to make, though time-consuming; we usually sit around the kitchen counter as a family and make several dozen at a time. Once they're wrapped, you can freeze them to steam and fry later. We give our pot stickers a local wrinkle by using spicy Italian sausage in place of the usual ground pork. Just be sure the sausage is on the lean side.*

DUMPLINGS

1 lb. spicy Italian sausage, removed from casings, or ground pork

3 green onions, finely chopped

1 small can of water chestnuts, drained and chopped

2 Tbsp. soy sauce

1 tsp. Asian fish sauce

2 Tbsp. Chinese rice wine or dry white wine

1 cup fresh spinach, washed, cooked, and coarsely chopped

1 Tbsp. cornstarch mixed with 1 Tbsp. water.

2 eggs, beaten

1 package of round won-ton wrappers (about 40)

Vegetable oil, for frying


SAUCE

¼ cup soy sauce

2 Tbsp. Chinese red pepper oil

2 Tbsp. rice wine vinegar

2 large cloves garlic, minced

1 green onion, finely chopped

1. In a skillet, combine all the dumpling ingredients up to and including the wine. Sauté over medium heat, breaking up the sausage or ground pork as it cooks to prevent clumping. Cook until no longer pink. Pour off any excess fat.

2. Stir in the spinach, then the cornstarch-water mixture, and then, gradually, about two-thirds of the beaten egg. Remove the skillet from the heat, transfer the mixture to a bowl, and set aside to let the filling cool.

3. Separate a few won-ton wrappers and place them on a cutting board. Brush the remaining egg along the top margin of each wrapper. Spoon a scant teaspoon of the filling into the center, carefully fold the wrappers over the filling to create a half-circle, and then press the edges together to seal. Place the finished dumplings on a platter and cover them with a damp cloth to keep them from drying out while you assemble the rest.

4. You can boil the dumplings in about an inch of simmering water, but steaming them over a simmering pot works better. In either case, cook only until the wrappers become translucent, about 2–3 minutes. At that point, the dumplings are ready to be eaten, but you can add further excitement with the "pot-sticking" trick.

5. Heat 1½ tablespoons of vegetable oil in a nonstick skillet over medium-high heat. Space out as many dumplings as the pan will hold and cook until they're crispy brown on one side. (This is when they'd start to stick to a regular pot.) Turn them to crisp the other side, then remove and keep warm. Add a little more oil between each batch and continue cooking until all are done.

6. Mix the sauce ingredients in a bowl. Serve the sauce on the side. MAKES FORTY DUMPLINGS.

# Broiled Mushrooms with Italian Sausage

*This was a clean-out-the-refrigerator dish we threw together one night when friends suddenly came over. Like us, they'd recently been to Italy, so this naturally came to mind. It's delicious and simple to prepare on short notice.*

4 links hot or sweet Italian sausage
¼ tsp. crushed red pepper
½ tsp. dried oregano
½ tsp. salt
10 sprigs flat-leaf parsley,
    leaves only, chopped

⅔ cup bread crumbs
1 lb. medium whole white
    mushrooms, stemmed
⅓ cup shredded Fontina or
    mozzarella cheese

1. Preheat the broiler. Remove the sausage from the casings. Place the sausage meat in a large skillet over medium heat and cook, breaking up the sausage with a kitchen fork until it begins to brown. Pour off any excess fat.

2. Add the crushed red pepper, oregano, salt, and ½ cup of water, and continue to cook until the sausage meat is no longer pink. Add the parsley and bread crumbs, and mix in well. Add a little more water, if needed, to keep the mixture from being very dry. (It should not be very wet, either.) Remove from the heat.

3. Slice off a sliver the size of a dime from the top of the mushroom cap to make a flat area. Stuff a heaping teaspoon of the sausage mixture into the cavity of each mushroom. Place the mushrooms, stuffing side up, on a baking pan. Place a generous pinch of the shredded cheese (as much as you can get to stay put) on top of the stuffing. Broil until the cheese melts and begins to brown. SERVES EIGHT TO TWELVE.

# Boudin Blanc

*White boudin is a rice-and-pork sausage found everywhere food is sold in Cajun country, from gas stations to fancy restaurants. Spicy with red pepper and enriched with a little bit of pork liver, this is the more familiar form of boudin (as opposed to the hard-to-find boudin noir, a blood sausage).*

*This is not a hard recipe to make, but some of the ingredients and equipment you'll need may not be easy to come by. Finding sausage casing can be a challenge unless you want a mile of it. I beg a supermarket that makes its own sausages (as most of the big ones do) to give me 10 or 20 feet of it. Then there's the pork liver, which is a special-order item in most markets. You'll need a meat grinder, although a food processor will do a passable job. Finally, if you want to stuff the sausage in the casings, you need the gizmo for doing that. An easier alternative is to forgo the casings and make boudin balls instead.*

*My contribution to this traditional recipe is the concentrated chicken-and-pork stock that makes the rice part of the filling taste especially good. Use short-grain rice, which has the slightly sticky texture you need.*

3–4 yards of medium sausage casing

STOCK
4 chicken-leg quarters
1 small pork shoulder (Boston butt), about 3–4 lb.
1 large onion, cut into eighths
2 bay leaves
2 ribs celery, chopped
Stems from 1 bunch of flat-leaf parsley
½ tsp. thyme
½ tsp. marjoram
1 tsp. black peppercorns

FILLING
4 slices bacon
1 lb. pork liver, cut into ½-inch-thick slices
1 medium onion, coarsely chopped
½ bell pepper, coarsely chopped
1 rib celery, coarsely chopped
1½ tsp. cayenne, plus more to taste
4½ tsp. salt, plus more to taste
3 cups uncooked short-grain rice (not parboiled or converted)
1 bunch of flat-leaf parsley, leaves only, finely chopped
2 bunches of green onions, green parts only, finely chopped
1 tsp. freshly ground black pepper

*(continued)*

1. Unroll the sausage casing and soak it in cold water for an hour or so. Pull it open and run water through the casing for a few seconds. Keep moist.

2. Put all the stock ingredients into a large pot and add enough water to cover—at least a gallon (16 cups) of water. Bring to a light boil and cook, uncovered, for 2 hours. Skim the fat and foam off the surface as the stock cooks.

3. To make the filling: Fry the bacon in a large skillet until crisp. Remove the bacon and reserve for another use. Add the pork liver and all the other filling ingredients up to (but not including) the rice to the drippings, and sauté over medium heat until the liver is tender. Add ½ cup of the simmering stock and cook 10 minutes more. Transfer to a bowl, let cool, and then refrigerate.

4. Remove the chicken and pork from the stockpot and set aside. Strain the stock and discard the solids. Return the stock to a light boil and reduce to 2 quarts.

5. Reserve two of the chicken-leg quarters for another purpose. Skin and bone the other two and dice the meat. Dice the pork shoulder, cutting across the grain of the meat. Refrigerate all this when finished.

6. When the stock is reduced, pour 5 cups into a large saucepan. Add the rice, bring to a boil, then reduce heat and simmer, covered, about 25 minutes, or until the rice is very tender and borderline gummy. Fluff and set aside.

7. If you have a meat grinder, fit it with the coarse blade or ¼-inch die. Combine the diced chicken, pork, and liver, and run the mixture through the grinder once. If you don't have a grinder, use a food processor, but stop short of mincing the ingredients.

8. Combine the ground meat mixture with the rice, chopped parsley, green onions, and black pepper. Add 1–2 cups of the stock, a little at a time, and mix well. You've added enough stock when you can easily form the mixture into a ball that doesn't stick to your fingers. Add more cayenne and salt to taste.

9. At this point, you can either stuff the boudin into the casing, or you can make boudin balls without casing. Either way, microwave until quite warm inside before serving. MAKES ABOUT TWENTY-FOUR 4-INCH LINKS.

# New Orleans Shrimp Spring Rolls

*It may seem strange, but rémoulade sauce and pasta (and shrimp, of course) go well together. This is especially true of the rice noodles used in Southeast Asian cooking.*

**SHRIMP**
Leafy tops from a bunch of celery
1 bay leaf
1 Tbsp. Tabasco
½ lemon, sliced
2 Tbsp. salt
1 lb. medium shrimp (25–30 count)

**ROLLS**
8 oz. rice stick noodles, soaked in cold water for about 45 minutes
12 round rice-paper wrappers
½ cup red rémoulade sauce (see Shrimp Rémoulade with Two Sauces, page 13)

**GARNISH**
Asian-style chili-garlic sauce
2 green onions, finely chopped

1. To prepare the shrimp: Bring ½ gallon (8 cups) of water to a boil in a pot. Add all the ingredients up to (but not including) the shrimp. Boil the water for 5 minutes, then add the shrimp. Remove the pot from the heat immediately and allow the shrimp to steep for 4 minutes, or until the shell separates from the meat easily.

2. Drain shrimp in a colander and set aside until cool enough to handle. Peel and devein the shrimp.

3. Bring a small pot of water to a boil. After the noodles have soaked for about 45 mintues, drain them, then plunge them in the boiling water for about a minute. Drain again and let cool.

4. Brush the rice-paper wrappers with water and let them soften. When the rice paper is stretchy, lay about 3 tablespoons of the noodles in a line about two-thirds of the way down the rice paper. Drizzle about a tablespoon of the rémoulade sauce across the noodles. Place 4–6 shrimp on top of the noodles, then roll up the rice paper. When the noodles and shrimp are covered, tuck in the loose ends of the rice paper and finish rolling.

5. Garnish rolls with squirts of the chili-garlic sauce and chopped green onions.
MAKES TWELVE ROLLS.

# Savory Waffles

*This started as another way to serve caviar at my big charity dinners (see Caviar on Savory Lost Bread, page 17). I'd make a little waffle with just one big depression in the center, and that was where the sour cream and caviar would go. Then I started snacking on the extra waffles and realized that they could be served with all sorts of other dishes, from seafood to eggs. They're not bad all by themselves, either, as an alternative to bread. Where this recipe deviates from the standard waffle is in substituting savory flavors for sweet.*

1 cup self-rising flour
½ tsp. granulated onion
¼ tsp. dry dill
½ tsp. salt
3 Tbsp. extra-virgin olive oil or melted butter
1 egg, beaten
1 cup half-and-half

1. Preheat a waffle iron.

2. In a small bowl, mix all the dry ingredients.

3. In a larger bowl, whisk together all the wet ingredients.

4. Add the dry ingredients to the wet ingredients and whisk slowly until all the flour is wet. Don't eliminate all the lumps.

5. Pour about 3 tablespoons of the batter into the center of each half of the waffle iron, covering only one square completely and allowing the batter to flow into the surrounding squares. Close the cover and cook according to the manufacturer's instructions. The top of the waffle need not brown entirely.

6. Flip the waffle over, browned side up, and fill the center square with sour cream, soft-scrambled eggs, crabmeat with hollandaise, or whatever else you might think of. MAKES ABOUT A DOZEN WAFFLES.

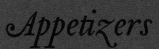

# Appetizers

In too many restaurants, the appetizers are dramatically better than the much more expensive entrées. Here's why I think this is: most chefs make up their menus from the top down. By the time they get to the main courses, they often have used up all their inspirations on the first courses. And they revert to mere trend-following when they get to the steaks, chicken, and fish. The best chefs have enough in their heads to devise menus full of interesting food. But the less-than-best chefs are also out there, working.

Also, chefs like to play around with very expensive ingredients. You can make a legitimate dish of mostly jumbo lump crabmeat if the serving is appetizer size. It's quite another matter when you need to put a half-pound of crabmeat on the plate.

Finally, appetizers must be brilliant. A meal that starts with a hit has a man on base, and you can figure out the rest of this metaphor. A spectacular first course often casts a glow on an underperforming entrée that might disguise its shortcomings. At least in the mind of the beholder.

No course lends itself more readily to invention and rule breaking than the appetizer. You can go hot or cold or in between. Use any method of cooking any ingredient in any presentation. Your guests may well be turned on by some fantastic creation. But even if they aren't, the risk to their appetites is small. You have the entire remainder of the meal to make up for it with safer dishes. So go nuts on the first course.

# Beyond Shellfish

The most pervasive appetizer tradition is to center it on seafood. There is a logic to this: Seafood is light, much of it can be served cold, and you can use intense, palate-perking sauces.

Louisiana seafood is a great resource for creating appetizers. The number of oyster dishes alone is dizzying (as I will prove shortly). The local crabmeat is almost absurdly delectable, even when eaten straight out of the container. The three major varieties of shrimp are all the equals of any other in the world.

When seafood will be the entrée, the meal is more interesting when it starts with something else. So we welcome duck breasts, sausages, sweetbreads, meat-filled dumplings, and other light meat dishes into the appetizer universe.

# Hot and Cold, Soft and Crunchy, Mild and Spicy

A chef I know uses a predictable pattern in all his wine-dinner menus. He starts with something cold, then serves a hot dish, then another cold item, followed by another hot item. If he could get away with it, he'd keep the pattern going all the way through the dessert.

My suspicion is that he does this mainly for logistical reasons. A cold dish can be prepared in advance, shoved into the refrigerator, and pulled out when it's time to send it out. This gives him more time to get the hot dishes ready. But there's a good taste reason for the strategy: contrast. Creating contrasts among flavors, spice levels, textures, colors, temperatures, and ingredients is a fine art. It's one of the things that separates the great chefs from the ordinary ones.

Since you have much more latitude in the appetizer course than in any other, think about what will follow it and create an appetizer that will force a gustatory shift when you and your guests move on.

# Crabmeat St. Francis

*Crabmeat St. Francis was created by the legendary New Orleans chef Warren Leruth, whose restaurant in Gretna was the premier haute-Creole place to eat in the 1960s and 1970s. Warren once told me that the biggest thing he missed about not having the restaurant anymore was that he couldn't eat crabmeat St. Francis whenever he wanted to. It was one of the most celebrated of his dishes, a fantastic appetizer.*

| | |
|---|---|
| 4 cups heavy whipping cream | ½ tsp. thyme |
| 2 cups crab stock (see recipe, page 312) | Generous pinch of celery seed |
| ¼ cup dry white wine | 1¼ tsp. salt |
| 4 bay leaves | ¼ tsp. cayenne |
| 1½ sticks (12 Tbsp.) butter | ¼ tsp. ground white pepper |
| 1 large green onion, finely chopped | ½ cup flour |
| 2 large cloves garlic, chopped | 1 Tbsp. chopped flat-leaf parsley leaves |
| ¼ cup chopped white onion | 4 egg yolks |
| ¾ cup hearts of celery, chopped | 2 lb. fresh jumbo lump crabmeat |
| | ½ cup bread crumbs |

1. Preheat the oven to 425 degrees. In a saucepan, bring the cream, crab stock, wine, and bay leaves to a simmer and hold there.

2. Melt the butter in a medium skillet over medium heat. Add the remaining ingredients up to (but not including) the flour and sauté until the vegetables are translucent.

3. Make a blond roux by adding the flour to the vegetables and cook, stirring often, for about 5 minutes, or until the flour is no longer raw and just starting to brown.

4. Whisk in the cream-and-stock mixture. Lower the heat, add the parsley, and gently simmer for about 15 minutes. Remove and discard the bay leaves.

5. Remove the skillet from the heat and whisk in the egg yolks, one at a time.

6. Place 2 oz. of the lump crabmeat in each of 16 ramekins or baking shells. Top each with a ½ cup of the sauce, sprinkle lightly with the bread crumbs, and bake until the top is browned and bubbly, 10–12 minutes. SERVES SIXTEEN.

# Crabmeat Ravigote

*This and shrimp rémoulade (see Shrimp Rémoulade with Two Sauces, page 13) are the most popular cold appetizers in traditional New Orleans restaurants. The word "ravigote" means "revived," the original idea being that you could add this tangy sauce to some crabmeat or fish that was on the edge of freshness and resurrect it. Of course, it was quickly noticed that it also tasted great with vividly fresh crabmeat.*

½ cup mayonnaise
2 Tbsp. cider vinegar
1 Tbsp. Creole mustard
¼ cup heavy whipping cream
1 green onion, green parts only, finely chopped
3 sprigs flat-leaf parsley, leaves only, chopped
2 Tbsp. small capers, drained
½ tsp. dried dill
½ tsp. dried tarragon
⅛ tsp. salt
Pinch of ground white pepper
Dash of Tabasco
1 lb. fresh jumbo lump crabmeat

1. Whisk all of the ingredients except the crabmeat together in a bowl.

2. Gently stir the crabmeat into the sauce. It's best if you let the mixture sit for an hour or two, refrigerated, before serving. SERVES EIGHT.

# Crabmeat West Indies

*One of my radio listeners once told me that in his opinion the ultimate way to eat jumbo lump crabmeat was to open the box, reach in, and just start eating. I really cannot argue with that, but it doesn't make for much of a recipe. Here, however, is a popular dish all along the Gulf Coast that is about as close to naked as a lump of crabmeat can get.*

1 lb. fresh jumbo lump crabmeat
1 small white onion, chopped
½ cup olive oil
6 Tbsp. cider vinegar
1 Tbsp. small capers, drained
¼ cup water
¼ tsp. salt
4 dashes of Tabasco
2 ripe tomatoes, thickly sliced

Gently blend together all of the ingredients except the tomatoes in a non-metallic bowl. Cover and refrigerate for at least 2 hours or overnight. Serve cold over slices of ripe tomato. SERVES FOUR TO SIX.

# Crabmeat Cannelloni

*Here's a rich crabmeat-and-pasta dish that makes a good appetizer or entrée. Resist the temptation to roll these things up so tight that the crabmeat can't escape; you want to see some of it wandering around on the plate. Do you know how you can tell that this is a New Orleans recipe and not one from Italy? The cheese. Italians would never put this much cheese (if any) in a seafood dish. In New Orleans, not adding the cheese would be unthinkable.*

Fifteen 4-inch pasta squares, preferably fresh, or 15 big pasta tubes, such as cannelloni or manicotti (include a few extra squares or tubes, since some will inevitably break as you roll or stuff them)
3 cups heavy whipping cream
½ cup grated Parmesan cheese
⅛ tsp. ground white pepper
½ tsp. chopped garlic
¼ tsp. salt
¼ tsp. crushed red pepper
1 lb. fresh jumbo lump crabmeat
1 Tbsp. fresh chopped basil
¼ cup shredded mozzarella

1. Preheat the oven to 400 degrees. Cook the pasta in salted boiling water until al dente. Drain and set aside.

2. Boil the cream in a large saucepan and reduce by half. (Don't let it foam over.) Pour about two-thirds of the reduced cream into a skillet. To the cream remaining in the saucepan, whisk in the Parmesan cheese and white pepper to finish the sauce. Keep warm on the side.

3. Add the garlic, salt, crushed red pepper, and crabmeat to the cream in the skillet. Simmer over low heat, stirring until the crab is well incorporated. Add the basil and mozzarella, and stir very lightly until the cheese begins to melts. Remove from the heat.

4. Spoon about 3 tablespoons of the crab mixture onto the lower third of each pasta sheet. Roll them into tubes about an inch in diameter and place seam side down in a large baking dish. If using pasta tubes, spoon about 3 tablespoons of the crab mixture into the tubes. Spoon about 2 tablespoons of sauce over each cannelloni.

5. Bake the cannelloni until the sauce starts to bubble and the pasta edges brown lightly, 3–5 minutes. SERVES TWELVE AS AN APPETIZER OR SIX AS AN ENTREE.

# Deviled Crab

*Although the crab cake (an import from Maryland, rarely seen in New Orleans before about 1990) has largely overshadowed similar local dishes, these are not half bad when made with the kind of good crabmeat we have around here. A case in point is this recipe, which I like to serve as a side dish to pasta, entrée salads, or fried seafood. It is also one of the relatively few dishes in this collection that begin with what is known around New Orleans as the holy trinity: yellow onions, bell peppers, and celery.*

1½ sticks (12 Tbsp.) butter
¼ cup chopped yellow onion
¼ cup chopped celery
¼ cup chopped red bell pepper
¼ cup dry white wine
1 Tbsp. lemon juice
1 tsp. yellow mustard
¼ tsp. Worcestershire sauce
¼ tsp. curry powder

1 lb. fresh jumbo lump crabmeat
3 Tbsp. chopped green onion
2 tsp. salt-free Creole seasoning
1 tsp. salt
1½ cups bread crumbs
2 lemons, cut into wedges
White rémoulade sauce (see Shrimp
    Rémoulade with Two Sauces,
    page 13) or tartar sauce

1. Preheat the oven to 375 degrees. Melt 1 stick (8 tablespoons) of the butter in a skillet until it bubbles. Add the onion, celery, and bell pepper, and sauté until soft.

2. Add the wine, lemon juice, yellow mustard, Worcestershire sauce, and curry powder, and bring to a boil, stirring to blend. When the liquid is reduced by half, add the crab, green onion, Creole seasoning, and salt. Stir gently, trying not to break up the lumps of crabmeat too much. Remove the skillet from the heat. Add the bread crumbs and gently stir until just mixed.

3. At this point, you can either put the mixture into clean crab shells or gratin dishes, or make them into cakes or balls. Place whatever you come up with on a buttered baking sheet. Top each piece with about a teaspoon of the remaining butter. Bake until the tops bubble and brown, 10–12 minutes

4. Serve with lemon wedges and white rémoulade sauce or tartar sauce. SERVES SIX TO EIGHT.

# Oysters Rockefeller

*Perhaps the strangest request for a recipe I've ever received came from Bernard Guste, the fifth-generation proprietor of Antoine's. He wanted my recipe for oysters Rockefeller. His reason was that since Antoine's own recipe (remember, they invented the dish) is a secret, they needed something to give the many people who ask for it. He told me that my recipe is embarrassingly close to the real thing. I'm flattered. And if I say so myself, he's right. It took me about 50 tries to create a match for the flavor of Antoine's great specialty.*

*Oysters Rockefeller never did include either spinach or Mornay (white cheese) sauce, which most recipes call for. It does include green food coloring—an atrocity now but common a century ago, when this dish was created. The Peychaud's bitters, a New Orleans specialty, can be ordered from the Sazerac Company (www.sazerac.com/bitters.html).*

*Oysters Rockefeller has always been among my favorite Creole-French dishes and one that creates its own special occasion whenever you make it.*

4 dozen fresh, shucked oysters, with their liquor
2 cups chopped celery
2 cups chopped flat-leaf parsley leaves
1½ cups chopped green onion, green parts only
1 cup chopped fresh fennel
1 cup chopped watercress
½ tsp. chopped fresh garlic
3 anchovy fillets
¼ cup ketchup
1 Tbsp. Worcestershire sauce
1 tsp. sugar
1 tsp. salt
1 tsp. ground white pepper
½ tsp. cayenne
2 dashes of Peychaud's bitters (optional; see headnote)
2 drops of green food coloring (optional, but authentic)
2 sticks (16 Tbsp.) butter
1 cup flour
1½ cups very fine, fresh bread crumbs

*(continued)*

1. Preheat the oven to 450 degrees. Drain the oysters, reserving the liquor. Pour the oyster liquor into a 2-cup measuring cup, add enough cold water to make 2 cups, and set aside.

2. Working in small batches, process the vegetables and anchovies together in a food processor to a near-puree, using the oyster water to help things along.

3. Combine the vegetable puree and any remaining oyster water in a saucepan and cook over low heat, stirring occasionally, until the excess water has evaporated but the greens remain very moist. Stir in the ketchup, Worcestershire sauce, sugar, salt, pepper, cayenne, bitters, and food coloring.

4. Make a blond roux by heating the butter in a medium saucepan over medium-low heat. Add the flour and cook, stirring often, until the mixture just begins to brown. Add the roux to the greens and stir until the sauce takes on a different, lighter texture. Then mix in the bread crumbs.

5. Place the oysters on individual half shells or in small ovenproof ramekins or gratin dishes. Top each oyster with a generous tablespoon (or more) of the sauce. Bake until the sauce just begins to brown, about 15 minutes. Serve immediately.

If you are using oyster shells, serve on a bed of rock salt or on a napkin to keep the shells from rocking. SERVES EIGHT.

# Oysters Rockefeller Flan

*Every food writer of my generation has a Julia Child story. Mine involves this dish. Chef André Poirot at Begue's at the Royal Sonesta Hotel cooked it for a small dinner party for Julia in the mid-1980s. I sat across the table from her and heard her declare, in her distinctive voice, "Divine! Very creative!" (We were not to hear any more such praise during the remainder of that meal.)*

*A savory custard holds together the traditional ingredients for oysters Rockefeller.*

OYSTERS

1 lb. fresh spinach, well washed, stems removed
1¼ tsp. salt
2 Tbsp. dry white wine
2 dozen fresh, shucked oysters, with their liquor
1 Tbsp. butter, softened
5 eggs
3 cups heavy whipping cream
2 Tbsp. Pernod
Pinch of nutmeg
Pinch of ground white pepper

SAUCE

6 Tbsp. dry white wine
2 Tbsp. chopped shallots
1 cup heavy whipping cream
1 stick (8 Tbsp.) butter, melted
Juice of 1 lemon
Salt and ground white pepper to taste

1. Preheat the oven to 325 degrees. Blanch the spinach for 1 minute in 2 quarts of boiling water seasoned with 1 teaspoon of the salt. Drain and douse the spinach with cold water. Drain again and set aside.

*(continued)*

2. Bring the white wine and oyster liquor to a light boil in a medium skillet and poach the oysters in it for about 2 minutes. Remove from the heat, let the oysters cool a bit, and chop coarsely. Strain the poaching liquid and reserve.

3. Lightly grease the insides of six 6-ounce ramekins with the butter. Line the insides of these with leaves of cooked spinach, draping the ends of the leaves over the sides. Divide the chopped oysters among all the cups.

4. Whisk the poaching liquid, eggs, cream, Pernod, nutmeg, pepper, and remaining ¼ teaspoon of salt together in a bowl. Pour the mixture over the oysters in the cups. Fold the spinach leaves over the custard.

5. Arrange the ramekins in a large baking dish. Pour in enough hot water to come halfway up sides of ramekins. Bake until the custard is just set, about 40 minutes.

6. While the flans are baking, make the sauce. Boil the wine and shallots together in a saucepan until the wine is reduced to 1 tablespoon. Add the heavy whipping cream and reduce until sauce is thick enough to coat the back of a spoon. Whisk in the butter, lemon juice, and season to taste with salt and white pepper. Strain the sauce, discarding solids, and keep warm.

7. Allow the soufflé dishes to cool for a few minutes after baking, then unmold onto serving plates. Spoon the sauce over the flans. SERVES SIX.

# Oysters Bienville

*Not enough restaurants make oysters Bienville anymore, which is a shame. This classic baked-on-the-shell dish, named for the founder of New Orleans, is seriously delicious. However, there's no gold standard for the dish. Nobody is sure who invented it, in fact. Arnaud's, Antoine's, and Commander's all make claims. Pascal's Manale and Delmonico are also famous for their versions.*

*I'm persuaded that the ingredient list must contain bacon, shrimp, mushrooms, bell peppers, sherry, a light roux, Parmesan cheese, a milder cheese, and bread crumbs. Other ingredients lurk in the background. You can bake oysters Bienville classically on the shells, but I find they're just as good made in a small casserole or gratin dish. I serve them that way at Thanksgiving instead of oyster dressing.*

*When cooking, oysters release a lot of water, resulting in a watery sauce. The solution is to use more bread crumbs than looks or feels right. And to have the sauce fully cooked and hot before it goes into the oven, so that the dish is cooked mostly by heat from above.*

4 dozen fresh, shucked large oysters, with their liquor

1 stick (8 Tbsp.) butter

1 lb. small shrimp (50 count), peeled, rinsed, and coarsely chopped

1 rib celery, coarsely chopped

1 large red bell pepper, seeded and coarsely chopped

½ lb. small white mushrooms, coarsely chopped

¼ cup dry sherry

4 strips lean bacon, fried crisp and crumbled

2 green onions, finely chopped

½ cup flour

⅔ cup milk, hot

2 egg yolks

⅔ cup finely shredded mozzarella cheese

1 cup bread crumbs

¼ cup grated Parmesan cheese

1 tsp. salt-free Creole seasoning

¼ tsp. salt

*(continued)*

1. Preheat the oven to 450 degrees. Drain the oysters, reserving the liquor. Put the oyster liquor into a 1-cup measuring cup and add enough water, if necessary, to make 1 cup liquid.

2. Heat 1 teaspoon of the butter in a medium skillet until it bubbles. Sauté the chopped shrimp until it just turns pink. Remove and set aside. Add 2 tablespoons of the butter to the skillet and heat until it bubbles. Add the celery, bell pepper, and mushrooms. Sauté until they get tender. Add the sherry and bring to a boil for about a minute.

3. Add the bacon, green onions, and reserved shrimp. Cook for another minute, then add the reserved oyster liquor. Bring the mixture to a boil and cook for about 2 minutes more. The sauce should be wet but not sloshy. Remove from heat.

4. Heat the remaining butter in a medium saucepan over medium-low heat. Add the flour and cook, stirring constantly, to make a blond roux. When you see the first hints of browning, remove from the heat and whisk in the milk to form a béchamel. (It will have the texture of mashed potatoes.) Add the egg yolks to the béchamel, stirring quickly to combine it before the eggs have a chance to set. Add the mozzarella slowly to the béchamel, stirring until the cheese melts.

5. Add the béchamel to the shrimp mixture in the skillet and stir to combine.

6. Mix the bread crumbs, Parmesan, Creole seasoning, and salt together in a bowl. Stir two-thirds of this mixture into the sauced shrimp. Set the remaining bread-crumb mixture aside.

7. Cover the bottom of a shallow baking dish with oysters, leaving just a little space between them. Top with the Bienville sauce. Sprinkle the top with the remaining bread-crumb mixture. Bake until the sauce is bubbling and the top is browned, 15–20 minutes (depending on the size of the baking dish). SERVES EIGHT TO TWELVE.

# Creole-Italian Oysters

*After Bienville and Rockefeller, this garlic-and-bread-crumby concoction is the most popular in the pantheon of local oyster dishes. The most famous version of the dish is Oysters Mosca, named for the restaurant that made it popular, but every restaurant that's even slightly Italianate makes a version of it, plus plenty of others. My version is a little spicier than most, inspired by the recipe used at La Cuisine. The ideal side dish with this is Pasta Bordelaise (see recipe, page 230).*

⅓ cup extra-virgin olive oil
24 fresh, shucked large oysters, partially drained
2 Tbsp. finely chopped garlic
2 Tbsp. chopped flat-leaf parsley leaves
1 Tbsp. fresh lemon juice
½ tsp. crushed red pepper
2 cups bread crumbs
⅔ cup grated Parmesan cheese
1 Tbsp. Italian seasoning

1. Preheat the oven to 400 degrees. Pour a little of the olive oil into the bottom of a baking dish of almost any size, from a small gratin dish to a pie plate. Arrange the oysters in the dish, leaving about ½ inch of space between them.

2. Sprinkle the oysters with the garlic, parsley, lemon juice, and crushed red pepper. Combine the bread crumbs, Parmesan, and Italian seasoning in a bowl and sprinkle evenly over the oysters.

3. Bake until the sauce is bubbling and the bread crumbs on top brown, about 10–15 minutes (depending on the size of the baking dish). SERVES SIX.

# Oysters Dunbar

*Next to the Holy Grail, the most difficult thing in the world to find is a recipe from a restaurant that is no longer in business. I'm asked for them at the rate of about one a week. I think I have been asked for this one at least a hundred times.*

*Corinne Dunbar's was a unique restaurant on St. Charles Avenue that operated more like a private home. It had a fixed menu each day, and you never knew what you'd be served. But you hoped it would be oysters Dunbar, the restaurant's most famous dish. It was an oyster-and-artichoke casserole, and although I have never been able to obtain an authentic recipe from original sources, I've managed to piece together enough facts about it to come up with this one. At the very least, it seems close to what I remember from the one time I went to Dunbar's in the early 1970s.*

2 dozen fresh, shucked oysters, with their liquor
2 Tbsp. salt, plus more to taste
Juice of 1 lemon
4 large artichokes
1 stick (8 Tbsp.) plus 2 Tbsp. butter
2 Tbsp. flour
¼ cup finely chopped green onion
1 cup sliced fresh mushrooms
¼ tsp. Tabasco
Freshly ground black pepper to taste
½ cup bread crumbs

1. Preheat the oven to 350 degrees. Drain the oysters, reserving the liquor. Put the oyster liquor into a 1-cup measuring cup and add enough water, if necessary, to make 1 cup liquid.

2. Bring a large pot of water to a boil with the 2 tablespoons of salt and half the lemon juice. Cook the artichokes until tender, then remove from the water and set aside to cool.

3. Using a spoon, scrape the meat from the tough outer artichoke leaves into a bowl and discard the leaves. Pull off the tender inner leaves and reserve them whole. Remove the fuzzy "choke" from the artichoke bottom, chop the bottom into medium dice, and reserve.

4. In a skillet, melt the stick of butter until it bubbles. Add the flour and cook, stirring often, to form a loose blond roux. Add the green onion and cook until tender.

5. Add the reserved oyster liquor and mushrooms. Bring to a light boil, reduce heat to a simmer, and cook until the mushrooms are tender and the liquid is very thick. Add the oysters and cook for 2 minutes more. Season to taste with Tabasco, salt, and pepper.

6. Scatter the reserved artichoke leaves and meat evenly in a baking dish. Pour the sauced oyster mixture over the artichokes and top with bread crumbs. Dot the top with the remaining butter and bake until the bread crumbs are browned and the rapid bubbling of the liquid contents has begun to slow, 12–15 minutes. Allow to cool for about 5 minutes. SERVES FOUR TO SIX.

# Oysters Jaubert

*Among the most distinctive of New Orleans dishes are oysters served with various kinds of brown sauces. There must be a dozen such dishes, and I've never met one I didn't like. This one is my attempt to recapture a dish served at a long-gone Central Business District café called Guertin's.*

1 quart fresh, shucked oysters, with their liquor
1½ sticks (12 Tbsp.) butter
1 medium onion, chopped
2 green onions, green parts only, finely chopped
½ very ripe green bell pepper, chopped
½ stalk celery, chopped
3 cloves garlic, chopped
2 Tbsp. Worcestershire sauce

1 Tbsp. Louisiana hot sauce, such as Crystal Hot Sauce
1 tsp. fresh lemon juice
1 Tbsp. salt-free Creole seasoning
½ tsp. salt
¼ cup flour
1 cup chicken stock, warm (see recipe, page 312)

1. Drain the oysters, reserving the liquor. Put the oyster liquor into a 1-cup measuring cup and add enough water, if necessary, to make 1 cup liquid.

2. Melt the butter in a large skillet over medium heat until it bubbles. Sauté the vegetables until they turn tender, then add the oysters. Cook until the edges begin to curl, 3–4 minutes.

3. Add the Worcestershire sauce, hot sauce, lemon juice, Creole seasoning, and salt, bring to a boil, and hold there for about a minute.

4. Sprinkle the flour into the skillet and gently stir until the flour is fully incorporated into the sauce. This should make for a very thick mixture.

5. Warm the reserved oyster liquor in a small saucepan and gradually add it to the skillet. Add just enough warm chicken stock, again gradually, until the mixture has a stewlike consistency. Adjust seasonings and serve immediately over toast or pasta. SERVES EIGHT AS AN APPETIZER OR FOUR AS AN ENTREE.

# Oysters au Poivre

*In 1997, my wife ordered me to enter the National Oyster Cooking Competition with this dish. The event takes place in St. Mary's County, Maryland, where the Chesapeake Bay oysters are almost identical to the ones we have in Louisiana. I came in second. But I think you'll enjoy this, one of my favorite fancy ways to eat oysters. The sauce is the best part, so make sure you provide lots of fresh, hot French bread to sop it up.*

2 dozen fresh oysters, the larger the better, preferably freshly shucked, with their liquor
2 cups heavy whipping cream
2 tsp. mixed dried peppercorns (black, white, green, pink)
8 sprigs fresh thyme
Pinch of saffron threads
¼ tsp. salt

1. Drain the oysters, reserving the liquor. Pour the oyster liquor into a 1-cup measuring cup and add enough water, if necessary, to make 1 cup liquid. Set oysters aside.

2. Combine the cream, peppercorns, 2 sprigs of the thyme, and the saffron in a stainless steel or porcelain 2-quart saucepan. Bring to a gentle simmer. (Watch to make sure the pan doesn't boil over, which cream likes to do.) Add the reserved oyster liquor and return to a simmer. Cook until the liquid is reduced to about 1 cup, about 30 minutes.

3. Add 6 oysters to the reduced sauce and let them cook until the sauce resumes bubbling, about 2–3 minutes. Using a slotted spoon or a skimmer, remove the oysters from the pan and keep warm while you cook the remaining oysters in batches of 6.

4. When all the oysters are cooked, plunge them back into the sauce for a few seconds to warm them back up. Arrange 3–6 oysters (depending on size) on plates. Spoon a little extra sauce over the oysters, stirring the pan to distribute the peppercorns and herbs. Garnish each plate with the remaining thyme sprigs. SERVES FOUR TO EIGHT.

# Oysters en Brochette

*This is the first dish I ever impressed anybody with. Even if you feel yourself very maladroit in the kitchen, you can get the same effect. This is a very easy dish to prepare. All you need is fat, fresh oysters and thick-sliced, smoky bacon.*

2 sticks (16 Tbsp.) butter
Vegetable oil, for frying
1 cup flour
1 Tbsp. salt
½ tsp. salt-free Creole seasoning
4 dozen fresh, shucked large oysters, drained
12 slices bacon, each cut crosswise into quarters
Juice of ½ lemon
1 tsp. Worcestershire sauce

1. Melt the butter in a small saucepan over very low heat. Once the bubbles subside, skim the foam off the top. Keep the butter over the lowest possible heat on your stovetop.

2. Pour the oil into a deep, wide pan, to a depth of about an inch. Heat over medium-high heat until temperature reaches 375 degrees.

3. Meanwhile, combine the flour, salt, and Creole seasoning in a wide bowl.

4. Skewer the oysters and bacon on 8-inch-long metal or bamboo skewers, alternating each oyster with a square of bacon. Arrange them so they're barely touching. Coat the brochettes with the seasoned flour and shake off the excess.

5. Fry the brochettes, turning once, until the oysters are golden brown, about 2 minutes per side. Keep them warm while you cook the remaining brochettes.

6. Carefully add the lemon juice and Worcestershire sauce to the warm butter in the skillet. Careful! This may make the butter foam up again and perhaps splatter.

7. Use a fork to unskewer the brochettes onto serving plates. Stir the butter sauce to get some of the browned solids at the bottom and spoon about 2 tablespoons of the sauce over each brochette. MAKES EIGHT APPETIZERS.

# Shrimp Limone

*This is a dazzling dish for shrimp lovers. The lemon really stands out, and the bit of smoky richness from the ham and the touch of red pepper at the end bring it to the culinary border of Italy and Louisiana.*

½ cup extra-virgin olive oil
2 cloves garlic, crushed
24 large shrimp (16–20 count), peeled and deveined
½ stick (4 Tbsp.) butter
¼ cup chopped shallots
10 sprigs flat-leaf parsley, leaves only, chopped
2 oz. lean, smoky ham, thinly sliced and cut into ribbons
½ cup dry white wine
¼ cup lemon juice
2 dashes of Tabasco
½ tsp. salt
8 thin slices French bread, toasted
8 thin slices lemon, for garnish

1. Heat the olive oil in a large skillet over medium heat until it shimmers. Add the garlic cloves and sauté until the garlic begins to brown. Remove and discard garlic.

2. Add the shrimp to the oil and sauté over medium-high heat until they just begin to turn pink. Add the butter, shallots, parsley, and ham, and cook until the shallots are soft.

3. Add the wine and lemon juice, season with the Tabasco and salt, and bring to a boil. Reduce the liquid by about two-thirds.

4. Place the French bread on individual plates. Place 3 shrimp on each slice and spoon the sauce over all. Garnish each serving with a lemon slice. SERVES EIGHT.

# Shrimp with Fennel and Herbs

*The flavors of shrimp and fennel have always worked well together for my palate. This is a great light appetizer with a big and slightly offbeat flavor.*

3 Tbsp. olive oil
1 lb. large shrimp (16–20 count), peeled and deveined
1 fennel bulb, finely sliced
2 cloves garlic, chopped
2 shallots, finely chopped
½ cup dry white wine
2 Tbsp. Herbsaint or Pernod
1 tsp. dried thyme
1 tsp. dried chervil
½ tsp. salt
¼ tsp. freshly ground black pepper
4 dashes of Tabasco
1 tsp. lemon juice
Chopped flat-leaf parsley, for garnish

1. Heat the oil in a skillet until it shimmers. Sauté the shrimp and fennel until the shrimp just begin to turn pink. Add the garlic, shallots, white wine, and Herbsaint or Pernod. Boil for about a minute.

2. Lower the heat to maintain a simmer. Add the thyme, chervil, salt, pepper, Tabasco, and lemon juice. Cook until the sauce thickens. Garnish with the parsley.
SERVES SIX.

# Spicy Garlic Shrimp

*Every summer the Upperline Restaurant has a Garlic Festival—a terrific menu of original dishes using garlic in all its delightful gustatory guises. This one is from the event's early days, compliments of the deft hand of the late chef Tom Cowman.*

GARLIC MAYONNAISE

½ cup mayonnaise
2 Tbsp. Dijon or Creole mustard
1 Tbsp. red wine vinegar
2 Tbsp. chopped garlic

SHRIMP

¼ cup vegetable oil
1 Tbsp. chili powder
½ tsp. salt
¼ tsp. cayenne
1 tsp. chopped garlic
½ lb. small-to-medium shrimp, peeled and deveined
½ medium onion, sliced thinly
Four 2-inch squares Jalapeño-Cheese Cornbread (see recipe, page 296)
¼ cup garlic mayonnaise

1. To make the garlic mayonnaise: Whisk all of the ingredients together in a bowl. It's better to make this a day ahead of time and refrigerate to let the flavors blend.

2. To prepare the shrimp: Mix the oil, spices, and garlic together in a bowl. Add the shrimp and toss to coat. Cover and let marinate in the refrigerator for 1–2 hours.

3. Heat a medium skillet over medium-high heat. Add the shrimp, the marinade, and the onion, and cook until the shrimp are pink and firm, 4–5 minutes, depending on the size of the shrimp.

4. Split the cornbread squares and spread both halves with the garlic mayonnaise. Put 2 cornbread halves on each of 4 plates and spoon the shrimp over the bread. SERVES FOUR.

# Tasso Shrimp

*The late chef Jamie Shannon's too short career brought many good dishes to the menu at Commander's Palace. This is one of his best. It looks simple, but it explodes with flavor. Tasso is a Cajun-style ham that is cured to be very spicy, smoky, and salty. It's used more as a seasoning than as a meat. I'd recommend chef Paul Prudhomme's brand, which is available in specialty food stores and by mail order (see Food Sources, page 327).*

6 Tbsp. butter, softened
Pinch of chopped garlic
Pinch of chopped shallots (or onion)
1 Tbsp. Louisiana hot sauce,
   such as Crystal Hot Sauce
1 tsp. heavy whipping cream
24 jumbo shrimp (20–25 count),
   peeled and deveined

4 oz. tasso, cut into
   matchstick-size pieces
Vegetable oil, for frying
1 cup flour
1 Tbsp. salt
¼ cup pepper jelly
Pickled okra or pickled green beans,
   for garnish

1. Melt 2 tablespoons of the butter in a medium skillet over medium-low heat. Sauté the garlic and shallots for a minute. Add the hot sauce and bring to a boil. Cook until very little liquid is left. Add the cream and cook about 1 minute more.

2. Remove from heat and gradually whisk in the remaining butter until it takes on a creamy consistency. (This is a New Orleans version of beurre blanc.) Keep warm.

3. Cut a slit down the back of each shrimp and insert a strip of tasso. Close the slit with a toothpick.

4. Pour the oil to a depth of ½ inch into a large, deep skillet and heat to about 375 degrees. Meanwhile, mix the flour and salt together in a wide bowl. Dust the skewered shrimp with the seasoned flour. Fry the shrimp, in batches, until golden brown. Drain on paper towels.

5. Transfer the cooked shrimp to a bowl, add the sauce, and toss to coat.

6. Spread a thin film of pepper jelly on the bottom of each of 8 small dishes and arrange 3 shrimp on each plate. Garnish with pickled okra or pickled green beans. SERVES EIGHT.

# Crawfish Boulettes

*Crawfish bisque is traditionally served with stuffed crawfish heads, but I find both the stuffing (while making) and the unstuffing (while eating) of the heads to be inconvenient and messy. Instead, I make small boulettes, or balls, with all the same ingredients except the head shells. These also make great appetizers when served with hollandaise, white rémoulade (see Shrimp Rémoulade with Two Sauces, page 13), or tartar sauce.*

| | |
|---|---|
| 1 cup cooked crawfish tails, peeled | 1 tsp. chopped green onion tops |
| 1 egg yolk | 1 cup bread crumbs |
| 1 Tbsp. olive oil | 1 cup flour |
| 1 tsp. chopped celery | 1 Tbsp. salt |
| 1 tsp. chopped flat-leaf parsley leaves | 1 Tbsp. salt-free Creole seasoning |
| 1 tsp. chopped red bell pepper | Vegetable oil, for frying |

1. Chop the crawfish tails very fine in a food processor. Add the egg yolk and process to blend.

2. Heat the olive oil in a medium skillet over medium heat. Add the celery, parsley, bell pepper, and green onion, and sauté until tender. Add the crawfish-egg mixture and warm through.

3. Add the bread crumbs a little at a time to stiffen the mixture. (You may not need all the bread crumbs.) Transfer the crawfish mixture to a bowl and set aside.

4. Mix the flour, salt, and Creole seasoning together in a wide bowl.

5. Pour the oil into a large, deep skillet to a depth of ½ inch and heat over medium-high heat until the temperature reaches 375 degrees. Divide the crawfish mixture into 16 equal portions and shape them into balls. Roll them in the seasoned flour and shake off the excess. Fry until golden brown. Drain on paper towels.

    If you're serving this in Crawfish Bisque (see recipe, page 69), drop 1–2 boulettes into each serving of bisque at the table or serve the boulettes on the side. MAKES ABOUT SIXTEEN BOULETTES.

# Crawfish with Morel Mushrooms

*Chef Raymond Toups—then the executive chef of the Rib Room at the Omni Royal Orleans hotel—prepared this recipe once on my old television show. Afterward, so many people came in to order it that the kitchen nicknamed it the "TV Special." It's a terrific combination of flavors. I wouldn't bother making it except at the height of crawfish season, March through June. It's best served with rice, but it's also good with pasta.*

1 oz. dried morel mushrooms
   (or 4 oz. fresh, if you're lucky enough to have them)
2 Tbsp. butter
1½ lb. fresh crawfish tails
1 Tbsp. chopped shallots
1 tsp. chopped fresh tarragon
1 tsp. chopped fresh chives
¼ tsp. salt
Pinch of cayenne
1½ cups cooked long-grain rice

1. Soak the morels in water to reconstitute them. Change the water several times to remove any sand.

2. Melt the butter in a large skillet. Add the crawfish meat and morels, and cook until they're hot all the way through—about 2 minutes. Add the shallots, tarragon, chives, salt, and cayenne, and cook for about 1 minute more.

3. Divide the rice among 8 plates and spoon the crawfish mixture over it.
SERVES EIGHT.

# Gratin of Crawfish Tails

*This is what I came up with when I tried to build my favorite aspects of some of my favorite crawfish appetizers into a single dish. Don't attempt this when crawfish are out of season. Freshness is essential. Best: crawfish you boil (without crab boil) and peel yourself. Worst: imported thawed, frozen, cooked crawfish.*

MARINADE
¼ cup dry white wine
Juice of ½ lemon
2 dashes of Worcestershire sauce
1 tsp. yellow mustard
1 tsp. Tabasco Garlic Pepper Sauce

CRAWFISH
1½ cups cooked crawfish tails, peeled
½ stick (4 Tbsp.) butter

3 Tbsp. flour
1 tsp. minced garlic
2 Tbsp. brandy
1 cup half-and-half, warmed
½ tsp. dried tarragon
½ tsp. dried chervil
½ tsp. dried dill
½ tsp. salt
¼ tsp. ground white pepper
18 slices French bread, toasted

1. Preheat the oven to 400 degrees. Whisk all of the marinade ingredients together in a bowl. Add the crawfish meat and toss to coat. Marinate for about 5 minutes.

2. Heat the butter in a medium saucepan over medium heat until it bubbles, then stir in the flour and cook, stirring constantly, to make a light roux. Cook until the texture changes, about 5 minutes, but don't allow the roux to brown.

3. Add the garlic and stir for about 30 seconds. Lower the heat to the lowest setting, stir in the brandy, and cook for about a minute. Add the half-and-half and whisk until the sauce thickens. Add all of the remaining ingredients except the French bread and simmer, stirring once or twice, for about 2 minutes.

4. Stir in the crawfish gently. Continue to simmer until the crawfish is heated through.

5. Divide the crawfish mixture among 4–6 ramekins or gratin dishes. Bake until the sauce begins to bubble and brown around the edges, 3–5 minutes. Serve immediately with the French bread. SERVES FOUR TO SIX.

# Asparagus and Crawfish with Glazed Hollandaise

*The best time to make this dish is April and early May, when both crawfish and asparagus are excellent and inexpensive. The flavor blend, enriched by the hollandaise, is remarkable.*

1 lb. asparagus, the tough bottom inch or two cut off
½ cup cooked crawfish tails, peeled
2 Tbsp. finely shredded Parmesan cheese
1 cup Hollandaise (see recipe, page 315)
Cayenne

1. The best way to cook the asparagus is in a steamer, but it can also be done in a large skillet. If you're using a skillet, bring ½ inch of water to a slow boil and drop in the asparagus. Let the asparagus cook about 2 minutes, until crisp-tender, then remove, being careful not to break them. Run cold water over the asparagus to stop the cooking, then drain.

2. Preheat the broiler. Arrange the asparagus in a single layer, all parallel to one another, on a broiler pan. Sprinkle the crawfish and the Parmesan across the centers of the asparagus spears. Pour the hollandaise over the centers of the spears, leaving the tips clean.

3. Broil the asparagus until the hollandaise begins to turn light brown on top, about 3 minutes. Remove from the oven. Use a long metal spatula to transfer 6–10 spears at a time to a serving dish, making sure the topping stays intact. Sprinkle lightly with cayenne. SERVES EIGHT.

# Seared Scallops with Artichokes

*This is a signature dish at the Pelican Club, where chef Richard Hughes calls it by the misleading name scallop-stuffed artichokes. (The recipe uses only the artichoke bottoms and some of the leaves; the rest of the artichoke can be used for other recipes.) Sophisticated in both flavor and appearance, this dish is best made with dry-pack (also known as day-boat) scallops, which have not been processed for a long shelf life. Be careful not to overcook the scallops. Use high heat and get them out of the pan while they're still bulging.*

4 small whole artichokes

GARLIC BEURRE BLANC
½ cup dry white wine
1 Tbsp. white vinegar
1 Tbsp. heavy whipping cream
1 head garlic, roasted until semisoft
1½ sticks (12 Tbsp.) butter, softened
Salt and freshly ground black pepper to taste

SCALLOPS
¼ cup clarified butter (see recipe, page 314)
1 lb. day-boat sea scallops, medium-large

VINAIGRETTE
1 Tbsp. balsamic vinegar
1 tsp. chopped fresh tarragon
1 Tbsp. chopped flat-leaf parsley leaves
1 tsp. grated Parmesan cheese
¼ cup extra-virgin olive oil

GARNISH
1 tomato, finely diced

*(continued)*

1. Wash and then steam the artichokes until tender, 20–30 minutes. Pull off and save 24 perfect leaves. Clean and remove the artichoke bottoms and set aside.

2. To make the garlic beurre blanc: Bring the wine and vinegar to a boil in a medium skillet. Lower the heat to a low simmer and add the cream. Puree the roasted garlic with the side of a kitchen knife and add to the skillet. Whisk in the softened butter, a little at a time, until the mixture takes on a creamy consistency. Add salt and pepper to taste. Remove from heat and reserve.

3. Heat 2 tablespoons of the clarified butter in a medium skillet over high heat. Add the sea scallops, in batches, and sauté until they are lightly browned but still bulging, about 1½ minutes per side. Add more butter to the skillet, as needed, to complete the cooking.

4. Combine all the vinaigrette ingredients except for the olive oil in a bowl. Gradually whisk in the oil.

5. Place an artichoke bottom on each of 4 plates. Surround each bottom with 8 artichoke leaves. Drizzle some of the vinaigrette over the artichokes. Divide the scallops among the 4 plates and spoon 2 tablespoons of the garlic beurre blanc over each. Garnish with the diced tomato. SERVES FOUR.

# Chicken Livers with Bacon and Pepper Jelly

*It's time for chicken livers to return to the menus of New Orleans restaurants. We used to get them all the time in all sorts of dishes but rarely anymore. A particular favorite of mine was the chicken liver omelet at the Coffee Pot. The Praline Connection made a hit with pepper jelly–coated fried chicken livers. I borrowed that idea as well as the old rumaki concept from Chinese restaurants to give you this dish. It's absolutely spectacular served over a plate of red beans and rice.*

24 chicken livers
12 slices bacon
¼ cup pepper jelly
1 Tbsp. lemon juice
1 green onion, finely chopped
½ tsp. salt

1. Preheat the broiler. Bring a pot of water to a rolling boil.

2. Rinse the chicken livers. Cut the bacon strips, crosswise, in half. Cook the livers and bacon in the pot of boiling water for about 2 minutes. Remove, drain, and cool for a few minutes on paper towels. Roll the chicken livers and bacon on the paper towels to dry them.

3. Whisk the pepper jelly, lemon juice, green onion, and salt together in a small bowl. Roll the chicken livers in the pepper-jelly mixture to coat well. Place each liver atop a half-slice of bacon and roll it up. Skewer 4–6 bacon-wrapped livers together on metal or bamboo skewers, leaving about ½ inch between each liver.

4. Place the skewers on the broiler rack and broil until the bacon is crispy on one side, about 4 minutes. Turn and broil for another 3–4 minutes, or until the second side turns crispy.

5. Remove livers from skewers and serve, as is, as an appetizer. Or unload the skewers on top of red beans and rice for a unique alternative to sausage. SERVES FOUR TO SIX.

# Frog's Legs Persillés

*Frog's legs are delicious, mild, and easy to love, even on a first try. The smaller they are, the better. I like to marinate them in buttermilk, like fried chicken, before cooking.*

FROG'S LEGS
8 pairs of small fresh frog's legs
1½ cups buttermilk
1 tsp. Tabasco Green Pepper Sauce
1 cup flour
1 Tbsp. salt
¼ tsp. ground white pepper
¼ tsp. dried thyme
½ cup clarified butter
   (see recipe, page 314)

1 clove garlic, crushed
1 tsp. red wine vinegar
2 lemons, halved, for garnish

PERSILLADE SAUCE
2 Tbsp. extra-virgin olive oil
6 cloves garlic, chopped
Leaves from 15 sprigs flat-leaf parsley,
   chopped
¼ tsp. salt

1. Rinse the frog's legs, then place them in a food storage bag with the buttermilk and green pepper sauce, and let marinate in the refrigerator for 2 hours.

2. To make the persillade sauce: Heat the oil in a small saucepan over medium-low heat. Add the chopped garlic and parsley, and cook until the parsley is wilted and the garlic is fragrant. Remove from heat. Transfer the parsley mixture to a small food processor or blender. Add the ¼ teaspoon salt and puree. Transfer the mixture into one corner of a small plastic sandwich bag.

3. Combine the flour, 1 tablespoon salt, pepper, and thyme in a wide bowl. Shake the excess buttermilk off the frog's legs and coat them lightly with the flour mixture.

4. Heat the clarified butter in a medium skillet over medium-high heat. Add the crushed garlic. When the butter is bubbling, add the frog's legs and sauté until golden, turning once. Transfer the frog's legs to paper towels to drain. Carefully add the vinegar to the skillet and whisk to make a sauce.

5. Arrange a frog's leg on each of 4 plates. Spoon some of the butter sauce over the legs, trying to avoid picking up the solids on the bottom of the pan. With scissors, snip off the corner of the plastic bag with the parsley sauce. Squeeze out lines of the persillade across the frog's legs. Garnish with lemon halves. SERVES FOUR.

# Abita Springs Stuffed Quail

*Seafood and birds rarely taste especially good together. We get around that here by having smoky andouille sausage make the introductions. As quails never seem substantial enough for a dinner entrée, I say serve this as an appetizer, especially if the main course is fish.*

STUFFED QUAILS

¼ lb. andouille (see page 326) or other smoked sausage

4 green onions, finely chopped

½ red bell pepper, diced

1 tsp. dried basil

1 cup jumbo lump crabmeat

1 cup shrimp, crab, or chicken stock (see recipe, page 312)

2 cups bread crumbs

2 eggs, beaten separately

8 baby quails, rib and backbones removed

4 tsp. butter, softened

EGGPLANT

1 eggplant, at least 2½ inches in diameter, peeled and cut into
    ¼-inch-thick rounds

1 cup flour

1 Tbsp. salt-free Creole seasoning

1 Tbsp. salt

¼ cup milk

¼ cup extra-virgin olive oil

SAUCE

2 green onions, chopped

½ cup dry white wine

2 cups chicken stock

1 Tbsp. tomato paste

Pinch of dried sage

Pinch of dried thyme

Salt and freshly ground black pepper to taste

*(continued)*

1. Preheat the oven to 400 degrees. Cook the andouille, green onions, bell pepper, and basil in a large skillet over medium heat until the sausage is lightly browned. Pour off any excess fat.

2. Add the crabmeat and stock, and bring to a boil. Gently stir to combine everything without breaking up the crab lumps. Over medium-high heat, reduce the liquid by about one-third.

3. Remove the skillet from the heat and stir in the bread crumbs to make a thick stuffing. Cool the stuffing in the refrigerator for 20 minutes. Then mix one of the eggs into the stuffing.

4. Fill each of the quails with some of the stuffing and arrange them in a roasting pan, breast side up. Dot each quail with ½ teaspoon of the butter. Roast until golden brown, 12–15 minutes. (If you have a convection oven, set it to convect.)

5. Meanwhile, cut each slice of eggplant into perfect circles with a 2-inch cookie or biscuit cutter and set aside. Combine the flour, Creole seasoning, and salt in a wide bowl. Whisk the milk and remaining egg together in another bowl. Dip eggplant rounds into the egg mixture, then into the flour mixture.

6. Heat the olive oil in a medium skillet over high heat and sauté the eggplant until golden brown on both sides. Drain the eggplant on paper towels and keep warm.

7. Transfer the roasted quail to a platter and keep warm. To make the sauce: Place the roasting pan over a burner on medium-high heat. Add the green onions and cook until they begin to brown. Add the wine and bring it to a boil, whisking to dissolve the crusty bits stuck to the bottom of the pan. Add the chicken stock, tomato paste, and herbs, and return to a boil. Reduce to about 1 cup. Season to taste with salt and pepper, and strain the sauce through a fine sieve.

8. Spoon some of the sauce over each of 8 warmed dinner plates. Arrange a few eggplant rounds on the sauce and top with a stuffed quail. SERVES EIGHT.

# Gumbos, Bisques, and Other Soups

The most famous soup in Louisiana is gumbo, in its endless isotopes. But there's plenty more where that came from. You would think that in a place with as much heat and humidity as New Orleans sweats through, the soups would be light, maybe even cold. In fact, they're among the heaviest in the soup world. Gumbo—especially the way it's made these days—is so substantial that a bowl of it needs only a length of French bread on the side to be a meal unto itself. That is also true of crawfish bisque, which is more often served as an entrée than as a preliminary.

However, if you turn back the hands of time about 30 years, you find that soups weren't nearly as thick or rich as they are today. The gumbos I grew up with in the 1960s had every bit as much flavor as those today, but the broth was much lighter. The original oyster artichoke soup that Chef Warren Leruth pioneered back then was not the thick, creamy potage we get under the same name today. But nobody ever pushed it off the table.

Seafood is a main ingredient of many Creole soups. A common starting point for many of them is stock made from shrimp, crab or crawfish shells, or fish bones. Stocks are not essential, but they're so easy to make and they add so much flavor that I highly recommend them. Just remember to keep the boil very low.

The element that makes the difference in many a New Orleans soup is oyster liquor. With a little advance notice, you can get oyster liquor in the quantities you need from your oyster dealer.

Cold soups, which seem so appealing in the summer, are rarely found in New Orleans restaurants. I like them, though, and so I've included a couple you probably haven't had before.

# Seafood Gumbo

*When I was growing up, my mother made gumbo every week, usually twice—chicken-filé gumbo on Wednesdays and seafood-okra gumbo on Fridays. Her special touch was sautéeing the okra before adding it to the pot, thereby avoiding the texture problems some people have.*

*The great truth about gumbo is that no two chefs make it alike. Anybody who tells you that there's only one right way to make gumbo is nuts. A few points about my version: not all recipes for seafood gumbo call for making a stock, but I always do. Usually I buy a package of "gumbo crabs," little crabs picked of their big lumps but with enough meat to make a good stock. (These are available in every supermarket's freezer in Louisiana but maybe not elsewhere.) The remnants of big boiled crabs also work, as do shrimp shells or crawfish shells. Or oyster liquor. Use what's available to make some kind of shellfish stock.*

*Also, following the technique of many restaurant chefs, I make the roux separately and add it to the broth well into the process, rather than at the start. My mother (and many other mothers) literally think this is crazy. But that's how chefs almost always do it.*

STOCK

6 gumbo crabs, and/or 4 cups shrimp or crawfish shells, and/or ½ gallon (8 cups) oyster liquor, strained
1 small onion, cut up into chunks
2 ribs celery, cut up into chunks
1 bunch of flat-leaf parsley, stems only
1 Tbsp. black peppercorns
2 bay leaves
½ tsp. dried thyme

GUMBO

3 Tbsp. vegetable oil
2 lb. fresh okra
2 medium yellow onions, chopped
1 very ripe (turning red) green bell pepper, seeded and chopped
2 ribs celery, chopped

8 sprigs flat-leaf parsley, chopped
½ tsp. dried oregano
1 Tbsp. salt-free Creole seasoning
Salt and freshly ground black pepper to taste
Louisiana hot sauce, such as Crystal
Pick 2 (or more, using less of each):
   2 lb. peeled, boiled, large shrimp
   1 lb. claw crabmeat
   2 cups cooked crawfish tail meat
   3–4 dozen fresh, shucked oysters

ROUX

½ stick (4 Tbsp.) butter
⅔ cup flour
¼ cup sliced green onion

*(continued)*

1. To make the stock: Bring about a gallon (16 cups) of water (including oyster liquor, if available) to a light boil in a large pot. Add all of the remaining stock ingredients. Return to a bare simmer and cook for about 30 minutes. Strain the stock into another large pot and discard the solids.

2. To make the gumbo: Heat the oil in a large skillet until the oil shimmers. Add the okra and cook, stirring, for about 3 minutes. Remove the okra and set aside. Add the onions, bell pepper, celery, parsley, and oregano, and sauté until the vegetables are soft. Add the vegetables, including the okra, to the stock and bring to a simmer. Add the Creole seasoning.

3. Meanwhile, make the roux by melting the butter in a small saucepan over medium heat until it sizzles. Add the flour and whisk until it changes texture. Shift to a spoon and stir frequently until the roux reaches the desired color. For me, that would be the color of a pecan shell. Remove from the heat and stir in the sliced green onion. Keep stirring because the heat of the roux can still result in burning.

4. Whisk half of the roux into the gumbo. It will rise to the surface and appear not to blend in, but if you keep whisking, it will. Add some of the remaining roux until the color and consistency of the gumbo are the way you want.

5. Simmer the gumbo for about an hour. Season to taste with salt, pepper, and hot sauce. Just before serving, add the shrimp, crabmeat, crawfish tails, and/or oysters. Simmer 2–3 minutes, until the seafood is heated through. Serve with cooked long-grain rice. SERVES EIGHT TO TWELVE.

# Chicken-Andouille Gumbo

*This is my favorite style of gumbo. I've enjoyed it literally all my life, as it is basically my mother's recipe, a regular part of her weekly cooking regimen. This gumbo is made in the old style, which is to say that the broth is not as thick as has come to be the vogue in most restaurants these days. We called it filé gumbo because Mama put filé (powdered sassafras leaves) only in chicken gumbo and okra only in seafood gumbo. The filé goes in at the table, and then just a pinch for aroma.*

*This is one of those soups that gets better after it sits in the refrigerator for a day. This recipe also reduces the amount of time needed on the stove by about a third.*

One 6-lb. stewing chicken
½ cup vegetable oil
½ cup flour
1 large onion, chopped
1 red bell pepper, chopped
2 cloves garlic, chopped
3 sprigs flat-leaf parsley, chopped
12 cups chicken stock (see recipe, page 312) or water
1 Tbsp. salt
1 tsp. freshly ground black pepper
¼ tsp. Tabasco
2 bay leaves
¼ tsp. dried thyme
1 lb. andouille (see page 326) or other smoked sausage
2 green onions, chopped
2–3 cups cooked long-grain rice
Filé powder (see page 326)

1. Cut the chicken into 12 pieces. Sear them in 2 tablespoons of the oil in a large kettle or Dutch oven over fairly high heat. Keep turning the chicken pieces until they brown on the outside; they should not cook through.

*(continued)*

2. Remove the chicken and reserve. Add the flour and remaining oil to the pot and make as dark a roux as you can. The key to making a roux is to avoid burning it. This is accomplished by constant stirring and watching the heat.

3. When the roux is medium-dark, reduce the heat and add the onion, bell pepper, garlic, and parsley, and sauté until the onions are translucent and have begun to brown.

4. Return the chicken to the pot, along with the chicken stock or water, salt, pepper, Tabasco, bay leaves, and thyme. Bring to a simmer and cook for about an hour.

5. Slice the andouille into 1-inch-thick disks. Wrap them in paper towels and microwave them on medium power for about 3 minutes to remove excess fat. Add the sausage to the gumbo pot.

6. Cook the gumbo, stirring occasionally, until the chicken is tender, for 1–2 hours. If you plan to serve the gumbo the next day, cook it for just 30 minutes, let it cool to warm, cover, and refrigerate. You might want to strip the chicken meat (see next step) while waiting for the gumbo to cool.

7. When ready to serve, remove the chicken and strip the meat off if you haven't done so already. Slice the chicken into bite-size pieces and return to the pot. (You can also just leave the pieces as is if you're among family.) Add the green onions and simmer for another 3–4 minutes.

8. Serve over rice with a pinch or two of filé at the table. SERVES SIX TO TEN.

# Nouvelle Gumbo z'Herbes

*The past few years have seen a revival of this great old tradition—the green gumbo of Lent. It was almost dead, but now quite a few restaurants offer it.*

*The traditional gumbo z'herbes includes a large number (but always an odd number) of greens, cooked down in a broth that, in its most stringent form, is nothing more than the water in which the greens and some savory vegetables were cooked. Most cooks, however, use a stock made with seafood or even seasoning meats. (The most famous local version, at Dooky Chase, uses both beef brisket and sausage.)*

*My thinking with this recipe is that there's no reason why we have to limit ourselves to ancient traditions. So I've added a few vegetables I've never seen in a gumbo z'herbes recipe before. The recipe also turns out a more elegant soup than usually goes under this name. My wife suggested I take it a step further and add heavy cream, but I can't bring myself to do that during Lent.*

STOCK

6 medium gumbo crabs, crushed
1 small onion, cut up
1 tsp. black peppercorns
2 bay leaves

GREENS

1 bunch of collard greens
1 bunch of mustard greens
12 Brussels sprouts
1 bunch of spinach
1 bunch of flat-leaf parsley,
  stems trimmed
Top 5 inches of a bunch of celery, cut
  into thin sticks, with leaves

GUMBO

1 stick (8 Tbsp.) butter
1 cup flour
5 green onions, finely chopped
2 cloves garlic, chopped
½ green bell pepper, finely diced
1 cup dry white wine (preferably
  Chenin Blanc)
1 Tbsp. lemon juice
1 head broccoli, broken up,
  stems removed
1 lb. fresh asparagus,
  bottom 2 inches cut off
1 tsp. Worcestershire sauce
1 Tbsp. Tabasco Green Pepper Sauce
¼ tsp. filé powder (see page 326)
Salt to taste

*(continued)*

1. Put the stock ingredients into a large saucepan with 1 gallon (16 cups) of water. Bring it to a boil, lower the heat, and simmer for 45 minutes. Strain the broth, discarding the solids, and set aside.

2. Pick through all of the greens to eliminate yellow or bruised parts and thick stems. Wash very well in several changes of water until there's no grit left.

3. Bring a large pot of water to a boil. Add the collard greens, mustard greens, and Brussels sprouts, and cook until they are completely soft, about 20 minutes. Add the spinach, parsley, and celery, and cook another 3 minutes at most. Drain the greens, reserving the cooking water. Once cool enough to handle, chop all of the greens and set aside.

4. Melt the butter in a clean, large pot over medium-high heat. Add the flour and cook, stirring constantly, until the roux turns a pale brown. Add the green onions, garlic, and bell pepper, and sauté until tender. Add the wine and lemon juice, and bring to a boil while whisking to dissolve the roux into the wine. Reduce the heat and whisk until what's left begins to resemble very runny mashed potatoes. Then whisk in the crab stock and bring to a simmer.

5. Cut the broccoli and the asparagus into small pieces and add to the soup. Add the chopped greens and the Worcestershire and green pepper sauces. Bring the mixture to a light boil and cook until the broccoli and asparagus are just tender, 5–7 minutes. If the soup is too thick, add some of the reserved greens cooking water.

6. Add the filé and salt to taste. Serve as is or over boiled long-grain rice. SERVES EIGHT TO TWELVE.

# Crawfish Bisque

*Crawfish bisque—one of the greatest dishes in all of Cajun cooking—is not like any other bisque. It's not creamy or thickened with rice, as in the classic French style, but it is made with a dark roux. Most of the ingredients, even the crawfish, are combined to form a rough puree, which further thickens the soup. This may seem like a long, involved recipe, but there are no great challenges in it. What comes out is something unforgettable, especially when served with Crawfish Boulettes (see recipe, page 51).*

5 lb. boiled crawfish
½ medium onion, chopped
2 cloves garlic, crushed
1 rib celery, chopped
½ red bell pepper, chopped
½ cup dry white wine
½ cup brandy
1 small lemon, sliced
½ stick (4 Tbsp.) butter
⅔ cup flour
5 sprigs flat-leaf parsley, leaves chopped
2 green onions, finely chopped
Salt to taste
Tabasco to taste
12 Crawfish Boulettes (optional; see recipe, page 51)

1. Rinse the boiled crawfish with lukewarm water to remove some of the salt, which will otherwise get concentrated later. Peel all of the crawfish and reserve the tail meat and the shells separately. Try to enlist a helper to pull off all the claws from the shells. Put the claws into a heavy plastic bag and bash with a meat mallet to break most of them.

2. Place the onion, garlic, celery, and bell pepper into an 8-quart (or larger) saucepan and sweat over medium heat until the vegetables begin to brown a little around the edges.

*(continued)*

3. Add the crawfish claws, shells, and wine, and bring to a boil. When most of the liquid has evaporated, pour the brandy over the shells. If you are comfortable with flaming dishes and have a fire extinguisher nearby, carefully touch a flame to the brandy. Let the flames die out. Otherwise, just let the brandy boil away.

4. Add the lemon and enough water to cover all the shells. Bring to a boil, reduce the heat, and simmer for 30 minutes, spooning off the foam that rises to the top every now and then.

5. Strain the stock into another saucepan and discard the solids. Simmer the stock until reduced to about 12 cups. Strain through a fine sieve. (At this point, the stock can be refrigerated for up to 3 days or frozen for later use.)

6. Make a dark roux by melting the butter in a medium saucepan over medium-low heat. Add the flour and cook, stirring constantly to avoid burning, until the roux turns the color of chocolate. Whisk the roux into the crawfish stock and continue whisking until completely blended.

7. Add the parsley and green onions. Reserve 6 large crawfish tails per person for garnish. In a food processor, chop the rest of the crawfish tail meat to a near-puree. Add this to the soup and simmer for 5 minutes. Season to taste with salt and Tabasco.

8. Place a crawfish tail in each of 6 soup plates and ladle in the bisque. If desired, add crawfish boulettes to the bisque at the table. SERVES SIX.

# Crabmeat and Corn Bisque

*Crabmeat and corn bisque is a big hit anywhere it's served. This is my own version, distilled from recipes learned at Commander's Palace, Vincent's, Dakota, and a few other places.*

*The recipe begins with instructions for making crab stock. If you already have it (or shrimp or crawfish or lobster stock), just plunge ahead. When crawfish are in season, try substituting a similar amount of crawfish tails for the lump crabmeat. You can also make this bisque in greater quantities and freeze it for use in other recipes.*

6–8 gumbo crabs or picked crab shells
1 jigger (1½ oz.) brandy
1 medium yellow onion, coarsely chopped
2 ribs celery, coarsely chopped
1 bay leaf
½ tsp. dried thyme
½ tsp. black peppercorns
1 stick (8 Tbsp.) butter
4 Tbsp. flour
2 cloves garlic, chopped
⅓ cup dry vermouth
2 ears fresh corn, kernels shaved off the cobs
2 cups heavy whipping cream
1 cup chopped green onion, green parts only
½ tsp. salt
¼ tsp. Tabasco
½ lb. lump crabmeat, carefully picked through

1. Make the stock by putting the crabs or the shells into a large, heavy saucepan over high heat and cooking them until the edges of the shells brown a little.

2. Lower the heat and add the brandy. If you're comfortable with flaming dishes and have a fire extinguisher nearby, carefully ignite the brandy. Otherwise, just let it cook and boil the alcohol away. Add the onion, celery, bay leaf, thyme, peppercorns, and 8 cups of water, and bring to a boil. Reduce the heat and simmer for 30 minutes.

*(continued)*

3. Strain the stock and discard the solids. Return the stock to a boil and reduce to about 2 cups. You can make this ahead and freeze it.

4. Make a blond roux by melting the butter in a medium saucepan over medium-high heat. Add the flour and cook, stirring constantly until roux just begins to turn light brown. Add the garlic and sauté until fragrant, about a minute.

5. Whisk in the vermouth and bring to a boil. Add the crab stock and simmer, stirring occasionally, for about 15 minutes. Add the corn and simmer 5 minutes more. Add the cream, green onion, salt, and Tabasco. Stir until smooth and bring back up to a simmer.

6. Add the crabmeat and blend it in gently, so as not to break the lumps. Adjust the seasoning and serve hot. SERVES FOUR TO SIX.

# Crab and Brie Soup

*This is the signature soup of Dakota Restaurant in Covington, but calling it a soup is a stretch. It's so thick that you could turn a spoonful upside down and it might not come out. I'd recommend serving it only when you can afford to put a lot of lump crabmeat in it.*

1½ sticks (12 Tbsp.) butter
8 gumbo crabs (small hard-shell crabs)
1 medium onion, chopped
1 medium carrot, chopped
3 ribs celery, chopped
1 clove garlic, crushed
2 bay leaves
¼ cup brandy

1 cup dry white wine
4 cups heavy whipping cream
¾ cup flour
8 oz. Brie cheese, rind removed
¼ tsp. salt
⅛ tsp. ground white pepper
½ lb. jumbo lump crabmeat
Pinch of cayenne

1. Melt 1 stick of the butter in a heavy kettle over medium heat. Crack the crabs with a meat mallet, add them to the butter, and sauté for 5 minutes. Add the onion, carrot, celery, garlic, and bay leaves, and cook until the vegetables soften.

2. Add the brandy, bring it to a boil, then carefully touch a flame to it. After the flames die down, add the wine and boil for 2 minutes. Add 8 cups of water and simmer for about 30 minutes.

3. Strain the stock and discard the solids. Return the stock to a cleaned pot, add the cream, and bring the soup base back to a simmer.

4. Make a blond roux by melting the butter in a saucepan over medium-high heat. Add the flour and cook, stirring constantly until the roux just barely starts to brown. Whisk into the soup base.

5. Slice the Brie into small pieces and add it to the pot. Stir until the cheese melts in completely. Add the salt and pepper.

6. Right before serving, divide the lump crabmeat among 6–8 bowls and ladle in the hot soup. Sprinkle on a little cayenne and serve. SERVES SIX TO EIGHT.

# Oyster and Artichoke Soup

*The idea of making a soup from oysters and artichokes belongs to chef Warren Leruth, who may not have discovered how well the two things go together, but who surely made the most of it. Leruth's original potage had no cream, and neither does this one.*

| | |
|---|---|
| 4 fresh artichokes | 2 bay leaves |
| 1 pint fresh, shucked oysters | 1 tsp. salt, plus more to taste |
| 1 quart oyster liquor (if available) | ¼ tsp. freshly ground black pepper |
| 1 lemon, quartered | ½ stick (4 Tbsp.) butter |
| 1 small onion, sliced | 2 Tbsp. flour |
| 2 sprigs fresh thyme | ½ tsp. Tabasco |

1. Trim off the thorny tips from the artichoke leaves. Remove all of the bruised leaves. Cut the artichokes in half and wash well. Drain the oysters over a bowl to catch the oyster liquor. Rinse the oysters and set aside. Measure the oyster liquor and pour into a saucepan. Add enough water or additional oyster liquor, if available, to make a total of 6 cups liquid. Add the artichokes, lemon, onion, thyme, bay leaves, salt, and pepper. Simmer until the artichokes are tender, about 40 minutes.

2. Lift the artichokes from the pot and set aside to cool. Strain the cooking liquid into a clean, small saucepan, discarding solids, and bring to a simmer. Meanwhile, separate all of the leaves from the artichokes. Using a spoon, scrape the meat from the leaves, transfer to a food processor or blender (discard leaves), puree until smooth, and set aside. Remove the choke and dice the hearts; set aside separately.

3. Make a blond roux by melting the butter in a saucepan over medium-high heat. Add the flour and cook, stirring constantly, until the roux just barely begins to brown. Whisk the roux into the simmering liquid and return to a boil. Add the pureed artichokes and boil for 10 minutes.

4. Set aside 12 of the biggest, best-looking oysters. Chop the remaining oysters.

5. Strain the soup through a fine sieve into a clean pot. Add the chopped oysters, the diced artichoke hearts, salt to taste, and Tabasco. Heat to a simmer, then add the whole oysters. Simmer 2 minutes more. Put 2 oysters into each of 6 soup bowls and ladle in the broth. SERVES SIX.

# Old-Style Oyster Stew

*This is the oyster stew that was once common in the casual seafood restaurants of New Orleans, especially around West End. Like West End itself—which was totally destroyed by Hurricane Katrina—this dish is little more than a memory. But it's a very good memory, and one that's easily revived in a home kitchen.*

1 stick (8 Tbsp.) butter
1 small yellow onion, chopped
2 Tbsp. chopped celery
4 cups oyster liquor, strained well
2 cups half-and-half
¼ tsp. black peppercorns
1 sprig fresh thyme (or ¼ tsp. dried)
3 dozen fresh, shucked oysters
4 green onions, chopped
Salt to taste

1. Melt the butter in a large saucepan. Add the onion and celery, and sauté until tender.

2. Add the oyster liquor, half-and-half, peppercorns, and thyme. Bring to a very light simmer and cook slowly for 15 minutes.

3. Add the oysters and green onions, and cook until the oysters are plumped up and the edges are curly, 3–5 minutes. Add salt to taste. (You may not need any salt, depending on the saltiness of the oysters and oyster liquor.) SERVES FOUR.

# Mirliton and Shrimp Soup

*Mirliton (pronounced in New Orleans with a slight French accent, MILL-ee-tahn) is the local name for the vegetable also known as a chayote or vegetable pear. They are much liked around town and used in many different ways. This is one of the most interesting: a great light soup that Le Parvenu's chef Dennis Hutley—who dreamed it up—describes as "cappuccino style." By that he means a thin layer of nonsweet whipped cream floats on top.*

2 medium mirlitons (chayotes)
1 lb. medium shrimp, with heads
1 bay leaf
¼ cup (2 Tbsp.) butter
¼ cup flour
¼ cup diced carrots
¼ cup thinly sliced leeks
2 Tbsp. diced celery

2 Tbsp. diced yellow onion
4½ tsp. chopped garlic
½ cup sweet white wine (German Riesling, sweet Chenin Blanc)
½ tsp. liquid crab boil
1 cup heavy whipping cream, warm
¾ tsp. salt
¼ tsp. ground white pepper

1. Peel the mirlitons and the shrimp. Put the mirliton trimmings, shrimp shells and heads, and bay leaf into a small saucepan with 2 cups of water. Bring the mixture to a light boil, reduce the heat, and simmer the stock for 20–30 minutes, during which time you can do the next step.

2. Dice the mirlitons and set aside. Melt the butter in a large saucepan, add the flour, and cook, stirring constantly, until the mixture begins to just turn a light brown. Add all the vegetables except the mirlitons and cook over low heat until the vegetables are soft, about 5 minutes.

3. Stir the shrimp and mirlitons into the vegetables. Add the wine and bring to a boil for 2 minutes. Strain the stock from the shrimp shells into the saucepan with the shrimp and vegetables, and discard the stock solids. Add the crab boil and heavy cream, and simmer 30 minutes more. Season with the salt and pepper and serve. SERVES FOUR.

# Lobster Bisque

*I offer this more-or-less classic recipe for lobster bisque for two reasons. First, because I like it. Second, to offer a contrast with crawfish bisque, which could not be more different, even though for all the world, crawfish look like small lobsters.*

*Lobster bisque is essentially a dish made from leftover lobsters. Use the tail meat for an appetizer or entrée and save everything else for this. The amount of flavor you can get from those shells is astonishing.*

½ cup vegetable oil  
Shells and claws from four  
   1–2-lb. lobsters  
⅓ cup brandy  
2 large tomatoes, peeled, seeded,  
   and finely chopped  
2 large carrots, coarsely chopped  
2 ribs celery, coarsely chopped  
1 medium onion, coarsely chopped  
1 Tbsp. chopped garlic  

1 tsp. crushed red pepper  
2 cups dry white wine  
3 bay leaves  
½ tsp. dried tarragon  
1 Tbsp. salt, plus more to taste  
¼ tsp. ground white pepper,  
   plus more to taste  
½ cup cooked long-grain rice  
¼ tsp. cayenne  
2 cups heavy whipping cream  

1. Heat the oil in a large saucepan over high heat. Remove the meat from the claws and reserve. Add the shells to the hot oil and sauté until the edges begin to turn dark brown. Pour off the excess oil.

2. Remove the pot from the heat and very carefully add the brandy. (You can flame it if you like, but be careful.) Return the pot to the heat and cook, tossing around, until the alcohol in the brandy evaporates.

3. Add the tomatoes, carrots, celery, onion, and garlic, and continue to cook over high heat, stirring often, until the vegetables are tender. Add the crushed red pepper and white wine, and bring to a boil.

4. Add the bay leaves, tarragon, salt, pepper, and 8 cups of cold water. Bring to a boil, reduce heat to low, and simmer for 1 hour.

*(continued)*

5. Put the rice into a food processor or blender, add ½ cup of the lobster stock, and puree until smooth. Add the puree to the stock and continue to simmer for 30 minutes more.

6. Strain the soup base through a colander. Puree the solids in a food processor with a little stock and strain this once again into the soup base.

7. Add the cream to the soup base and return to a simmer. Adjust seasonings with salt, pepper, and the cayenne. I think this soup's flavor should have a noticeable pepper glow.

8. Divide the reserved claw meat among 4–6 soup plates. Ladle the soup over the claw meat. SERVES FOUR TO SIX.

# Turtle Soup

*New Orleans–style turtle soup is as unique to our cuisine as gumbo. Unlike the clear turtle soup eaten in most other places, Creole turtle soup is thick and almost a stew. The most widely served style of turtle soup in the area is descended from the one served at Commander's Palace, which is distinctive in that it uses as much veal shoulder as turtle and includes spinach as an ingredient.*

*My recipe is influenced by that old style, as well as by the incomparable (and quite different) version at Brennan's. The hardest part of any turtle soup recipe is finding turtle meat; if you can't, using veal shoulder turns out a very credible mock-turtle soup.*

*It is traditional to serve turtle soup with sherry at the table, but I've never liked the resulting alcoholic taste and aroma. I add the sherry into the recipe early to get the flavor but not the bitter alcohol.*

3 lb. turtle meat or veal shoulder
   or a combination of the two,
   including any bones available

3 bay leaves

3 whole cloves

Peel of 1 lemon, sliced

1 Tbsp. salt, plus more to taste

½ tsp. black peppercorns

2 sticks (16 Tbsp.) butter

⅔ cup flour

2 ribs celery, chopped

2 medium yellow onions, chopped

1 small green bell pepper, chopped

2 cloves garlic, finely chopped

½ tsp. dried thyme

½ tsp. dried marjoram

1 cup tomato puree

1 cup dry sherry

2 Tbsp. Worcestershire sauce

1 Tbsp. Louisiana hot sauce,
   such as Crystal

1 tsp. freshly ground black pepper,
   plus more to taste

2 hard-boiled eggs, chopped

1 bunch of flat-leaf parsley,
   leaves only, chopped

Half a 10-oz. bag of spinach,
   well washed and chopped

*(continued)*

1. Put the turtle meat and/or veal with bones into a large pot. Add the bay leaves, cloves, lemon peel, salt, peppercorns, and 1 gallon (16 cups) water. Bring to a boil, reduce heat, and simmer very slowly for about 2 hours.

2. Strain the stock, reserving the liquid and the meat. If you don't have at least 3 quarts of stock, add water or veal stock to get up to that quantity. Chop the meat into small pieces and set aside.

3. Make a medium-dark roux by melting the butter in a large saucepan. Add the flour and cook, stirring constantly, until the mixture turns the color of a well-used penny. When the roux is the right color, add the celery, onions, bell pepper, and garlic, and cook until the vegetables are soft. Add the thyme, marjoram, tomato puree, sherry, and Worcestershire sauce, and bring to a boil.

4. Add the hot sauce, pepper, and diced meat, and simmer for 30 minutes. Add the eggs, parsley, and spinach, and simmer 10 minutes more. Adjust the seasonings with salt and pepper and serve. SERVES SIX TO EIGHT.

# Red Bean Soup

*I've been predicting for years that our allegiance to red beans would result in its being served widely as a soup instead of a main course. This has not come to pass. But I love a good red bean soup. I always order it when it's on the menu. And when it isn't, I make it myself.*

2 Tbsp. olive oil
1 cup thinly sliced carrots
1 cup finely chopped celery
½ cup chopped yellow onion
1 tsp. dried summer savory
½ cup brandy
4 cups beef broth
6 cups cooked red beans (or 3 cans Blue Runner red beans if you're rushed)
¾ lb. andouille (see page 326) or other smoked sausage,
   very thinly sliced
½ tsp. salt
Freshly ground black pepper to taste
1 Tbsp. Louisiana hot sauce, such as Crystal
2 green onions, chopped, for garnish

1. Heat the oil in a large saucepan over medium heat until it ripples. Add the carrots, celery, onion, and savory, and cook until the vegetables are tender. Add the brandy and bring it to a boil for about a minute. Add the beef broth and bring to a simmer.

2. Meanwhile, puree the red beans in a food processor. Stir the puree into the pan with the vegetables and return to a simmer.

3. Microwave the andouille on paper towels for 1 minute on high to remove the excess fat. Add the andouille to the soup and cook for at least 10 minutes more.

4. Season with the salt, pepper, and hot sauce. Serve the soup garnished with the green onions. SERVES SIX TO EIGHT.

# White Bean Soup with Ham

*My wife and I are both nuts for white beans in any form, but I'm especially partial to a light, peppery soup made with them and an inexpensive shank or bottom part of a smoked ham.*

STOCK

3–4-lb. ham shank or smoked
    pork shoulder
1 medium onion, coarsely chopped
Stems from 1 bunch of
    flat-leaf parsley
1 bay leaf
8 black peppercorns
¼ tsp. dried thyme
¼ tsp. dried marjoram

SOUP

2 Tbsp. olive oil
2 ribs celery, chopped
1 medium onion, chopped
2 cloves garlic, chopped
1 lb. white beans (navy beans),
    sorted and soaked overnight
½ tsp. Worcestershire sauce
1 tsp. salt
½ tsp. Tabasco Green Pepper Sauce
2 green onions, thinly sliced,
    for garnish

1. Put all the stock ingredients into a stockpot with 20 cups of water. Bring to a boil, reduce heat, and simmer, uncovered, for 2–3 hours, or until the ham comes easily off the bone.

2. Remove the ham from the pot. Strain the stock and discard the solids. Pick the ham from the bone and set aside.

3. Rinse the stockpot and wipe dry. Return the pot to medium-high heat and add the oil. Add the celery, onion, and garlic, and sauté until the onion browns slightly. Drain the beans and add to the pot, along with the Worcestershire sauce, salt, green pepper sauce, and a little less than 8 cups of the strained stock. Simmer, covered, until the beans are tender, about 2 hours.

4. Strain the soup. Puree the solids in a food processor, then add it back to the broth. Shred as much ham as you'd like in your soup and add it. Adjust seasonings. Garnish with green onions.

5. Reserve the rest of the ham and stock (you can reduce the stock to make it easier to store) for other purposes (jambalaya or pasta dishes, for example). SERVES EIGHT.

# Split-Pea Soup

*I loved my mother's split-pea soup as I was growing up, but when I tried to cook it, I couldn't get it right. Then I parted with tradition by leaving out the ham that's in every recipe and using a vegetable stock. This meatless, fatless soup turned out to be just what I remembered. (No surprise that my frugal mom made hers without meat.) The cilantro gives it a great fresh flavor, but if you don't like cilantro, use parsley. This soup is better the second day.*

**STOCK**

3–4 carrots, coarsely chopped

2 ribs celery, coarsely chopped

1 large onion or 1 large leek, coarsely chopped (if using the leek, wash it very well after pulling it apart)

Stems from a bunch of cilantro or flat-leaf parsley

3 cloves garlic, peeled and crushed

2 bay leaves

1 Tbsp. mixed peppercorns (black, red, white, and green)

1 tsp. dried thyme

1 tsp. dried marjoram

**SOUP**

1 lb. split peas, sorted through and soaked at least 4 hours or overnight

20 sprigs cilantro or flat-leaf parsley, leaves only, chopped

1 rib celery, sliced into narrow, short sticks

1 green onion, finely chopped

½ tsp. turmeric

Dash of Worcestershire sauce

1 Tbsp. salt, plus more to taste

½ tsp. freshly ground black pepper, plus more to taste

1 Tbsp. Tabasco Green Pepper Sauce, plus more to taste

1. Put all of the stock ingredients and 12 cups of water into a large stockpot. Bring to a boil, lower the heat, and simmer for about an hour. Strain the stock into a clean pot and discard the stock vegetables.

2. Drain the peas and add to the vegetable stock. Add all of the remaining soup ingredients. Bring to a boil, reduce the heat, and simmer, uncovered, for 2 hours.

3. Pass the soup through a food mill or push through a coarse sieve. You can also strain the soup and process the solid parts with a food processor, stopping short of a puree. Add the near-pureed peas to the soup. Adjust seasoning with salt, pepper, and green pepper sauce to taste. SERVES EIGHT.

# Eggplant and Tomato Soup

*Now and then and here and there, a soup of eggplant and tomato is the soup of the day. It's always so good—no matter who cooked it—that it must be one of those ideal flavor combinations. Here's my take on it.*

⅓ cup extra-virgin olive oil
3 cloves garlic, crushed
¼ tsp. crushed red pepper
1 large eggplant, peeled and cut into large dice
2 sprigs fresh thyme, leaves chopped
4 leaves fresh rosemary (only 4 leaves!)
Three 28-oz. cans whole plum tomatoes, crushed by hand, juice reserved
1 tsp. lemon juice
1½ tsp. salt

1. Heat the oil in a large saucepan over high heat. When the oil shimmers, add the garlic and crushed red pepper, and cook until the garlic is browned at the edges. Remove and discard the garlic. Add the eggplant, cooking until it's browned on the edges.

2. Reduce the heat to medium-low and add the thyme, rosemary, tomatoes, and 1½ cups of the reserved tomato juice. Bring to a boil, reduce the heat, and simmer, uncovered and stirring occasionally, for 45 minutes.

3. Roughly puree the soup in a food processor, leaving small chunks of eggplant. Return to the saucepan. Add the lemon juice and salt, and bring to just a boil. Add a little water or chicken stock, if necessary, to lighten the texture. SERVES SIX TO EIGHT.

# Pumpkin Soup with Tasso

*Every October people begin asking me what they can cook with all those beautiful and inexpensive pumpkins out there. Jack-o'-lantern pumpkins are wrong for pie, but they do make interesting savory dishes. This rich soup gets a bit of spice and smokiness from the tasso— Cajun-style cured ham. (Buy the very dry, crusty, peppery kind.)*

1 medium–large pumpkin, 5–7 lb.
2 Tbsp. butter
2 medium yellow onions, chopped
3 Tbsp. bourbon
1 tsp. dried marjoram
½ tsp. Tabasco Garlic Pepper Sauce, plus more to taste

4 cups chicken or vegetable stock (see recipe, page 312)
4 oz. tasso (see page 326) or other smoked ham, finely chopped
2 cups heavy whipping cream
Salt to taste
1 green onion, green part only, chopped, for garnish

1. Cut a round hole about 5 inches in diameter in the top of the pumpkin. Scrape out the seeds and juicy membranes and discard. Then scrape out the flesh of the pumpkin, leaving about a 1-inch-thick shell if you plan to use it as a soup tureen.

2. Chop the pumpkin flesh roughly in a food processor. Measure out 4–5 cups' worth, saving the rest for another use.

3. Melt the butter in a large saucepan over medium heat. Add the onions and sauté until soft. Add the bourbon and bring to a boil. (Careful—it might catch fire if a flame touches it. This is not undesirable, but use caution.) Add the pumpkin, marjoram, garlic pepper sauce, and stock. Bring to a boil, reduce heat, and simmer until the pumpkin is very tender, about 30 minutes.

4. Puree the saucepan contents in a food processor (in batches, of course). Strain through a coarse-mesh strainer back into the rinsed saucepan. Add the tasso and cream, stir, and return to just below a simmer. Cook for about 10 minutes more, then add the salt and more garlic pepper sauce to taste, and a little water to thin out the soup if necessary. (Note: Tasso is salty and peppery, so taste before seasoning.)

5. Serve the soup out of the pumpkin shell if you like. Garnish with green onion. SERVES EIGHT.

# Soup of Seven Onions and Seven Peppers

*This is a classic French onion soup, with a spicy twist. Try really hard to find the oxtails to make it. They're not essential, but they give the soup an ideal mouthfeel and flavor. Include a mix of hot peppers (e.g., Serrano, jalapeño, cayenne, cascabel) and mild (red and green bell, wax, poblano). And make sure you remember which seven onions and seven peppers you use, because someone will want to know.*

3 lb. oxtails or meaty beef soup bones
3 bay leaves
1 tsp. dried marjoram
¼ cup olive oil
1 each large yellow, red, and white onion, thinly sliced
1 bunch of green onions, finely chopped
1 leek, cut open, well cleaned, and thinly sliced

Enough of 7 varieties of peppers to yield 1½ cups when seeded and thinly sliced
4 cloves garlic, chopped
½ cup tawny port or sherry
Salt to taste
4 Tbsp. chopped chives, for garnish
2 cups shredded Gruyère cheese, for garnish

1. Heat a large soup pot over high heat. Add the oxtails or beef bones and brown until rather dark. Add the bay leaves, marjoram, and 1 gallon (16 cups) of water. Bring to a boil, lower the heat, and simmer for 2 hours (or longer if possible). Strain the stock and set aside, discarding the solids. (You can do this a day or two ahead and refrigerate the stock, which will congeal.)

2. Heat the oil in a large, heavy pot over medium-high heat until it shimmers. Add all the yellow, red, and white onions, green onions, and sliced leek, and cook, stirring occasionally, until the onions have browned rather darkly. This will take as long as 30 minutes but is essential to getting the sweetness of the onions. Then add the peppers and garlic.

3. Add the port or sherry and cook until most of the liquid is gone. Add the reserved beef stock and boil for about 30 minutes. Season to taste with salt. Serve the soup garnished with snipped chives and shredded cheese. SERVES EIGHT.

# Cream of Garlic Soup

*Susan Spicer, the chef-owner of Bayona, has been a friend since before she became a chef. She has one of the surest senses of taste I've ever encountered. This soup has been on all her menus since her earliest restaurant days and with good reason: It's irresistible and not all that hard to make. For a great garnish, fry a few morsels of garlic in butter and float them on the soup.*

2 Tbsp. butter

2 Tbsp. olive oil

2 lb. onions, peeled and roughly chopped (about 4 cups)

2 cups garlic cloves, peeled and chopped

6 cups chicken stock (see recipe, page 312)

1 bouquet garni (parsley stems, thyme sprigs, and bay leaf tied together
   with kitchen twine)

2 cups stale French bread, cut into ½-inch cubes

1 cup half-and-half

Salt and ground white pepper to taste

1. Heat the butter and oil together in a 1-gallon, heavy-bottomed pot over medium heat. Add the onions and garlic, and cook, stirring frequently, until they turn a deep golden brown, about 30 minutes.

2. Add the chicken stock and bouquet garni, and bring to a boil. Stir in bread cubes and simmer 10 minutes, until the bread is soft.

3. Remove the bouquet garni and puree the soup in a blender, carefully. Strain it back into the saucepan. Add the half-and-half and season to taste with salt and pepper. Add a little water or chicken stock if soup is too thick. Bring to just a boil and serve. SERVES SIX TO EIGHT.

# Guacamole Soup

*I came up with this one for a midsummer dinner party in very warm weather. I was think-ing about a cold gazpacho, but while shopping, I saw some nice avocados and thought, Why not? This is more than just watery guacamole. You need to puree the avocado, which you shouldn't for guacamole. Also, although you want to serve the soup cold, chilling avocados for any length of time causes them to turn very dark. So you must make the soup right before serving. And while I won't even try to make guacamole without Hass avocados, this soup works well with even the big, shiny Florida avocados—as long as they're completely ripe.*

3 tomatillos, husks removed
1 medium sweet onion, chopped
10 sprigs cilantro, leaves chopped
¼ cup lime juice
2 Tbsp. olive oil
2 small cloves garlic
3 large ripe tomatoes, skinned and
    seeded (depending on size)
1 tsp. salt, plus more to taste
2 Tbsp. Tabasco Green Pepper Sauce,
    plus more to taste

5 medium Hass avocados
    (or 3 Florida avocados), fully ripe
2 cups light chicken stock (see recipe,
    page 312) or water

GARNISH
Sour cream
Chopped red onion
Chopped cilantro leaves
Chopped fresh tomato

1. Microwave the tomatillos on 70 percent power for 4 minutes. Let them cool, then peel them and cut into quarters. Remove the seeds and chop.

2. In a non-metallic bowl, combine the tomatillos with all the other ingredients except the avocados and chicken stock. Then scoop the meat out of the avocados and add it to the mix. Stir.

3. Working in batches, process the mix in a food processor to a rough puree.

4. Whisk in the chicken stock (or water). Adjust the seasonings with salt and green pepper sauce.

5. Place a piece of plastic wrap over the surface of the soup and refrigerate for no more than an hour. Serve in chilled bowls. Garnish with sour cream, red onion, cilantro, and tomato. SERVES EIGHT.

# Red Pepper Vichyssoise

*Despite the French name, vichyssoise was invented in America at a New York French restaurant. Another surprise (to me, anyway): All the versions of vichyssoise I've ever loved had ham in the recipe, although not visibly in the soup.*

*Classic vichyssoise is a cold leek-and-potato soup. But we don't always have to do the classics. The late chef Tom Cowman used to do variations with watercress, bell peppers, and other colorful infusions when he was at Restaurant Jonathan and, later, the Upperline. That is the inspiration for this recipe.*

2 lb. white potatoes, peeled and cubed
½ red bell pepper, stemmed, seeded, and chopped
1 leek, white part only, washed well and chopped
4 cups vegetable stock (see recipe, page 312)
⅓ cup finely chopped ham
2 cups half-and-half, hot
¼ cup sour cream
Snipped chives, for garnish

1. Prepare the vegetables carefully. Leave no peel or spots on the potatoes, seeds or membranes in the pepper, or dirt in the leeks.

2. In a large stockpot, bring the stock to a light boil. Add the vegetables and the ham, and cook until the potatoes are soft, about 25 minutes.

3. Puree the stock and vegetables in a food processor. Strain the mixture through a sieve or food mill and return to the pot. Add the hot half-and-half and the sour cream, and stir until well mixed. Refrigerate until cold. Serve chilled, garnished with chives. SERVES FOUR TO SIX.

# Brisket and Vegetable Soup

*I love homemade vegetable soup. My mother used to make this from time to time, and it was never often enough. I rediscovered this style of vegetable soup when I started going to old places like Tujague's, Galatoire's, and Maylie's, where they used the stock from boiling briskets to make the soup.*

*What gives this soup a great edge is boiling all the vegetables except the carrots (which lend a nice color to the soup) separately, not in the soup itself. That way, when you add them right before serving, they're all vivid and firm and full of flavor.*

1½ gallons brisket stock (see Boiled Brisket of Beef, page 160)

One 28-oz. can whole tomatoes, crushed by hand, with juice

1–2-lb. boiled brisket (optional)

1 small cabbage, cored and coarsely chopped

1 large yellow onion, coarsely chopped

1 turnip, peeled and cut into ½-inch cubes

2 lb. carrots, cut into ½-inch-thick slices

2 lb. red potatoes, peeled and cut into ½-inch cubes

1 lb. fresh green beans, trimmed and cut into 1-inch pieces

4 ribs celery, cut into 3-inch-long, narrow sticks

2 ears corn, kernels shaved off the cobs

½ tsp. dried basil

¼ tsp. dried thyme

2 Tbsp. salt, plus more to taste

Freshly ground black pepper to taste

½ tsp. Tabasco, plus more to taste

1. Put the brisket stock, crushed tomatoes, and juice into a kettle or stockpot. Bring to a boil. Meanwhile, cut the brisket (if using) into large cubes, removing any interior fat. Add the meat to the stock. Reduce the heat and simmer.

2. Bring a separate stockpot three-quarters full of water to a light boil. As you cut the vegetables in the order given in the ingredients list, add them to the pot. (Some vegetables take longer to cook than others.)

3. When the carrots and potatoes have lost all crispness, drain the vegetables and add them to the brisket stock, along with the basil and thyme. Lower the heat to a simmer and cook for at least 30 minutes. Adjust seasonings with salt, pepper, and Tabasco. SERVES ABOUT EIGHT, WITH LOTS OF LEFTOVER SOUP FOR THE NEXT DAY.

# Petite Marmite

*A marmite is a covered crock, usually made of earthenware, designed to hold a soup or a stew that will be baked. Petite marmite has come to mean an intense, clear soup based on a consomme, with beef and vegetables. The best of these has an amazing flavor, especially when infused with a good shot of black pepper. I love this version. It's no small project to make it. (In fact, cooking schools give this to chefs as a test of their skills.) But the results are wonderful, and you will have really accomplished something elegant and special.*

STOCK

6 lb. oxtails
1 large onion, coarsely chopped
2 ribs celery, coarsely chopped
1 carrot, coarsely chopped
1 bay leaf
¼ tsp. dried thyme
¼ tsp. dried marjoram
1 tsp. black peppercorns

CONSOMME

1 lb. ground round, chilled
1 medium carrot, chopped
1 rib celery, chopped
1 small onion, chopped
2 egg whites
4 eggshells, well crushed
1½ tsp. salt
¼ tsp. Tabasco

SOUP

Green onions or chives to tie beef bundles
4 small carrots, cut into thin sticks
4 small potatoes, cut into ½-inch dice
2 ribs celery, cut into thin sticks
Salt and freshly ground black pepper to taste

*(continued)*

1. To make the stock: Brown the oxtails in a large kettle over high heat until rather dark. Add the onion, celery, carrot, bay leaf, thyme, marjoram, and peppercorns, along with 1 gallon (16 cups) of water (or more, if necessary, to cover). Bring the pot to a low boil. Cook for 2 hours (or longer, if possible). Skim the fat and foam that rises to the surface as the stock cooks.

2. Strain the stock. Remove the oxtails and reserve. Discard the vegetables. Set the strained stock aside to cool. (You can do this a day or two ahead and refrigerate the stock. It should congeal into a jelly, so any remaining fat can be easily removed from the surface.)

3. To make the consomme: Return the strained stock to a clean pot and heat over medium heat. Meanwhile, combine the ground round, carrot, celery, and onion in a bowl. Flatten the mixture out into a sort of gigantic hamburger patty. Float this on top of the stock—this is called a raft, and its purpose is to clarify the stock. (It might sink, but the boiling will make it rise.) Pour the egg whites over this raft and break the eggshells on top of that.

4. When the pot comes barely to a boil, punch a few holes in the raft so that the stock bubbles up and over the raft. Keep the stock at a very light boil for about 2 hours, gently submerging the raft every now and then. Add the salt and Tabasco.

5. Meanwhile, pick the lean meat from the oxtails and make small bundles of it, tying them with a thin green onion or a chive. Set aside.

6. Remove the raft and anything else floating in the stock, which should now be clear or close to it. Carefully skim the fat from the top of the pot. Strain the soup through a very fine sieve or (better) double cheesecloth.

7. About 30 minutes before serving, bring the consomme to a simmer. Add the carrots and potatoes, and cook until tender. Ten minutes after adding the carrots and potatoes, add the celery. Season to taste with salt and pepper.

8. Place a bundle or two of the oxtail meat on a soup plate and ladle in the broth with its vegetables around it. SERVES EIGHT TO TWELVE.

# ſhellfiſh Entrées

**A**lthough the Gulf and lake waters are full of first-class finfish, when someone from South Louisiana thinks of seafood, he's probably thinking of a crustacean or a mollusk. The crawfish really should be on the official seal of the state of Louisiana.

It's hard to imagine Creole cooking without crabs, shrimp, oysters, and crawfish. They're all used in both starring and supporting roles in all kinds of dishes. Featured in this chapter are recipes in which our best local shellfish (along with a few exotic ones) are the centerpieces.

But first get to know these delicacies a little better.

# Shrimp

Few foods inspire more culinary creativity than shrimp. You can cook shrimp just about any way you can think of, and thousands of ways have yet to be invented.

Louisiana shrimp are the standard of the world. They are caught in tremendous numbers from several species, with seasons so complicated that only fishermen seem to know exactly when they come and go. Anyway, shrimp stand up to freezing better than any other seafood, so they're available almost all the time. (If you buy them frozen, thaw them in the refrigerator as slowly as possible.)

The two most common varieties are the brown shrimp and the white shrimp. The argument as to which is the better has been going on for a long time. I say they're both spectacular and just leave it at that.

Shrimp come in sizes from tiny (60 or more to the pound) to real monsters (3–4 to the pound). The size is usually specified by the "count": 16–20 count means 16 to 20 to the pound. I always buy shrimp whole, with the heads on; the flavor is much better, and it gives you shrimp shells for making stock for gumbo and all sorts of other dishes.

Shrimp cook very rapidly. When they overcook, the shrimp can stick to the shells or get mushy. Another problem that occasionally turns up with shrimp is a strong flavor of iodine. This is usually blamed on a lack of freshness, but in fact, it's due to the shrimp's diet. When acorn worm—which concentrates iodine in its tissues—is around in large numbers, the shrimp that eat them pick up the iodine flavor. It's objectionable but harmless.

# Crabs

Adding a sprinkling of lump crabmeat to a dish that needs just a little something is a favorite trick of New Orleans chefs. But that's a cliché and a waste of good crabmeat. The best crabmeat dishes employ the biggest lumps with the lightest of sauces. The flavor of the local blue crab is so distinguished that it needs no help. And it's so subtle that it's easy for a sauce to get in the way.

Louisiana crabs are the same species found throughout the Gulf and up the Atlantic seaboard. All forms of blue crabs are best and least expensive in the warm months. Crabmeat is always available, but its price skyrockets in the winter.

Picked crabmeat comes already cooked in containers of a half-pound to a pound. Pasteurized crabmeat has largely supplanted the superior fresh crabmeat, and crabmeat from Southeast Asia has become common. Read labels carefully before buying.

When you add picked crabmeat to a dish, you only need to warm it through. So add it last to the pan. Here are the most common forms of Louisiana crabmeat:

JUMBO LUMP (ALSO KNOWN AS BACKFIN). This is the big lump of meat from just below the point where the claws are attached. There's a little sliver of thin shell in there that's almost impossible to remove without breaking the lump. Restaurants buy almost all the jumbo lump in the market, at the highest prices. But it can usually be found in season in the better grocery stores and markets.

LUMP. This is from the same part of the crab as the jumbo lump but from smaller crabs or perhaps broken jumbo lumps.

WHITE. The white meat from inside the crab, but in large flakes and shreds instead of lumps. The flavor is not bad, but the look isn't as good, and the quality is inconsistent. It's best for soups and sauces.

CLAW. The big lump of meat from inside the claws actually has the most pronounced flavor in the crab. It doesn't look as good—the meat is darker and stringy. It's the cheapest variety of crabmeat but perfectly fine for stuffings.

WHOLE BOILED HARD CRABS. This form may be the ultimate way to eat crabmeat because all of the above is packed securely within that shell. At the peak of the season, they can't be beat—even though the work expended in opening and picking the crabs is not replaced by the calories in the crabmeat.

And then there's the miracle of . . .

# Soft-Shell Crabs

Soft-shells are almost absurdly delectable. During the warm months, particularly in late spring, the blue crabs that live around New Orleans shed their old hard shells. For a brief time afterward, they can be eaten almost whole. The process is closely monitored by crab farmers, who know when the crabs are about to molt. They remove the crabs from the water as soon as that happens, before the new shell stiffens.

A crab grows so much in the minutes after it sheds that it seems impossible that it ever could have fit in the old shell. If the crab is taken before it sheds and pumps up, and the shell is removed by hand, the meat is richer and more intense. That's what is done to "buster" crabs, which usually lose their legs and claws in the process.

Crabs get better as they get bigger. A gigantic soft-shell crab (known as a "whale" in the trade) contains massive jumbo lumps. I'd prefer one whale to two smaller crabs, even if the two weighed more.

Without a doubt, the best way to cook soft-shell crabs is to fry them. You might marinate or smoke a crab before and sauce it after, but if you do anything but fry it in between, you'll wish you hadn't. You can make the crab look really good by just dipping its legs in the hot oil for a few seconds before putting the rest of the crab in.

# Oysters

Oysters are, to my palate, the finest of local seafood. Gulf oysters are among the best in the world, available in tremendous quantity at very low prices throughout most of the year. Creole cooks have dreamed up hundreds of ways to prepare them.

For all that culinary exploration, connoisseurs agree that oysters are at their best cold and raw on the half shell. The health risk you're constantly told about actually affects only a small number of people. Even for those who are advised to stay away from raw seafood, properly cooked oysters are quite safe to eat.

Oysters are somewhat seasonal. Although refrigeration has largely eliminated the risk of eating oysters in months without an "R," there is a grain of truth to the old myth. In early summer, oysters change sex (!) and spawn, resulting in a harmless but off-putting milky liquid in the shell. In early fall, oysters are lean and can shrink a lot when cooked.

In New Orleans, wholesale and retail oyster houses shuck and package fresh oysters in pints, quarts, and gallons on a daily basis. The freshest and best oysters are those you shuck yourself, since the oyster is still alive until you open it. But shucking oysters is hard and borderline dangerous work. I have a short list of friends who have the knack; I invite them to all our oyster dinners and keep them well supplied with beer or wine as they perform their unenviable task (which they seem to like, for some reason).

One rule applies to all oyster dishes: Don't overcook them! When the edges get curly and the oyster plumps up, it's cooked. Get it out of the pot or pan!

One other thing. Never, ever just throw away the liquor in which oysters are packed. Strain it and add it to whatever you're cooking for another burst of flavor.

# Crawfish

People who don't eat crawfish call them "crayfish" or "crawdads," two other names for these small, lobsterlike crustaceans. The crawfish season begins around Thanksgiving in a good year, reaches a peak in April and May, and tapers off around the Fourth of July. Crawfish tail meat is available most of the year, but outside the season, it's usually the much inferior imported product. I recommend eating crawfish only in season

In recent years, the popularity of Cajun cooking has brought about a large increase in the annual consumption of crawfish in America. Crawfish tail meat is usually available in one-pound frozen packages. In gourmet stores, you can sometimes even find live or boiled whole crawfish, much of which comes from China. I would strongly recommend looking for the Louisiana crawfish, which has more fat.

The peak revelry involving crawfish is a crawfish boil. It happens only when crawfish are at peak. Mounds of the red mudbugs are piled on newspapers, and the eaters go through fantastic numbers of them with potatoes, corn, and beer.

Crawfish are the official food of Cajun country, where hundreds of dishes utilize them. The important issue is that crawfish have a rather mild taste and require a lot of help from the seasonings and sauces. That done, they're delicious.

# Barbecue Shrimp

*Barbecue shrimp, one of the four or five best dishes in all of New Orleans cooking, is completely misnamed. They're neither grilled nor smoked, and there's no barbecue sauce. The dish was created in the mid-1950s at Pascal's Manale Restaurant. A regular customer came in and reported that he'd enjoyed a dish in a Chicago restaurant that he thought was made with shrimp, butter, and pepper. He asked Pascal Radosta to duplicate it, and the result, said the customer, was not quite the same, but actually even better.*

*The dish is simple: huge whole shrimp in a tremendous amount of butter and black pepper. The essential ingredient is large, heads-on shrimp, since the fat in the shrimp heads provides most of the flavor. I know that the amount of butter and pepper in here is fantastic. But understand that this is not a dish you will eat often—although you will want to.*

3 lb. large (16–20 count) Gulf shrimp, with heads, preferably fresh
¼ cup dry white wine
1 Tbsp. lemon juice
2 tsp. Worcestershire sauce
2 cloves garlic, chopped
1 newly purchased 4-oz. jar ground black pepper
2 tsp. paprika
¼ tsp. salt
3 sticks (24 Tbsp.) butter, softened

1. Rinse the shrimp and shake off the excess water. Put them in a large skillet (or two) over medium heat, with the wine, lemon juice, Worcestershire sauce, and garlic. Bring to a light boil and cook, shaking the skillet, until the shrimp just turn pink.

2. Cover the shrimp with a thin but complete layer of black pepper. Be bold with this. Trust me, it's almost impossible to use too much pepper in this dish. Continue to cook another couple of minutes, then sprinkle on the paprika and salt.

3. Lower the heat to the minimum. Cut the butter into tablespoon-size pieces, and add three at a time to the skillet, swirling the butter over the heat as it melts. When the butter is completely melted, add another 3 pieces, continuing the process until all the butter is used. Keep shaking the skillet to make a creamy orange-hued sauce.

4. When all the butter is incorporated, place the shrimp and lots of the sauce in bowls and serve with hot French bread for dipping. (Don't forget to provide plenty of napkins and perhaps bibs.) SERVES FOUR TO SIX.

# Shrimp Clemenceau

*Clemenceau is the name of a classic Creole chicken dish. But if you take the same ingredients and substitute big shrimp for the chicken, you get a delicious dish that's very different from most other shrimp concoctions, with a great blending of flavors. It comes out best if you buy whole shrimp, peel them, and make a shrimp stock from the shells.*

Vegetable oil, for frying
2 large potatoes, peeled and cut into
   ½-inch dice
½ stick (4 Tbsp.) butter
32 medium (21–25 count) shrimp,
   peeled
½ tsp. crushed red pepper
¼ cup dry white wine
1 cup sliced fresh mushrooms

4 artichoke hearts, poached and cut
   into quarters (or use canned or
   jarred artichoke hearts, drained)
2 cloves garlic, chopped
1 cup shrimp stock (see recipe,
   page 312)
2 green onions, chopped
½ cup frozen petit pois peas
½ tsp. salt
¼ tsp. freshly ground black pepper

1. Pour the oil into a deep skillet to a depth of 1 inch. Heat until the temperature reaches 375 degrees. Fry the potatoes, in batches, until golden brown. Don't eat too many of them as you do.

2. Melt the butter in a large skillet over medium-high heat. Add the shrimp and crushed red pepper, and cook until the shrimp just turn pink. Remove the shrimp from the pan and set aside.

3. Add the wine and bring it to a boil. Add the mushrooms, artichoke hearts, garlic, and shrimp stock, and cook over medium-low heat, shaking the skillet to mix the ingredients. Reduce until the mixture is thick enough to coat the back of a spoon.

4. Add the green onions, peas, fried potatoes, salt, and pepper, and cook until everything is heated through. Adjust the seasonings and serve with hot French bread on the side. SERVES FOUR.

# Vol-au-Vent of Louisiana Seafood

*This is a delectable combination of fresh local shellfish in a rich, slightly spicy sauce. The vol-au-vent (a large version of what Orleanians call a patty shell) can be bought fresh from a French baker or frozen at supermarkets.*

2 Tbsp. olive oil
½ cup chopped green onion
1 Tbsp. chopped shallots
¼ cup dry white wine
2 cups heavy whipping cream
Pinch of saffron threads
½ tsp. salt
¼ tsp. ground white pepper
Pinch of cayenne

Pinch of ground ginger
1 lb. sea scallops
1 lb. large (16–20 count) shrimp,
  peeled and deveined
2 dozen fresh, shucked oysters
1½ tsp. fresh tarragon, chopped
  (or ½ tsp. dried)
6 large vol-au-vents
  (puff pastry shells)

1. Preheat the oven to 300 degrees. Heat the oil in a large skillet over medium heat. Add the green onion and shallots, and sauté until they're limp. Add the wine and bring it to a boil. Reduce until most of the liquid is gone. Add the cream, saffron, salt, pepper, cayenne, and ginger, and bring to a light boil. (Also add tarragon at this point if using dried.)

2. Add the scallops and shrimp, and cook for 4 minutes, then add the oysters and, if using, fresh tarragon. Cook until the edges of the oysters are curly, 3–5 minutes. Throughout the process, shake the pan to slosh the sauce over the seafood.

3. Bake the vol-au-vents until warmed through, about 2 minutes. Place the shells on individual plates and overfill each shell with seafood and sauce so that the mixture runs over the top and onto the plate. SERVES SIX.

# Soft-Shell Crab with Crabmeat Meunière

*Few dishes inspire the eye-popping anticipation that a large, golden brown soft-shell crab does. It's so intrinsically good that any fancy preparation diminishes it. The standard (and best) preparation is to dust the crab with seasoned flour and fry it. All it really needs in the way of a sauce is a little brown butter, and perhaps a topping of extra-jumbo lump crabmeat.*

4 large soft-shell crabs
Vegetable oil, for frying
1 tsp. salt
1 tsp. ground white pepper
2 cups flour
1 cup milk

1 whole egg
1 stick (8 Tbsp.) butter
1 Tbsp. lemon juice, freshly squeezed
½ tsp. Worcestershire sauce
½ lb. jumbo lump crabmeat

1. Rinse the crabs and shake off excess water. Using scissors, cut out the gills (the dead man's fingers) from under the shell and then cut off the eyes and mouthparts.

2. Pour the oil into a large, heavy kettle to a depth of ½ inch and heat to 375 degrees. Meanwhile, blend the salt and pepper into the flour in a wide bowl. Whisk the milk and eggs together in another bowl.

3. Lightly dredge the crabs in the flour mixture, then dip them into the egg mixture. Coat crabs again with the seasoned flour.

4. Place a crab, top shell side down, on the end of a long-handled cooking fork. (Do not skewer it.) Let the legs and claws dangle. Lower all but the body into the hot oil. Hold that position for about 15 seconds and then carefully flip the crab backward into the oil. Fry two at a time until golden brown and drain. (Let the heat of the oil recover before frying the next batch.)

5. Melt the butter in a small saucepan over low heat until it stops bubbling and the milk solids at the bottom just begin to brown. Carefully add the lemon juice and Worcestershire sauce—this will cause the butter to foam!—and cook until the foaming subsides. Add the crabmeat and sauté 30 seconds. Spoon the butter and crabmeat over the hot fried crabs. SERVES FOUR.

# Soft-Shell Crabs with Chinese Hot Garlic and Black Bean Sauce

*It surprises some Orleanians (who tend to think that all our favorite dishes originally came from our city) that crabs are also much enjoyed in Southeast Asian coastal cuisines, from Thailand to China, and throughout the Indonesian archipelago. And Southeast Asian cooks know what we know: that the crabs must be fried somewhere along the line. This is a spicy Chinese approach to the delectable beasts, with a sauce that doesn't overwhelm.*

4 large soft-shell crabs
1 egg, lightly beaten
2 Tbsp. cornstarch
1 tsp. chopped green onion
Pinch of freshly ground black pepper
½ cup vegetable oil
¼ cup soy sauce
1 Tbsp. rice wine vinegar

¼ cup dry white wine
1 Tbsp. sesame oil
4½ tsp. sugar
1 tsp. chopped garlic
¼ tsp. finely chopped fresh ginger
½ tsp. hot bean sauce
   (available at Asian markets)
¼ tsp. crushed red pepper flakes

1. Rinse the crabs and shake off excess water. Using a pair of scissors, cut off the eyes and mouthparts. Turn each crab on its back. Remove and discard the "apron"—the part of the shell in the rear. Carefully lift up the pointed ends of the bottom shell and remove the gills (the dead man's fingers) and the sand sac at the front. Push the shell back in place. Cut each crab in half, front to back.

2. Mix the egg, cornstarch, chopped green onion, and black pepper together in a wide bowl. Dip the crabs into the mixture to coat.

3. Heat the vegetable oil to almost smoking in a heavy skillet or wok over high heat. Fry the crab halves, two at a time, until crisp on the outside but still soft and moist inside. Remove from the pan, drain, and keep warm.

4. Pour out the oil from the pan but don't wipe. Add all the remaining ingredients and and boil, stirring, for about 1 minute.

5. Place 2 crab halves on each of 4 plates and spoon on the sauce. Serve immediately. SERVES FOUR.

# Crab Cakes

*Crab cakes are not native to New Orleans, but you would never know that to look at menus or recent local cookbooks. They moved in from Maryland in the early 1990s, replacing the good old stuffed crab and igniting the issue that rages wherever crab cakes are found: Which restaurant makes the best? Interestingly, every place claims its are self-evidently superior.*

*Most people will say that a great crab cake will contain as much jumbo lump crabmeat as possible while still sticking together as a cake. But clearly there should be other things in there, too. I like green onions, parsley, garlic, and red bell pepper. I use béchamel to hold the crabmeat together and a light dusting of bread crumbs so the things can be browned. Crab cakes should fall apart at the touch of a fork, not hold together like a hamburger.*

WHITE REMOULADE SAUCE
¼ cup mayonnaise
2 Tbsp. Creole mustard
1 Tbsp. lemon juice
1 tsp. Worcestershire sauce
Dash of Tabasco
¼ tsp. granulated garlic

CRAB CAKES
1 stick (8 Tbsp.) butter
½ cup flour
½ tsp. salt
¼ tsp. ground white pepper
1 cup warm milk
2 lb. lump crabmeat
⅓ cup finely chopped red bell pepper
2 green onions, thinly sliced
1 tsp. chopped fresh tarragon
   (or ½ tsp. dried)
½ cup plain bread crumbs
2 tsp. salt-free Creole seasoning
¼ cup clarified butter (see recipe,
   page 314)

1. To make the sauce: Mix all of the rémoulade ingredients in a bowl and set aside.

2. To make the crab cakes: Make a blond roux by melting the butter in a heavy saucepan over low heat. Add the flour, salt, and white pepper, and cook, stirring constantly, until the mixture just barely starts browning. Whisk in the warm milk until the blend has the texture of runny mashed potatoes. Cool to room temperature. (You've just made a béchamel.)

*(continued)*

3. Remove any shells from the crabmeat, trying to keep the lumps as whole as possible. In a large bowl, combine the crabmeat with the bell pepper, green onions, and tarragon. Add ¼ cup of the cooled béchamel and mix with your fingers, being careful not to break up the crabmeat.

4. Season the bread crumbs with Creole seasoning and spread the seasoned crumbs out on a plate. Use an ice-cream scoop to measure 12 balls of the crabmeat mixture. Gently form each into cakes about ¾ inch thick. Press them gently onto the bread crumbs on each side and shake off the excess.

5. Heat the clarified butter in a medium skillet. Sauté the crab cakes until they are golden brown on the outside and heated all the way through. (The way to test this is to push the tines of a kitchen fork into the center of the cake, then touch the fork to your lips. That will tell you whether the heat has penetrated all the way through.) Serve crab cakes with the rémoulade on the side. MAKES TWELVE LARGE CRAB CAKES.

# Crabmeat Imperial

*Crabmeat Imperial is an old local favorite that has fallen on hard times. It's as good as ever—about the only way one could dislike it would be to dislike crabmeat—but few restaurants serve it. I like the very simple way it's prepared at the Bon Ton Café, the city's oldest Cajun restaurant. The crabby flavor fairly explodes in your mouth. This is my variation on Bon Ton's recipe.*

6 Tbsp. butter
½ cup chopped green onion
¼ cup sliced mushrooms
1 lb. jumbo lump crabmeat
¼ of a roasted red bell pepper (pimiento), chopped
¼ cup dry sherry
4 slices toasted French bread
¼ cup chopped flat-leaf parsley, for garnish
Pinch of cayenne, for garnish

1. Preheat the broiler. Melt 3 tablespoons of the butter in a large skillet over medium-low heat. Add the green onion and mushrooms, and sauté until the green onion becomes limp but not brown.

2. Add the crabmeat, red bell pepper, and sherry, and turn the heat up a bit. Cook, shaking the skillet (don't stir), until the sherry is boiled away.

3. Melt the remaining 3 tablespoons of butter into the crabmeat mixture and pile it onto rounds of toasted French bread on ovenproof dishes. Run the plates under the broiler, about 5 inches from the heat, for 2–3 minutes, or until the crabmeat sizzles. Garnish with the parsley and cayenne. SERVES TWO TO FOUR.

# Crabmeat au Gratin

*As widely as this is thought to be true,* au gratin *does not mean covered with a thick layer of Day-Glo melted cheese. All it means is that there's some kind of crust on top. In this recipe, the crust is mostly bread crumbs, although there's some Parmesan cheese both in the crust and in the sauce. You will thank me for not ruining the taste of the crabmeat with melted Cheddar or the like.*

1 cup heavy whipping cream
½ medium yellow onion, chopped
4 large mushrooms, sliced
2 Tbsp. green onion tops, chopped
1 Tbsp. chopped fresh flat-leaf parsley
1 tsp. salt-free Creole seasoning
1 tsp. lemon juice
5 Tbsp. grated Parmesan cheese
1 lb. jumbo lump crabmeat
2 Tbsp. plain bread crumbs

1. Preheat the broiler. Heat the cream in a small saucepan and reduce by about a third. Add all of the vegetables and return to a boil. Stir in the Creole seasoning, lemon juice, and 3 tablespoons of the Parmesan. Add the crabmeat and toss in the pan to combine with the sauce. Be careful not to break up the lumps.

2. Divide the mixture into 4 ovenproof dishes for appetizers, 2 dishes for entrées. Combine the bread crumbs and remaining cheese together and sprinkle over the top of each dish. Broil until the sauce begins to bubble, 3–5 minutes. Serve immediately. SERVES FOUR AS AN APPETIZER OR TWO AS AN ENTREE.

# Fettuccine Pontchartrain

*I'm not sure who thought of it first, but the combination of Louisiana crabmeat lumps with fettuccine and an Alfredo-style sauce is inspired and irresistible. This recipe takes it a step further, with a soft-shell crab (or even better, a buster crab) on top.*

6 small soft-shell crabs
Vegetable oil, for frying
1 cup flour
1 tsp. salt
¼ tsp. ground white pepper
2 Tbsp. butter
⅓ cup chopped yellow onion
1 clove garlic, chopped

1 cup heavy whipping cream
¼ tsp. salt
⅛ tsp. cayenne
⅔ cup shredded Romano cheese
1 lb. white crabmeat
1 lb. (precooked weight) fettuccine,
   cooked al dente

1. Rinse the crabs and shake off any excess water. Using scissors, cut off the eyes and mouthparts. Turn each crab on its back. Remove and discard the "apron"—the part of the shell in the rear. Carefully lift up the pointed ends of the bottom shell and remove the gills (the dead man's fingers) and the sand sac at the front. Push the shell back in place.

2. Dry the crabs very well with paper towels. Heat about 1 inch of the oil in a deep skillet or saucepan to 375 degrees. Season the flour with salt and pepper in a wide bowl. Dredge the crabs in the seasoned flour. Drop the crabs in the oil two at a time and fry until golden brown. Drain on paper towels and keep warm until serving.

3. Melt the butter in large skillet and sauté the onion for 1 minute, then add the garlic and sauté until fragrant. Add the cream, salt, and cayenne, and reduce for 1–2 minutes. Add the Romano cheese, stirring until it melts into the cream. Add the crabmeat and cook for another minute, shaking the skillet to mix the ingredients. Remove the sauce from the heat.

4. Add the cooked, drained fettuccine and toss with the sauce. Divide among 6 plates and top each with a fried soft-shell crab. SERVES SIX.

# Pasta with Cajun Crawfish Cream Sauce

*This is the most famous and the best of the many Louisiana pasta-and-seafood dishes, with suaveness and rambunctiousness playing off each other. It gets its distinctive pink-orange color from Creole seasoning. I add a little Cognac at the beginning and a little tarragon at the end. If I have crawfish stock around, I add some of that, too.*

2 Tbsp. butter
½ cup finely chopped green onion, plus more for garnish
1 clove garlic, finely chopped
2 Tbsp. Cognac or brandy
½ cup crawfish stock (optional; see recipe, page 312)
2 cups heavy whipping cream
4½ tsp. salt-free Creole seasoning
1 tsp. salt
¾ tsp. fresh tarragon, chopped (or ¼ tsp. dried)
2 lb. crawfish tail meat
1 lb. bowtie or other pasta, cooked al dente and drained

1. Melt the butter in a large stainless steel skillet until it bubbles. Add the green onion and garlic, and cook until the garlic is fragrant. Add the Cognac. Warm it and either boil it off or flame it (very carefully). If you have crawfish stock, add it and bring the mixture to a boil. Reduce it by half.

2. Add the cream, Creole seasoning, salt, and tarragon, and bring to a boil while shaking the skillet carefully to blend its contents. Reduce the cream by about a third (approximately 3 minutes over medium-high heat). Then add the crawfish tails and cook until heated through.

3. Add the pasta and toss with the sauce to distribute all the ingredients and sauce uniformly. Serve immediately, garnished with finely chopped green onion. (Resist the temptation to add Parmesan or Romano cheese.) SERVES FOUR.

# Aline's Crawfish Etouffée

Etouffée *means "smothered," and that's the idea. It's not a long-cooked stew. My mother's version of this Cajun classic is important to me not only because it's very good, but also because of a poignant memory it always triggers. One afternoon in 1984, I brought Mama a big bag of boiled crawfish, and she made a pot of this étouffée. My father, 75 and ailing, ate a big plate of it. He remarked how good he thought it was, then went off for a nap. He never woke up. It is my fondest wish that I shuffle off this mortal coil the same way.*

*It's best to make this from whole boiled crawfish, so when you peel them, you can extract the fat from inside the head. (Your finger will do the trick.) That adds lots of flavor to the étouffée. One more thing: Crawfish tails are addictive, so bring home lots of them.*

½ cup vegetable oil
½ cup flour
½ stick (4 Tbsp.) butter
1 small yellow onion, chopped
2 green onions, greens only, chopped
½ red bell pepper, chopped
2 cloves garlic, chopped
1 ripe tomato, coarsely chopped
2 Tbsp. chopped celery
4 sprigs flat-leaf parsley

1 basil leaf
1 bay leaf
3 cups crawfish tail meat from
  boiled crawfish
Fat from crawfish heads
3–4 dashes of Tabasco
Salt and freshly ground black pepper
2 cups cooked long-grain rice
¼ cup very finely chopped green
  onion, for garnish

1. Make a medium-brown roux by heating the oil in a large saucepan over medium-high heat. Add the flour and cook, stirring constantly, until the mixture turns the color of a fallen leaf. Add the butter, allowing it time to melt and mix in.

2. Add the yellow onion and sauté until it's barely brown around the edges. Add the green onions, bell pepper, and garlic, and cook until tender. Add the tomato and 2 cups of water. Bring to a boil, then add the celery, parsley, basil leaf, and bay leaf. Simmer for 10 minutes.

3. Add the crawfish tails, crawfish fat, Tabasco, and salt and pepper to taste, and simmer for 10–12 minutes more. Remember as you add the salt and pepper that the boiled crawfish already have a good bit of both. Serve over rice, topped with finely chopped green onion for garnish. SERVES FOUR TO SIX.

# Oysters Ambrosia

*This was created at Commander's Palace by Sebastian "Chef Buster" Ambrosia, who might have the best name I've ever heard for a chef. For many years, Chef Buster hosted a cooking show on WWL Radio, where I work. He has served oysters Ambrosia in every restaurant he's headed, and it was always the best dish in that restaurant at the time. It's as Creole as something can be: seafood with a brown sauce. "It's good, hearts!" as Chef Buster would say.*

4 dozen fresh, shucked large oysters, with their liquor
2 Tbsp. salt-free Creole seasoning
2 sticks (16 Tbsp.) butter
3 cups flour
2 cups red wine
4 cups rich beef stock (see recipe, page 312)
6 bay leaves
1 Tbsp. chopped garlic
¼ cup Worcestershire sauce
1 tsp. Louisiana hot sauce, such as Crystal
Salt and freshly ground black pepper to taste
Vegetable oil, for frying
1 Tbsp. salt
2 green onions, chopped, for garnish
8 sprigs flat-leaf parsley, chopped, for garnish

1. Drain the oysters, reserving the liquor. Sprinkle the oysters with the Creole seasoning and toss around to coat. Put them in the refrigerator while making the sauce.

2. Make a medium-dark roux by melting the butter in a medium saucepan. Add 1 cup of the flour and cook, stirring constantly, until the mixture turns the color of an old penny. When the roux has reached the right color, add the wine and bring it to a boil, stirring for about 1 minute.

3. Add the beef stock, strained oyster liquor, bay leaves, and garlic, whisking to dissolve the bits of roux that will be floating around. Bring the sauce up to a simmer and let it cook and thicken for about 45 minutes.

4. Add the Worcestershire sauce and hot sauce, and season to taste with salt and pepper. Simmer another 10 minutes, at most, while you prepare the oysters.

5. Pour the oil into a kettle to a depth of 1 inch and heat until the temperature reaches 375 degrees. Place the remaining 2 cups of flour in a large bowl and season with the tablespoon of salt. Dredge the oysters in the seasoned flour. Fry the oysters, in batches, until golden brown, about 2 minutes. Don't add so many oysters that the oil temperature drops radically. Drain after frying.

6. Spoon some of the sauce into a bowl and toss the oysters in the sauce to coat them well. Place 6 oysters (for an appetizer) or 12 oysters (for an entrée) on a plate and top with some green onions and parsley. (Note: For an opulent option, add some lump crabmeat to the bowl when tossing the oysters in the sauce and serve them both together.) MAKES EIGHT APPETIZERS OR FOUR ENTREES.

# Oysters and Pasta Creole Bordelaise

*A delicious and very simple combination: spaghetti aglio olio (or bordelaise, as we call it in New Orleans) with fresh Louisiana oysters.*

¼ cup extra-virgin olive oil
24 fresh large oysters
½ stick (4 Tbsp.) butter
2 Tbsp. finely chopped garlic
4 Tbsp. finely chopped green onion tops
½ tsp. crushed red pepper
¼ tsp. salt
1 lb. vermicelli, cooked al dente
8 sprigs flat-leaf parsley, chopped, for garnish

1. Heat the oil in a small skillet over medium-low heat. Add the oysters, cooking them by shaking the pan and making them roll around until they plump up and the edges curl up.

2. Add the butter, garlic, green onion tops, crushed red pepper, and salt, and cook, shaking the pan all the while, until the green onions have wilted. Don't cook more than a minute, or the garlic and green onions will lose their flavor.

3. Remove from the heat and add the cooked, drained pasta to the pan. Toss the pasta until well coated with the sauce. Garnish with the parsley. SERVES FOUR.

# Mussels in Ghent-Style Wine Sauce

*The best mussels I ever ate were in a big restaurant called Auberge de Fonteyne in the center of Ghent in Belgium on the third day of our honeymoon. The mussels were awash in what they called a wine sauce, although it seemed more like a cream sauce to me. It's a Belgian classic, and no place in the world is more enthusiastic about mussels than Belgium.*

*Mussels are very inexpensive, so buy plenty of them. The best are the black-shell mussels from Prince Edward Island in Canada. (I do not recommend the green-lipped mussels from New Zealand.) Mussels should be tightly closed; if the shell gapes a little, tap it. If it doesn't close, pitch it. Although most of the mussels I'm finding in stores these days are pre-washed, scrubbing them and removing the byssus (beard) is still essential. After the mussels pop open in the pan, check them to see whether they need to be washed inside even a little more because sometimes they do. Mussels cook very quickly, and they shrivel up if you cook them too long. So get them out of the pan as soon as they open and are heated through.*

MUSSELS

8 dozen mussels, scrubbed

1 yellow onion, coarsely chopped

1 Tbsp. coarsely cracked black pepper

1 tsp. dried thyme

Stems from 1 bunch of flat-leaf parsley

2 cups dry white wine

SAUCE

½ stick (4 Tbsp.) butter

1 heaping Tbsp. flour

1 small yellow onion, minced

2 cloves garlic, minced

¼ tsp. crushed red pepper flakes

1 cup heavy whipping cream

½ tsp. saffron

4 sprigs flat-leaf parsley, chopped

Salt and freshly ground black pepper to taste

2 green onions, chopped, for garnish

*(continued)*

1. Put the mussels into a very large, heavy pot with all the other non-sauce ingredients, plus ¼ cup of water. Bring to a boil over high heat. After a couple of minutes, vigorously shake the pot to allow the unopened mussels to work their way to the bottom and open. Steam for about 4 minutes, or until all the mussels have opened.

2. Remove the mussels to a strainer set over a bowl to catch all the juices. After they cool for 3–4 minutes, rinse the inside of the shells in a bowl of water and remove any beards that may remain. Strain the mussel juices back into the pot through a fine sieve or cheesecloth.

3. Make a blond roux by melting the butter in a large saucepan until it bubbles. Add the flour and cook, stirring constantly, until the mixture just barely begins to brown. Add the onion, garlic, and crushed red pepper, and cook until the garlic is fragrant, about 2 minutes.

4. Add the strained mussel juices and gently simmer for about 8 minutes. Add the cream, saffron, and parsley, and simmer 3–4 minutes more. Season the sauce with salt and pepper to taste.

5. Place a dozen mussels in a large, broad-rimmed soup bowl and ladle the sauce over them. Garnish with the green onions. Provide hot loaves of French bread, damp towels, and a bowl for the shells. SERVES ONE MUSSEL FANATIC OR FOUR NORMAL PEOPLE.

# Bouillabaisse, New Orleans Style

*Save this recipe for the day when you find yourself with a surplus of whole fresh fish. If you never have such a day, make crab or shrimp stock (see recipe, page 312) instead of the fish stock. The best fish to use, both for the stock and the big pieces that will make their way into the soup, are firm-fleshed white fish, such as redfish, red snapper, drum, grouper, and lemonfish. For something outrageously good, use pompano. For various reasons (texture and color, mostly), I would avoid catfish, escolar, salmon, or tuna.*

STOCK

Bones, heads, and scraps from 5–8 lb.
  white fish (see headnote),
  livers and gills removed
Top 4 inches of a bunch of celery,
  chopped
Stems from 1 bunch of flat-leaf parsley
1 yellow onion, chopped
1 Tbsp. black peppercorns
1 tsp. dried thyme

BOUILLABAISSE

½ cup extra-virgin olive oil
1 large yellow onion, coarsely chopped
1 fennel bulb, coarsely chopped
6 large cloves garlic, crushed
½ tsp. crushed red pepper
2 medium fresh tomatoes, skin, seeds,
  and pulp removed, coarsely chopped
2 canned whole Italian plum tomatoes,
  chopped
½ cup juice from canned tomatoes

⅔ cup dry white wine,
  such as Sauvignon Blanc
1 large bay leaf
2 lb. white fish (see headnote),
  cut into large pieces
½ pound squid, cleaned and bodies
  sliced into rings (optional)
4 dozen mussels,
  scrubbed and debearded
Pinch of saffron threads
16 large (16–20 count) shrimp, peeled
  except for tails (or take them off, too)
½ lb. lump crabmeat (optional)
2 green onions, finely chopped
8 sprigs flat-leaf parsley, leaves only,
  chopped
Salt to taste
Cayenne to taste
Parsley, for garnish

Toasted French bread rounds
½ cup Spicy Garlic Mayonnaise
  (see recipe, page 317)

*(continued)*

1. To make the stock: Put all of the fish bones, heads, skins, and scraps into a stock-pot and cover with cold water. Bring it to a boil, then dump the water, saving all the fish parts. Refill the pot with just enough water to barely cover the fish parts. Add all of the remaining stock ingredients and bring to just a simmer. Reduce the heat to low and very gently simmer for 30 minutes more, skimming the foam that rises to the top.

2. Strain the stock and discard the solids. Return the stock to the pot and simmer while you continue with the rest of the recipe.

3. To make the bouillabaisse: Heat the oil in another large kettle over medium-high heat. Add the onion, fennel, garlic, and crushed red pepper, and sauté until the onion turns translucent. Add the fresh and canned tomatoes and juice, and cook 1 minute more. Add the wine and bay leaf, and boil for 3 minutes.

4. Ladle ¼ cup of the fish stock into a skillet and set aside. Add the fish and squid and remaining vegetables to the kettle and return to a simmer.

5. Meanwhile, add the mussels to the skillet with the stock and cook for about a minute, by which time all of them should open. (Discard any that do not.) Turn the heat off and allow to cool while shaking the pan so that the stock sloshes inside the mussels. Remove the mussels to a bowl. If any of the mussels appear to have grit or beard inside, clean them. Strain the liquid from the pan and the bowl through a fine sieve into the kettle with the fish.

6. Add the saffron and shrimp to the kettle and cook for about a minute. Add the crabmeat, mussels, and green onions, and cook for another minute, gently stirring to distribute the ingredients. Season to taste with salt and cayenne.

7. Divide the seafood equally among 4–6 bowls and ladle the broth and vegetables over everything. Garnish with parsley. Serve with toasted French bread slices spread with spicy garlic mayonnaise. SERVES FOUR TO SIX.

# Cajun Seared Scallops with Near-Guacamole

*Save this recipe for occasions when you find those sea scallops that are almost the size of filets mignons. Sea scallops that size are delicious and lend themselves particularly to pan-searing. In our part of the world, this verges on blackening and that's just fine, assuming the pan is really hot and you don't let the scallops sit there too long. The salsa is essentially my recipe for guacamole but with the avocados sliced on top instead of blended in.*

SCALLOPS

1 lb. sea scallops, the bigger the better

Salt-free Creole seasoning

Salt to taste

½ stick (4 Tbsp.) butter, melted

SALSA

2 tomatillos, peeled and
    coarsely chopped

1 medium sweet onion,
    coarsely chopped

Juice of 1 lime

1 Tbsp. red wine vinegar

1 Tbsp. olive oil

2 tsp. Tabasco Green Pepper Sauce

2 large tomatoes, peeled, seeded,
    and chopped

¼ tsp. salt

¼ tsp. coarsely ground black pepper

2 tsp. Vietnamese fish sauce

2 Hass avocados, ripe but not soft,
    each cut into 8–12 slices

8 sprigs cilantro, leaves only, chopped,
    for garnish

1 green onion, tender green part only,
    sliced, for garnish

1. Heat a black iron skillet over high heat. Check the sea scallops to make sure they've been well trimmed. (Sometimes you'll find some fibrous stuff at the edge; remove and discard this.) Coat the sea scallops generously with the Creole seasoning and a little salt. Add the butter to the skillet, then add the scallops and sear them for about 2 minutes on each side.

2. Blend all the salsa ingredients up to (but not including) the avocados in a food processor.

3. Spoon about ¼ cup of the salsa onto each of 4 plates. Place 4–6 scallops on the salsa (depending on size). Put 2–3 avocado slices between the scallops. Garnish with the cilantro and green onion. SERVES FOUR.

# Louisiana Seafood Pasta

*Here's my take on the very rich Creole-seasoned, chock-full-of-seafood pasta dish that became popular in the early 1980s and remains so today. When crawfish are in season, use them instead of the scallops.*

2 Tbsp. butter
½ cup chopped green onion
1 Tbsp. chopped shallots
¼ cup dry white wine
2 cups heavy whipping cream
Pinch of saffron threads
½ tsp. salt, plus more to taste
¼ tsp. ground white pepper
Pinch of cayenne
Pinch of ground ginger
1 lb. sea scallops, halved crosswise
1 lb. medium (20–25 count) shrimp, peeled and deveined
2 dozen fresh, shucked oysters
½ tsp. fresh tarragon (or ¼ tsp. dried)
1 lb. lump crabmeat
2 lb. farfalle pasta, cooked al dente
Dash of Tabasco or pinch of crushed red pepper (optional)

1. Melt the butter in a large skillet over medium heat. Add the green onion and shallots, and cook until they're limp. Add the wine and reduce until most of the liquid is gone. Add the cream, saffron, salt, pepper, cayenne, and ginger, and bring to a light boil. (Also add tarragon at this point if using dried.)

2. Add the scallops and shrimp, and cook for 4 minutes. Add the oysters and fresh tarragon, if using. Cook until the edges of the oysters are curly, then add the crabmeat. Throughout the process, shake the skillet to slosh the sauce over the seafood.

3. Taste the sauce and add salt if necessary. You can also spice it up with a bit of Tabasco or crushed red pepper. Remove from the heat. Add the cooked and drained pasta, and toss until well combined. SERVES EIGHT.

# Finfish Entrées

The most fundamental change on New Orleans menus during my years of covering restaurants was in the fish department. Until the mid-1980s, speckled trout was the default fish everywhere. Also commonly available were pompano, redfish, flounder, and catfish. And that was really about it.

Then the market changed. The blackened redfish craze decimated that species. Trout became scarce, too. Restaurants began resorting to fish only fishermen know about. This meant not only introducing customers to new flavors and textures but coming up with new recipes designed for unfamiliar species. The silver lining here is that we are now cooking and eating a far greater variety of fish than ever before.

Most of the finfish used in New Orleans cooking are saltwater fish. Among the popular local wild fish, only catfish is a freshwater species.

Here's a quick guide to the most popular Louisiana fish. Notes on some other species are found with the recipes for them.

## Pompano

Full-flavored and on the high end of the fat scale, pompano is not for everyone. But to my palate, this is the most delicious fish there is. It's also a beauty. Perhaps the best way to prepare it is to clean it and grill it whole. Even if you fillet a pompano, leave the skin on; that's where the rich, flavorful fat is. The silvery flesh has an unusual texture that neither flakes nor shreds. Pompano is seasonal, and the seasons are peculiar. When you find it, get it. And keep it simple. There's no close substitute.

## Speckled Trout

The favorite fish in New Orleans white-tablecloth restaurants for decades, speckled trout suddenly became rare and we started appreciating it even more. The "spotted sea trout" (as ichthyologists call it) is a drum, not at all related to freshwater trout. The best speckled trout are the smallish ones, up to two pounds. Really small ones are excellent cooked whole—either fried or broiled. The fish lends itself to pan-sautéeing and deep-frying with a light dusting of seasoned flour. Speckled trout is the definitive fish for New Orleans–style meunière and amandine dishes. If speckled trout isn't available, substitute redfish, red snapper, drum, or striped bass.

# Tuna

Although a tremendous amount of tuna—both yellowfin (ahi) and the rarer bluefin—is caught in the Gulf of Mexico, fresh tuna is relatively new to New Orleans cookery. Tuna is unlike most of the other fish we consume. (And it's not much like the tuna we all know from cans, either.) It's an enormous fish, some weighing in the hundreds of pounds. Its flesh is red, not white, has the texture of meat, and is usually cut into steaks.

Tuna is best cooked using the same methods and sauces you would for beef. Never cook it all the way through; leave it red in the center. (Of course, a lot of tuna is eaten completely raw in sushi bars.) I recommend having tuna cut very thick—as much as three inches. Then hit it with very high heat. (Tuna lends itself exceptionally well to blackening.)

# Red Snapper

Red snapper is a favorite not only around New Orleans but all across America. That makes it a bit more expensive and spotty in its availability, even though fishermen catch a lot of it in nearby waters.

Red snapper has a tender texture that holds together well even though it's a flaky fish. Despite its relatively low oil content, red snapper has a delectable flavor. Some people like their snapper grilled, but I prefer it pan-sautéed or broiled. Red snapper also lends itself to being cooked whole, particularly if it's a smaller specimen. Substitutes include redfish, trout, and striped bass.

# Flounder

Flounder is a flatfish, like turbot, halibut, and sole. The few restaurants that specialize in this underappreciated fish sell lots of it because its fans know where to go.

Flounder is among the best fish to cook whole, either broiled or fried. Even for the uninitiated, it's easy to cook and eat that way, as long as you avoid the free-floating bones around the perimeter. Flounder is good with any butter sauce, particularly those involving lemon.

# Black Drum

I always order drumfish when it's the fish of the day unless there's something obviously better. Funny: The fish was once despised. But after its cousin, the redfish, was banned from commercial fishing, black drum took its place in restaurants and markets. And suddenly we found that drum wasn't so bad after all. Delicious, in fact.

Drum and redfish are similar in many ways. The right-sized drum is a two-to-four-pounder called a "puppy drum," and it's a nice fish indeed. It has the same white-with-a-tinge-of-gray color and flakes of about the same size and texture as speckled trout (another relative) and, in most cases, makes a good substitute for it.

# Sheepshead (Sea Bream)

Were it not for its unappealing name, sheepshead would be one of the best-liked fish in Louisiana. To that end, the authorities have applied the name "sea bream" to sheepshead, which helped a little. It's not a new fish to our tables: I've found it on menus from 100 years ago. Assuming you don't see its funny head or have to clean it (quite a job), it's a beautiful fish—white, firm, and flavorful without being oily. The larger ones are very good on the grill or blackened. Smaller ones can be pan-sautéed or broiled to resemble redfish or drum. Never hesitate to use sheepshead for any recipe that calls for a good white fillet.

# Fried Catfish

*It's gospel, as far as I'm concerned: No catfish you ever make will ever be as good as catfish rolled in cornmeal and deep-fried. If you want to give it some extra moxie, marinate it in something good, as I do in this recipe. The other article of faith is the great superiority of small, wild catfish to big, farm-raised ones. Unfortunately, the catfish you find in the store is almost certainly farm-raised, which not only has an off-taste to me but also is too big.*

*The essential trick in frying fish is to keep the oil at 375 degrees. Use a fat thermometer to monitor this. Whatever utensil you have that will keep the heat up is fine. I've had good luck with a black iron skillet with an inch of oil, a deep Dutch oven with a couple of quarts of oil, and a good electric fryer.*

| | |
|---|---|
| 2 lb. small catfish fillets | 1 tsp. Worcestershire sauce |
| 3 Tbsp. yellow mustard | 1 cup corn flour (Fish-Fri) |
| 2 Tbsp. lemon juice | 1 cup cornmeal |
| 1 Tbsp. juice from a jar of dill pickles | 1 Tbsp. salt |
| 2 tsp. milder Louisiana hot sauce, | ½ tsp. granulated garlic |
|   such as Crystal | Peanut oil, for frying |

1. Wash the catfish and remove the skin and any remaining bones. Unless the fillets are very small, cut them on the bias into strips about 1½ inches wide.

2. Blend the mustard, lemon juice, pickle juice, hot sauce, and Worcestershire sauce in a bowl. Put the catfish fillets into the bowl and toss to coat with the marinade. Let marinate for about 30 minutes, refrigerated.

3. Combine the corn flour, cornmeal, salt, and garlic with a fork in a large bowl. Put 4–6 pieces of catfish into the corn-flour mixture and toss around to coat the catfish. Repeat with the remaining fish.

4. Pour the oil into a cast-iron skillet or a Dutch oven to a depth of 1 inch and place over medium-high heat until the temperature reaches 375 degrees. Working in batches, fry the catfish until they turn golden brown. Remove with a skimmer (or, better, the spider utensil used by Asian cooks). Drain on paper towels.

5. Serve with tartar sauce and pickles and hot sauce. And don't forget the Hush Puppies (see recipe, page 232). SERVES TWO TO FOUR.

# Trout Meunière Old Style

*The word "meunière" is a reference to the miller of wheat, whose wife (according to French lore) cooked everything coated with flour. The original French style of trout meunière, then, was seasoned and floured, sautéed in butter, and then topped with the browned butter from the pan. This is still more or less how the dish is done in some restaurants—notably Galatoire's.*

*There is a New Orleans twist on this, however, and I think it's better than the French classic. It was invented by "Count" Arnaud, who while trying to standardize and stabilize the sauce so the fish could be fried instead of sautéed, added a bit of stock and roux to the butter and lemon. At its best, this sauce is incredibly good and works not just on trout but also on other fried seafood, notably oysters.*

| | |
|---|---|
| 1½ cups flour | 1 cup veal stock (see recipe, page 312) |
| 1 Tbsp. salt-free Creole seasoning | 2 Tbsp. lemon juice, strained |
| ¼ tsp. salt | 1 Tbsp. Worcestershire sauce |
| Six 8-oz. speckled trout fillets | 1 tsp. red wine vinegar |
| 1¼ sticks (10 Tbsp.) butter | Peanut oil, for frying |
| | Lemon wedges |

1. Combine the flour, Creole seasoning, and salt in a wide bowl. Rinse the trout fillets and pat dry. Dredge the fish in the seasoned flour and knock off the excess.

2. Make a medium-brown roux by melting the butter in a saucepan over medium heat. When it begins to bubble, add the remaining seasoned flour and cook, stirring constantly, until the mixture turns a medium brown.

3. Put the stock into another saucepan and place over medium-high heat. Whisk the roux into the stock until dissolved. Add the lemon juice, Worcestershire sauce, and vinegar, and simmer for 3 minutes, then remove the pan from the heat. Keep the sauce warm while you prepare the fish.

4. You can sauté the fish in butter if you like, but it's more common in New Orleans to fry it in about an inch of oil heated to 375 degrees. Either way, cook until golden brown (about 2 minutes per side).

5. Spoon the sauce over the fish and serve with lemon wedges. SERVES SIX.

# Trout with Pecans

*In the early 1980s, when trout amandine ruled the earth, Ella Brennan asked her chefs at Commander's Palace, "Why are we cooking trout with almonds like every other place in the world? Almonds don't grow around here. Why not use pecans?" The chefs got to work, and trout with pecans was born. This preparation also works very well with fried soft-shell crabs.*

**PECAN BUTTER**
3 Tbsp. butter
2 Tbsp. toasted pecans
3 Tbsp. lemon juice
1½ tsp. Worcestershire sauce

**SAUCE**
2 Tbsp. flour
½ cup shrimp or fish stock
   (see recipe, page 312)
½ cup Worcestershire sauce
3 Tbsp. lemon juice
2 sticks (16 Tbsp.) butter, softened

**TROUT**
2 cups flour
3 Tbsp. salt-free Creole seasoning
2 Tbsp. salt
2 eggs
½ cup milk
Six 6–8-oz. trout fillets
1 cup clarified butter (see recipe,
   page 314)
8 oz. toasted pecan halves

1. To make the pecan butter: Place all of the pecan butter ingredients into the container of a food processor or blender. Process to a smooth puree and set aside.

2. To make the sauce: Stir the flour and 2 tablespoons of water together in a heat-proof bowl to a smooth paste. Bring the stock, Worcestershire sauce, and lemon juice to a light boil in a small saucepan. Whisk about ⅓ cup of the hot stock mixture into the flour paste. Then gradually pour the flour mixture back into the saucepan and bring to a boil, stirring constantly with the whisk. Whisk in the softened butter, a tablespoon at a time. Keep the sauce warm.

3. Combine the flour, Creole seasoning, and salt in a wide bowl. Beat the eggs with the milk in another wide bowl. Dust the trout lightly with the seasoned flour. Pass it through the egg wash and then dredge it once more in the seasoned flour.

*(continued)*

4. Heat half of the clarified butter in a large skillet over medium-high heat until a sprinkling of flour sizzles in it. Add half of the fillets and sauté, turning once, until golden brown, 3–4 minutes. Transfer the fillets to a warm serving platter and keep warm. Repeat the process with the remaining clarified butter and trout.

5. Spread the pecan butter over the trout, sprinkle with roasted pecans, and top with the sauce. SERVES SIX.

# Trout Marigny

*This is a variation on the local classic trout Marguery, with a lighter and easier-to-make sauce. For once, this is a dish that's designed to be made with true trout, rather than the good fish we called speckled trout around here. (You could use specks, but I think rainbow or ruby-red trout or even salmon would be better.) Asparagus makes a great side vegetable for this.*

1 stick (8 Tbsp.) plus 1 Tbsp. butter
Four 6–8-oz. freshwater trout or salmon fillets
½ tsp. black peppercorns
2 slices lemon
1 cup Chardonnay
¾ cup sliced fresh mushrooms
2 Tbsp. shallots, chopped
¼ cup flour
¼ tsp. salt
Generous pinch of cayenne
Parsley, for garnish

1. Preheat the oven to 350 degrees. Grease the bottom of a glass or ceramic baking dish with 1 tablespoon of the butter. Arrange the fish side by side, but not touching, in the dish. Sprinkle the peppercorns over the fillets. Add the lemon and pour the wine over all. Bake for 20–25 minutes, depending on the thickness of the fish.

2. With a slotted turner, transfer the fish to a warm platter. Reserve the juices in the baking dish.

3. Melt the remaining butter in a saucepan over medium-low heat until it bubbles. Add the mushrooms and shallots, and cook until the mushrooms are soft, about 2 minutes.

4. Reduce the heat to low. Sprinkle in the flour and whisk until smooth. Add 1 cup of the fish-poaching juices, a little at a time, stirring lightly. Add the salt and cayenne, and continue to cook, stirring lightly, until the sauce blends and thickens.

5. Place a trout fillet on each of 4 plates and top with the sauce. Garnish with parsley. SERVES FOUR.

# Trout en Croute with Shrimp Mousse

*This dish looks and sounds much more difficult than it really is, but it is very impressive when served. The puff pastry can be found (probably frozen) at better food stores.*

Four 13 x 11-inch sheets puff pastry
5 eggs
½ tsp. salt
½ tsp. ground white pepper
¼ tsp. dry mustard
2 cloves garlic
½ lb. medium (20–25 count) shrimp, peeled and deveined
½ cup heavy whipping cream
4 slices lemon
½ cup dry white wine
Stems of 1 bunch of flat-leaf parsley
½ tsp. black peppercorns
Four 6–8-oz. speckled trout fillets (drum, redfish, sheepshead, rainbow trout, or salmon also work well for this dish)

1. Preheat the oven to 400 degrees. Unfold each sheet of puff pastry onto a lightly floured surface and trim to an approximately 10 x 10-inch square. Transfer the 4 pastry squares to a baking sheet and refrigerate until ready to use.

2. Put 4 of the eggs, the salt, pepper, dry mustard, and garlic into a food processor. Pulse the machine until the ingredients are well blended. Add the shrimp and, with the machine running, add the cream. Add a little water if the mixture seems to be very dry. Don't overdo it; it's okay for there to be small lumps.

3. Bring a wide, shallow pan of water to a simmer with the lemon slices, white wine, parsley stems, and peppercorns. Add the trout and poach for 6 minutes. Transfer the trout to a plate and discard the poaching liquid.

4. With a very sharp knife, butterfly the trout fillets into 2 thin halves. Put 1 trout half on each pastry square, moving the fish toward the bottom half of the pastry and leaving a ½-inch border of pastry around the perimeter. Spoon about 2 table-spoons of shrimp mousse over the trout. Top with the other half of the fish.

5. Beat the remaining egg and brush the edges of the pastry with it. Fold the pastry up and over the stuffed fish, pressing on the edges to seal. If you really want to get fancy, cut the pastry envelope in the shape of a fish. You can stick the parts of the dough you cut off back onto the fish to create fins. Make scalelike indentations on the side with the tip of a spoon.

6. Arrange the stuffed-pastry envelopes, at least 1 inch apart, on a lightly oiled baking sheet. Bake until the pastry has puffed and has just turned brown, 6–8 minutes. Serve immediately. This is good as is, but if you want a sauce, reduced cream with fennel or fresh thyme is delicious. SERVES FOUR.

# Redfish with Artichokes and Mushrooms

*This superb dish appears on the menus of quite a few New Orleans restaurants. Flounder, trout, lemonfish, sheepshead, or striped bass also work for this recipe. So do really big oysters.*

**FISH FILLETS**

Juice of ½ lemon, strained

Four 6–8-oz. redfish (or flounder, trout, lemonfish, etc.) fillets

1 cup flour

1 Tbsp. salt

¼ tsp. ground white pepper

3 eggs, beaten

½ stick (4 Tbsp.) butter

**SAUCE**

⅓ cup dry white wine

4 fresh artichoke bottoms, poached and cut into eighths (or use canned artichoke bottoms)

2 cups sliced white mushrooms

2 Tbsp. chopped green onion

¼ tsp. chopped garlic

½ tsp. chopped shallots

3 Tbsp. small capers

⅓ cup lemon juice

1½ sticks (12 Tbsp.) butter

1. Sprinkle the lemon juice over the fillets. Combine the flour, salt, and pepper in a large bowl. Dredge the fillets in the seasoned flour, shaking off excess. Dip the fillets in the eggs and then dredge once more in the seasoned flour, shaking off any excess.

2. Melt the 4 tablespoons of butter over medium-high heat in a large, heavy skillet. Sauté the fish fillets until cooked through, about 3 minutes per side. Remove and keep warm.

3. To make the sauce: Add the white wine to the pan in which you sautéed the fish and whisk to dissolve the pan juices. Bring to a boil until the wine is reduced by two-thirds. Lower the heat to medium and add all of the remaining sauce ingredients except the butter. Cook until the mushrooms are soft.

4. Reduce the heat to low and add the 12 tablespoons of butter, a tablespoon at a time, shaking the skillet until the butter has blended in completely.

5. Place a fillet on each of 4 warm serving plates and top with sauce. SERVES FOUR.

# Redfish with Sizzling Crabmeat and Herbs

*The surprise in this dish is based on the fact that you can get clarified butter extremely hot without burning it. Hot enough to sizzle anything it's poured over. The butter looks very harmless when I bring it to the table, but when I spoon it onto the fish and its topping . . . drama! Along with a wonderful aroma.*

⅓ cup chopped flat-leaf parsley (about half a bunch)
1 Tbsp. capers, chopped
2 tsp. chopped garlic
4 oz. white crabmeat
Dash of Worcestershire sauce
Juice of ¼ lemon
Four 8-oz. fillets redfish (or trout, drum, sheepshead, or other white fish)
Salt and freshly ground black pepper to taste
½ cup clarified butter (see recipe, page 314)

1. Preheat the broiler and broiler pan. Combine the parsley, capers, garlic, and crabmeat in a small bowl. Sprinkle in the Worcestershire sauce and lemon juice, and toss to combine.

2. Season the fish with salt and pepper. Broil about 4 inches from the flame for about 6 minutes, or until the slightest hint of browning is seen around the edges. Check the fish to see if it's cooked in the center of the thickest part. If not, broil just a minute longer or less.

3. Place the fish on a warm, heatproof serving platter. Top with a small pile (not a scattering) of the crabmeat-and-herb mixture.

4. In the smallest saucepan you have, heat the clarified butter until a flake of parsley immediately sizzles in it. Carefully spoon the very hot butter over the fish and its topping, which will sizzle when the butter hits it. It's most dramatic to do this at the table, but be very careful: The heat of the butter presents a burning hazard if splashed. SERVES FOUR.

# Redfish Herbsaint

*After an absence of several years from markets (though not from sports fishermen's ice chests), redfish is starting to reappear. This elegant, light dish shows off the quality of red-fish very well. You can substitute trout, black drum, or sheepshead for the redfish.*

*Herbsaint, an anise-flavored liqueur made in New Orleans, is responsible for the dish's delightful aroma. The original inspiration for the recipe came from chef Gunter Preuss, who made something much like this at the now gone Versailles. (Gunter is now in the kitchen at his French Quarter restaurant, Broussard's.)*

| | |
|---|---|
| 1½ cups dry white wine | 2 leeks, white part only, well washed |
| Juice of 1 lemon | and sliced into matchsticks (2 cups) |
| Four 6-oz. redfish fillets | ½ stick (4 Tbsp.) butter |
| 1 medium carrot, peeled and cut into | 1 cup heavy whipping cream |
| matchsticks (about ½ cup) | 4½ tsp. Herbsaint (or Pernod) |
| 1 rib celery, strings removed and cut | 1 tsp. salt |
| into matchsticks (about ½ cup) | ½ tsp. ground white pepper |
| 6 black peppercorns | ½ cup lump crabmeat |

1. Put 1 cup of the wine and all of the lemon juice in a stainless steel skillet and bring to just barely a simmer over low heat. Add the fish, carrot, celery, and peppercorns, and poach for 8–10 minutes. Check the fish after 5 minutes to make sure that it doesn't overcook. (The fish should not fall apart into flakes when done.)

2. While the fish is poaching, sauté the leeks in 1 tablespoon of the butter until soft, about 3 minutes. Add the remaining ½ cup of white wine and bring to a boil. Cook for another minute, then turn off the heat.

3. Remove the fish when done to a warm plate. To the fish-poaching liquid in the skillet, add the remaining 3 tablespoons of butter, the cream, Herbsaint, salt, and pepper. Reduce over medium heat until the sauce thickens, about 5 minutes.

4. Add the crabmeat and cook, gently shaking the skillet, until the crabmeat is heated through.

5. Divide the leeks among 4 warm serving plates. Place the fish, celery, and carrot over the leeks and top with the sauce. SERVES FOUR.

# Redfish Courtbouillon

*Here is a great, light, big-flavored, very traditional Creole dish that is served almost nowhere anymore. It's one of the few dishes that pair tomatoes with seafood that I actually think is good. In this case, very, very good.*

*Courtbouillon means brief boil, which describes the final step. However, I find I get much better results by finishing the dish in the oven instead of on top of the stove, and the process from there takes about an hour—which is not what I would call brief. My version veers further from the standard by lightening up on roux and adding a few flavors from the Italian spectrum. These add a taste dimension without deeply altering the dish.*

*You need to make fish stock (see recipe, page 312) for this, so wait until you have a whole fish to work with. You can make a courtbouillon of almost any white fish that poaches well— drum, sheepshead, lemonfish, and striped bass all work well—but for some reason, in these parts, you can't say courtbouillon without prefacing it with redfish.*

### STOCK

1 whole 2½-lb. redfish fillet

1 bunch of flat-leaf parsley, stems only

Tops from a bunch of celery

½ yellow onion, coarsely chopped

½ tsp. black peppercorns

### SAUCE

½ cup extra-virgin olive oil

¼ cup flour

2 medium yellow onions, coarsely chopped (about 1½ cups)

2 ribs celery, chopped

½ fennel bulb, chopped

1 small red bell pepper, seeds and membranes removed, coarsely chopped

2 cloves garlic, chopped

4 canned whole plum tomatoes, chopped

2 medium fresh, ripe tomatoes, seeded and chopped

½ cup juice from canned tomatoes

½ cup dry white wine, preferably Sauvignon Blanc

3 bay leaves

½ tsp. dried thyme

¼ tsp. allspice

1 tsp. salt-free Creole seasoning

Juice of 1 small lemon, strained

6 sprigs flat-leaf parsley, leaves only, chopped

1 Tbsp. Louisiana hot sauce, such as Crystal

1½ tsp. salt, plus more to taste

Freshly ground black pepper

2 green onions, green parts only, finely chopped, for garnish

*(continued)*

1. Preheat the oven to 375 degrees.

2. To make the fish stock: Fillet the fish and remove the skin from the fillets. Put the skinless fillets onto a plate and refrigerate until ready to use. Put all the fish bones, heads, skins, and scraps into a stockpot and cover with cold water. Bring it to a boil, then dump the water, saving all the fish parts. Refill the pot with just enough water to barely cover the fish parts. Add all of the remaining stock ingredients and bring just to a simmer. Reduce the heat to low and very gently simmer for 30 minutes, skimming foam that rises to the top.

3. To make the sauce: Make a blond roux by putting the oil in a large, stainless steel or enamel skillet (for which you have a cover, though you don't need it just now) and heating it over medium-high heat until it shimmers. Add the flour and cook, stirring constantly, until the mixture barely begins to turn brown. Add the onions, celery, fennel, bell pepper, and garlic, reduce heat to medium, and cook, stirring now and then, until the vegetables are soft.

4. Add the canned and the fresh tomatoes, tomato juice, and wine. Bring to a boil and cook, stirring occasionally, for about 2 minutes. Add all of the remaining ingredients except the green onions. Add 4 cups of fish stock, bring the sauce to a very light boil, and simmer for about 15 minutes.

5. Cut the redfish fillets into pieces about the width and length of 2 fingers. Place the fish pieces atop the sauce and season to taste with salt and pepper. Cover the skillet and bake for 20–25 minutes. The fish should be tender but not falling apart.

6. Adjust seasonings to taste. Serve with plenty of the sauce in wide bowls. Garnish with green onions. Garlic bread is great with this. SERVES SIX TO EIGHT.

# Nouvelle Pompano en Papillote

*There are few worse travesties than the pompano* en papillote *found in traditional New Orleans restaurants. It starts with the best fish there is—one I find so good that sauces tend to detract from, not add to, the flavor. Then this great fish goes into a parchment bag with the gloppiest kind of "light roux, white wine, three or four seafood" sauce.*

*I will admit, however, that the idea of the papillote—to keep the fish moist by cooking it essentially in its own steam in a parchment pouch—is a fine idea. Looks nice, too. So here's my take. It starts with flounder, a milder fish that steams well. Small salmon and freshwater trout also work well. Of course, you could use actual pompano.*

*The parchment paper you need for this is more easily available than it once was; you can always get it at kitchen-supply stores.*

| | |
|---|---|
| Four 6-oz. flounder fillets (or pompano, trout, or salmon) | 4 tsp. chopped fresh dill |
| 2 Tbsp. butter, softened | 1 tsp. chopped fresh tarragon |
| ½ cup green onion, green parts only, finely chopped | 2 Tbsp. dry white wine |
| ½ stalk celery, cut into matchsticks | 1 Tbsp. lemon juice |
| | ¼ tsp. Tabasco Green Pepper Sauce |
| | Salt |

1. Preheat the oven to 375 degrees. Cut 4 sheets of parchment paper large enough to enclose the fish completely, with enough overlap to fold over to make a tight seal.

2. After washing the fish fillets and checking for bones, generously butter each fillet. Place them on the parchment paper. Top each fillet with the green onion, celery, dill, and tarragon. Combine the wine, lemon juice, and green pepper sauce in a small bowl. Spoon the wine mixture over each fillet and season to taste with salt.

3. Fold the paper up and over the fish and fold the edges down hard, then fold down again to seal the pouch as securely as possible. Place the papillotes on a baking sheet and place them in the center of the oven. Bake for 15–18 minutes (longer if the fish is thick).

4. Remove the papillotes from the oven and place on serving plates. Serve immediately, along with a sharp steak knife for opening the bags. The fish should be eaten right out of the bag (set on a plate, of course). SERVES FOUR.

# Pasta Milanese with Pompano

*Get two older New Orleans–Italian ladies together, and you'll have argument about which is the right way to make Milanese, the name for one of the main dishes traditionally served in New Orleans Italian homes on St. Joseph's Day (March 19). Both ladies will hate this recipe—unless it's served on a day other than St. Joseph's and you don't call it Milanese. Then they'll love it, and they'll say it reminds them of Milanese.*

*The traditional fish used for Milanese is the strongly flavored Mediterranean sardine. It's good but hard to find. I substitute pompano, which has the flavor to carry the dish while adding a touch of class to it. The traditional pasta shape is bucatini: the thickest of the strand pastas. The topping is bread crumbs, a reminder of the sawdust of St. Joseph, the carpenter.*

1 bulb fennel
5 Tbsp. extra-virgin olive oil
5 green onions, trimmed and chopped
4 flat anchovy fillets, crushed
One 28-oz. can Italian plum tomato puree
1 Tbsp. chopped fresh oregano
2 small whole pompano, cleaned
2 cloves garlic, crushed
¼ cup dry white wine
¼ cup pine nuts
¼ cup dried currants
Salt and freshly ground black pepper to taste
1 lb. bucatini pasta
1 cup bread crumbs
1 tsp. Italian seasoning

1. Bring a large pot of water to a boil for the pasta. Cut the fennel bulb in half from top to bottom. Cut out the core and trim off the tough top parts, leaving about 3 inches of the stems intact. Coarsely chop and set aside.

2. Heat 3 tablespoons of the olive oil in a large saucepan. Add the the fennel and green onions and sauté until they soften. Add the crushed anchovies and cook another minute. Add the tomato puree and the oregano, and bring to a simmer. Cook, uncovered, for about 20 minutes.

3. Meanwhile, cut the tails and (if you like) the heads off the pompano. Heat the remaining 2 tablespoons of olive oil in a large skillet over high heat. Brown the crushed garlic, then add the pompano. Brown the pompano on both sides, cooking about 2 minutes on each side. Remove the garlic and discard.

4. Add the white wine and bring to a boil. Lower the heat to medium-low and add a cup of the tomato sauce from the other pot. Bring the sauce to a boil, then lower to a simmer. Shake the skillet to slosh the sauce inside the fish. Cover the pan and cook for 4–6 minutes. Remove the fish from the pan. Cut out the fillets, but leave the skin intact. Keep warm.

5. Pour the remaining fennel-tomato sauce into the skillet you just cooked the fish in. Add the pine nuts, currants, and salt and pepper to taste. Gently simmer the sauce while you cook the pasta.

6. Add a tablespoon of salt to the boiling water. Cook the pasta for 6 minutes, then drain. Add the pasta to the sauce and toss to coat. Serve alongside a pompano fillet. Sprinkle bread crumbs mixed with the Italian seasoning over everything. SERVES FOUR.

# Poached Fish with Cranberry Hollandaise

*I served this dish at one of my annual charity Christmas dinners. Its great hollandaise sauce takes advantage of the tartness and very light sweetness of cranberries. The best fish to use include redfish, drum, flounder, or salmon.*

¼ cup dry white wine
½ lemon, sliced
6 black peppercorns
4 sprigs flat-leaf parsley
½ tsp. salt
Four 6–8-oz. redfish, drum, flounder, or salmon fillets

SAUCE
2 egg yolks
2 sticks (16 Tbsp.) butter, softened
1 cup cranberry juice, boiled down to ¼ cup
Generous pinch of cayenne

1. Pour water to a depth of about ½ inch into a large stainless steel or enameled saucepan and bring to a simmer. Add the wine, lemon slices, peppercorns, parsley, and salt, and simmer for 5 minutes. Reduce the heat to maintain a gentle simmer while you make the sauce.

2. To make the sauce: Set a metal bowl over a saucepan of barely simmering water and vigorously whisk the egg yolks until they become thick and pale yellow. Whisk in the softened butter, a tablespoon at a time. (If the sauce shows any sign of curdling, remove the bowl from the saucepan and keep whisking until it cools.) Keep whisking in butter until half of it is incorporated, then add the reduced cranberry juice and a tablespoon of water from the fish pan. Whisk in the rest of the butter slowly until fluffy. Whisk in the cayenne. Set the sauce aside.

3. Add 2 fish fillets at a time to the gently simmering wine-and-lemon mixture and cook for 6–10 minutes, depending on the thickness of the fish. Remove the fish with a slotted turner and allow excess water to drain. Place a fillet on each of 4 plates and top with the cranberry hollandaise. SERVES FOUR.

# Broiled Fish with Beurre Orange

*Many different types of fish work for this recipe, among them redfish, flounder, trout, sheepshead, drum, or lemonfish. But the one I think looks and tastes best is salmon.*

½ cup freshly squeezed orange juice, strained through a fine sieve
1 tsp. lemon juice, strained through a fine sieve
1 Tbsp. red wine vinegar
1 small shallot, finely chopped
1 stick (8 Tbsp.) plus 1 Tbsp. butter, softened
Salt and ground white pepper to taste
Six 6-oz. skinless salmon fillets or other skinless fish (see headnote)
1 Tbsp. orange zest, for garnish

1. Preheat the broiler. Lightly grease a baking sheet and set aside.

2. Combine the orange and lemon juices, vinegar, and shallot in a small saucepan. Bring to a light boil over medium heat and reduce by about two-thirds.

3. Remove the saucepan from the heat and whisk in the stick of butter, a tablespoon at a time. Return the pan to very low heat for a few seconds, if necessary, to fully melt the last pieces of butter. Add the salt and pepper to taste, and strain the sauce through a fine sieve into a clean saucepan. Keep warm while cooking the fish.

4. Season the fish lightly with salt and pepper, and place on the prepared baking sheet. Dot each piece of fish with some of the remaining butter. Broil about 3 inches from the heat, for about 3 minutes.

5. Arrange a piece of fish on each of 6 plates and spoon on the sauce. Garnish each with a sprinkling of the orange zest. SERVES SIX.

# Fish in a Salt Dome

*The late chef Jamie Shannon prepared this dish for a dinner I had at the chef's table in the kitchen of Commander's Palace in 1992. It was as delicious as it was dramatic. The whole fish was presented on a pan covered with the mound of salt in which it had been baked. The salt formed a shell that had to be broken. Amazingly, the fish was not salty at all—just full of elemental fish flavor. For this recipe, I'd recommend pompano, red snapper, Spanish mackerel, or other nice fatty fish.*

One 2–4-lb. whole fatty fish (see headnote), gutted
2 boxes kosher salt

1. Preheat the oven to 375 degrees. The ideal pan for this is a heatproof 18 x 12-inch oval, about 3 inches deep. Cover the bottom with about ½ inch of salt and place the fish on top of it. Cover the fish with salt so that it forms a mound about ½ inch thick at its thinnest part.

2. Using a clean spray bottle, spray water all over the salt until it glistens with dampness. Bake for 40 minutes (for a 2-pounder) up to an hour (for a 4-pounder). You can test for doneness by inserting a meat thermometer through the salt into the fish when you think it's nearly done. Look for an internal temperature of 125–130 degrees.

3. Remove the fish from the oven and allow it to stand for 10–15 minutes. Break the salt shell, brush off the excess salt, and as you carve the fish, remove the skin. This fish will be so juicy and delicious that no sauce is needed. SERVES TWO TO SIX, DEPENDING ON THE SIZE OF THE FISH. (FIGURE ABOUT TEN OUNCES OF WHOLE FISH PER PERSON.)

# Sea Bream in an Envelope

*This recipe is very light—nothing like the oversauced* en papillote *dishes we often do around here. And instead of using parchment, you bake the fish in a tight envelope of foil.*

½ stick (4 Tbsp.) butter, softened
4 sprigs flat-leaf parsley
½ rib celery, cut into matchsticks
Eight 4-oz. sea bream (sheepshead) fillets (trout or flounder would also work)
⅓ cup tomato puree
12 large white grapes, peeled and thinly sliced
¼ cup dry white wine
Salt and freshly ground black pepper to taste

1. Preheat the oven to 400 degrees. Tear off four 12 x 18-inch sheets of aluminum foil. Rub the softened butter in the center half of each sheet.

2. Place a sprig of parsley and a fourth of the celery on the buttered side of each foil sheet. Place 2 fish fillets, head ends together, on top of the parsley and celery. Spoon the tomato puree lightly over the fish and top with the grape coins. Sprinkle a little white wine over the fish and season to taste with salt and pepper.

3. Fold the foil up and over the fish. Fold the edges and crimp to make a tightly sealed envelope. Repeat the process for the remaining fish. Place the envelopes on a baking sheet and bake for about 12 minutes. The envelopes should puff up somewhat. Serve the fish in their envelopes on plates so that when they're opened, the aroma will waft up right into the nostrils of the eater. SERVES FOUR.

# Sea Bream Nouvelle Creole

*I am usually not a fan of seafood dishes with tomato sauce. Sometimes, though, they can be spectacular. In this one, the combination of hollandaise with the tomato sauce is what makes the magic. You can prepare this recipe with many species of white fish. I recommend the inexpensive and excellent sea bream (the polite name for sheepshead), but redfish, trout, red snapper, and lemonfish would also be good.*

*This recipe begins with Creole sauce, which is actually seldom used in Creole cooking.*

**CREOLE SAUCE**

2 Tbsp. olive oil

1 large yellow onion, minced

1 green bell pepper, seeded and minced

2 ribs celery, chopped

2 tomatoes, diced

½ bunch of green onions, chopped

½ tsp. chopped garlic

2 bay leaves

1 sprig fresh thyme

½ tsp. Worcestershire sauce

2 leaves fresh basil, chopped

½ cup tomato puree

Salt and freshly ground black pepper

**FISH**

1 cup flour

1 tsp. salt

¼ tsp. freshly ground black pepper

1 egg

½ cup milk

2 Tbsp. butter

2 Tbsp. extra-virgin olive oil

Eight 4–6-oz. sea bream (sheepshead)
    fillets

**TOPPING**

4 large mushrooms, quartered

1 lb. white crabmeat

1 Tbsp. dry white wine

1 Tbsp. lemon juice

½ bunch of green onions, chopped

¼ tsp. salt

¼ tsp. Tabasco Green Pepper Sauce

1 cup Hollandaise (see recipe, page 315)

Pinch of cayenne

1. To make the Creole sauce: Heat the olive oil in a heavy saucepan. Add the onion, bell pepper, celery, tomatoes, green onions, and garlic, and cook until the onions are translucent. Add all of the remaining sauce ingredients except the basil and the tomato puree, and cook over medium-low heat until thickened, about 7 minutes. Add the basil, remove the bay leaves, and cook another 3 minutes. Season to taste with salt and pepper, remove from heat, and keep warm.

2. To prepare the fish: Combine the flour, salt, and pepper in a wide bowl. Whisk the egg and milk in a small bowl to make an egg wash. Dust the fish with a little of the seasoned flour. Dip into the egg wash, then dredge once more in the seasoned flour, shaking off the excess.

3. Heat the butter and oil together in a skillet over high heat. Add half of the fish and cook 2–3 minutes on each side, until golden. Remove the fish to a warm platter and keep warm. Repeat the process with the remaining fish, adding more butter and oil if necessary.

4. To make the topping: Pour off all but about 1 tablespoon of the butter and oil. Return the skillet to medium heat. Add the mushrooms and sauté until they soften. Add the remaining topping ingredients and sauté about 2 minutes, until warmed through.

5. Ladle some of the Creole sauce onto 4 plates. Place 2 fish fillets atop each. Add a heaping tablespoon of the topping over each fillet, then a stripe of hollandaise. Finish with a pinch of cayenne. SERVES FOUR.

# Whole Flounder Stuffed with Crabmeat

*Bruning's opened at West End Park in 1859 and remained popular and excellent, run by the same family, until it and everything else at West End were destroyed by Hurricane Katrina. Bruning's great specialty was stuffed whole flounder. The restaurant may be gone (although maybe not forever), but the dish lives on. Use the biggest flounder you can find. (Fishermen refer to those as doormats.) I use claw crabmeat for the stuffing because it has a more pronounced taste.*

| STUFFING | FISH |
|---|---|
| ½ stick (4 Tbsp.) butter | 4 large whole flounder |
| ¼ cup flour | 1 cup flour |
| 3 green onions, chopped | 1 Tbsp. salt-free Creole seasoning |
| 3 cups shrimp stock | 1 tsp. salt |
| (see recipe, page 312) | 2 eggs |
| 1 Tbsp. Worcestershire sauce | 1 cup milk |
| 1 lb. claw crabmeat | ½ cup clarified butter (see recipe, |
| (or crawfish in season) | page 314) |
| ¼ tsp. salt | 1 lemon, sliced, for garnish |
| Pinch of cayenne | Chopped flat-leaf parsley, for garnish |

1. Preheat the oven to 400 degrees.

2. To make the stuffing: Melt the butter in a saucepan. Add the flour and cook, stirring constantly, until the mixture just begins to brown. Stir in the green onions and cook until limp. Whisk in the shrimp stock and Worcestershire sauce, and bring to a boil, then add the crabmeat, salt, and cayenne. Gently toss the crabmeat in the sauce to avoid breaking the lumps. Remove the pan from the heat and set aside.

3. Wash the flounder and pat dry. Combine the flour, Creole seasoning, and salt in a wide bowl. Whisk the eggs and milk together in another wide bowl. Coat the outside of the flounder with the seasoned flour. Dip the flounder into the egg mixture, then dredge once more into the seasoned flour.

4. Heat the clarified butter in a large skillet over medium-high heat. Add the fish, one at a time, and sauté about 4 minutes on each side. Remove and keep warm.

5. Cut a slit from head to tail across the top of each flounder. Divide the stuffing among the fish, spooning it inside the slit and piling it on top. Place the flounder on a baking sheet and bake for 6 minutes, or until the stuffing is heated through.

6. Place the flounder on hot plates. Garnish with lemon slices and fresh chopped parsley. SERVES FOUR TO EIGHT.

# Blackened Tuna

*There's no better fish for blackening than tuna. By wonderful coincidence, no method of cooking tuna is better than blackening. The essential thing to know is that blackening fish creates a terrific amount of smoke and perhaps flames. It's best done outdoors over a very hot fire. And don't be shy about getting the heat up there—it can't possibly be too hot.*

Four 10-oz. tuna steaks, each about
   1 inch thick (the thicker the better)
½ cup dry white wine
2 Tbsp. lemon juice, strained
1 tsp. Worcestershire sauce

2 cloves garlic, finely chopped
¼ cup salt-free Creole seasoning
1 Tbsp. salt
½ stick (4 Tbsp.) butter, melted
6 Tbsp. butter, softened

1. Trim away any dark parts of the tuna and discard.

2. Blend the wine, lemon juice, Worcestershire sauce, and garlic together in a broad bowl. Place the tuna steaks in this mixture for about 30 seconds on each side. Shake off any excess marinade and set the tuna aside.

3. Strain the excess marinade into a small saucepan, discarding solids, and bring to a light boil. Reduce by half.

4. Place a large cast-iron skillet over the hottest heat source you have. The pan is ready when the oils that have soaked into the metal have burned off and the surface is smoking.

5. Combine the Creole seasoning and salt together in a bowl. Generously season both sides of the fish with the seasoning mixture. Spoon melted butter over both sides, enough for it to drip a bit. Place the fish into the hot skillet. WARNING! There is a very good chance that this will flame up briefly and a certainty that there will be much smoke. The fish will first stick to the skillet, but after about a minute or so, it will break free. Turn it and cook the other side for another minute or so. It should be red in the center.

6. Make a lemon-butter sauce for the tuna by heating the reduced marinade over medium-low heat. Add the softened butter, a tablespoon at a time, to make a creamy-looking sauce. SERVES FOUR.

# Grilled Tuna with Orange-Soy Sauce

*Fresh tuna is a natural for Asian-style sauces like this one. Use high heat and avoid over-cooking—the tuna steaks should be a little red at the center. This recipe pairs the natural juiciness of tuna with some crisp vegetables and a sharp, low-calorie sauce.*

**MARINADE**

¼ cup red wine vinegar
¼ cup orange juice
3 Tbsp. sugar
3 Tbsp. soy sauce
1 tsp. ground ginger
¼ tsp. crushed red pepper flakes

**FISH**

Four 8–10-oz. yellowfin tuna steaks, each at least 1 inch thick
3 Tbsp. butter
3 cups shredded cabbage
3 green onions, finely chopped
1 medium carrot, peeled and sliced into matchsticks
1 tsp. soy sauce
Salt and freshly ground black pepper

1. Combine all of the marinade ingredients in a broad bowl. Pass the tuna steaks through the marinade, wrap them (still dripping) with plastic wrap, and refrigerate for at least an hour. Save the remaining marinade.

2. Melt the butter in a skillet over medium-high heat. Add the cabbage, green onions, and carrots, along with the soy sauce, and stir-fry until the vegetables wilt. Remove from the heat.

3. Heat a cast-iron skillet until smoking. (You may also grill this over a very hot fire.) Season the tuna with salt and pepper. Cook the tuna for about 1½ minutes on each side. (Note: This will produce a great deal of smoke, so keep the exhaust fan on or cook the tuna outside.) Remove the tuna and keep warm.

4. Reduce the heat to medium. Add the reserved marinade to the skillet and bring to a boil. Slightly reduce it.

5. Divide the vegetables among 4 plates. Top each with a piece of tuna and spoon on the reduced sauce. SERVES FOUR.

# Tuna Puttanesca

*Puttanesca, you've probably heard, means in the style of prostitutes. See, the sauce is made with a bunch of powerfully flavored, salty ingredients, and . . . well . . . I get the implication, but . . . uh . . . it's very satisfying. I recommend getting the tuna cut as thick as possible, perhaps even in cubes or blocks three inches on a side.*

Four 8–10-oz. tuna steaks, each at least 1½ inches thick
3 Tbsp. extra-virgin olive oil
Salt and freshly ground black pepper to taste
One 10-oz. bag of fresh spinach, well washed and picked
12 black olives, pitted and coarsely chopped
12 green olives, pitted and coarsely chopped
1 tsp. chopped garlic
1 tsp. chopped anchovy fillet
1 tsp. chopped fresh oregano
¼ tsp. crushed red pepper
1 cup Fresh Marinara Sauce (see recipe, page 320)

1. Brush the tuna with some of the oil and season with salt and pepper. In a hot cast-iron skillet or over a hot grill, cook the tuna for 1–2 minutes on each side. Remove and keep warm.

2. Heat 1 teaspoon of the oil in a saucepan. Add the wet-from-washing spinach with a little salt and pepper until it just begins to wilt. Remove and set aside.

3. Heat the remaining oil in another saucepan over medium heat. Add the black and green olives, garlic, anchovy, oregano, and crushed red pepper, and cook until just heated through. Add the marinara sauce and bring to a boil. Lower heat to a simmer.

4. Divide the spinach among 4 serving plates. Top each with a piece of tuna, then spoon on the sauce. SERVES FOUR.

# Seared Tuna with Tomato-Lemon Vinaigrette

*Although the menu at Gautreau's is constantly changing, there always seems to be a great tuna dish on it. This is one I recall from the early 1990s. It involves tuna cut into thick blocks and finished almost in the style of a salad. I've been cooking this ever since, whenever I can find thick tuna.*

VINAIGRETTE

2 Tbsp. lemon juice
1 Tbsp. white wine vinegar
1 tsp. Dijon mustard
6 Tbsp. olive oil
2 Tbsp. vegetable oil
Salt and ground white pepper
2 large ripe tomatoes
1 clove garlic, chopped
Leaves of 1 sprig fresh thyme

TUNA

2 lb. thick tuna steaks, cut into 16 cubes
3 Tbsp. olive oil

6 oz. arugula or spring mix salad

1. To make the vinaigrette: Whisk the lemon juice, vinegar, and mustard together in a bowl. Add the oils in a slow stream, whisking vigorously, to form a light emulsion. Season to taste with salt and pepper, and set aside.

2. Bring a pot of water to a rolling boil. Cut the stem core out of the top of the tomatoes and cut an X in the bottom. Plunge the tomatoes into the boiling water for 15–20 seconds, then rinse under cold water. The peel can now be removed easily. Slice the tomatoes in half crosswise and remove the seeds and pulp.

3. Put the tomatoes, garlic, thyme, salt and pepper to taste, and the vinaigrette into a food processor or blender and process until well blended. Thin with a little vinegar if necessary.

4. Allow the tuna fillets to stand at room temperature for 15 minutes. Season all sides with salt and pepper.

*(continued)*

5. Heat the 3 tablespoons of olive oil in a large, heavy skillet until almost smoking. Place 4 tuna blocks at a time in the pan and cook over high heat for about 20 seconds per side, until all sides are lightly browned. Repeat until all of the tuna is cooked, adding more olive oil if necessary.

6. Toss the arugula or spring mix with enough vinaigrette to coat and arrange in the center of the plate. Place tuna around the salad and drizzle with more of the vinaigrette. SERVES FOUR.

# Horseradish-Crusted Grouper
# with Oysters and Saffron

*This is another creation of Commander's chef Jamie Shannon, who died tragically young but left behind many warm memories. The sauce is made with the most expensive ingredient in the world, saffron (don't worry—a little bit goes a long way) and fresh oysters.*

CRUST

1 stick (8 Tbsp.) butter
3 cups bread crumbs
3 Tbsp. finely grated fresh horseradish
1 bunch of flat-leaf parsley,
   leaves chopped
2 Tbsp. salt-free Creole seasoning
2 tsp. salt

Four 8–10-oz. grouper fillets

SAUCE

2 cups heavy whipping cream
1 Tbsp. butter
1 Tbsp. chopped yellow onion
1 Tbsp. chopped shallots
¼ tsp. chopped garlic
¼ tsp. saffron (about 10 threads)
½ tsp. salt
½ tsp. ground white pepper
1 dozen fresh, shucked large oysters

1. Preheat the oven to 400 degrees. Lightly oil a large baking pan and set aside.

2. To make the crust: Melt the butter and blend it with the remaining crust ingredients to form a pasty mixture. Divide this into 4 portions and cover the top of each fillet with a layer of the crust. With the back of a knife, make a crisscross pattern in the crust for eye appeal.

3. Place the encrusted fish in the prepared pan. Bake the fish until the crust is golden, 10–14 minutes.

4. To make the sauce: Place the cream in a saucepan over medium-high heat and reduce by a third. Melt the butter in a skillet over medium heat. Add the onion, shallots, and garlic, and cook until translucent. Add the reduced cream to the skillet and bring to a boil. Strain the cream back into the saucepan. Add the saffron, salt, pepper, and oysters, and gently simmer until edges of the oysters begin to curl.

5. Place the fish on serving plates and surround with 3 oysters per person. Pour the sauce onto the plate, around (but not over) the fish. SERVES FOUR.

# Salmon Florentine

*For this dish, buy the thickest salmon fillets you can, remove all the skin (not as hard as it looks—just have a sharp knife handy), and broil it just until it's warm all the way though.*

| SALMON | MARINADE |
|---|---|
| Two 10-oz. bags of fresh spinach | ¼ cup extra-virgin olive oil |
| Four 8-oz. salmon fillets | ¼ cup dry white wine |
| 6 Tbsp. butter | 1 Tbsp. lemon juice |
| ¼ cup heavy whipping cream | ½ tsp. Worcestershire sauce |
| ¼ tsp. dried dill | 1 tsp. soy sauce |
| Juice of ½ lemon | 2 dashes of Tabasco |
| ¼ tsp. salt | |
| Pinch of ground white pepper | |
| Pinch of nutmeg | |

1. Preheat the broiler. Lightly grease a baking sheet and set aside.

2. Pick stems from the spinach; discard bad leaves. Wash the spinach in several changes of water. Place the wet spinach in a large saucepan and cook, uncovered, over medium-low heat until wilted. Drain the spinach and set aside until cool enough to handle. Squeeze out excess water, coarsely chop, and return to pan. Set the spinach aside.

3. Combine the marinade ingredients in a wide bowl. Add the salmon fillets and marinate for a minute on each side. Lift the salmon from the marinade and place on the prepared baking sheet. Broil 3 inches from the heat for 3 minutes. Flip the fish, dot each with ¼ teaspoon of the butter and continue to broil for another 2–3 minutes. Loosely cover with foil to keep warm.

4. To the spinach, add the cream and cook over medium-low heat, stirring, until the spinach is heated through. Meanwhile, melt the remaining butter in a saucepan over low heat. Add the dill, lemon juice, salt, pepper, and nutmeg, and whisk constantly until a creamy sauce forms.

5. Divide the spinach among 4 serving plates. Arrange a salmon fillet on top of the spinach on each plate and spoon sauce over all. SERVES FOUR.

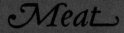

# Meat

New Orleans is so famous for seafood that one might assume it's not the place to eat meat. This is not the case. New Orleans is a steak town on a par with New York and Chicago, with a long tradition of using top grades of aged beef. Beyond that, the city has a distinctive style of serving a steak: in a sizzling pool of butter on a hot plate. Ruth's Chris Steak House, one of the major players in the deluxe steak category, started in New Orleans—and it wasn't the first great steak place in town.

Beyond beef, Creole chefs cook everything else from the butcher shop. The local cuisine includes many unique sausages and dishes made from them. There's even a meaty, traditional breakfast dish. All of this, of course, is done with a free hand with the seasonings and big, flavorful sauces.

# Strip Sirloin Steak Bordelaise

*My favorite cut of beef is a thick, 24-ounce bone-in strip sirloin. The best way to cook steak like this is on a very hot outdoor grill or in an equally hot cast-iron skillet. In either case, it will throw off a lot of smoke and perhaps even flames, so this is best done outside. You could also broil or pan-broil the steaks, but in either case, use the highest heat you can.*

*Bordelaise sauce in New Orleans usually means a garlic-and-parsley butter. This version is closer to the wine-based French original. Lyonnaise Potatoes (see recipe, page 217) make an excellent accompaniment for this steak.*

SAUCE
1 bottle red Bordeaux wine
   or Cabernet Sauvignon
1 sprig fresh thyme
10 black peppercorns
½ stick (4 Tbsp.) butter
4 cloves garlic, finely chopped

1 cup rich beef or veal stock (see
   recipe, page 312)
Salt

STEAKS
Four 24-oz. bone-in strip sirloin steaks
Salt-free Creole seasoning
Salt to taste
½ stick (4 Tbsp.) butter, melted

1. Make the sauce first, since it will take about an hour. Bring the wine, thyme, and peppercorns to a boil in a saucepan. Reduce heat to medium-low and simmer until the wine is reduced to ½ cup. Meanwhile, melt ½ teaspoon of the butter in a large skillet over medium heat. Add the garlic and sauté until it smells good. Strain the reduced wine into the skillet, add the stock, and bring to a boil. Reduce by half. Reduce heat to low and add the remaining butter, a tablespoon at a time, whisking constantly until a creamy sauce forms. Season to taste with salt. Keep warm.

2. Preheat the grill, cast-iron skillet, or broiler to as hot as you can get it. Dust the steaks generously with the Creole seasoning and salt. Brush the melted butter generously on both sides of the steaks and put them onto the grill or into the pan.

3. Turn the steaks only once, with tongs. For medium-rare, look for a meat thermometer reading of 130–135 degrees. As the steak will cook a little more in its own heat, pull it off a little early. Spoon the sauce over the steaks and serve with Lyonnaise Potatoes. SERVES FOUR TO EIGHT.

# Filet Mignon au Poivre

*My favorite fancy steak dish is steak au poivre ("with pepper"). Here's a simple version of that restaurant classic.*

*The method of cooking steaks in a skillet with butter is the one that most restaurants use. I find that it's the easiest way to cook a steak. But I also like the appearance and the flavor it gives and the uniform brown crust it produces. This technique works better for a filet than for other cuts.*

| | |
|---|---|
| Four 8–10-oz. filets mignons | ¼ cup brandy |
| Salt and freshly ground black pepper | 1 cup heavy whipping cream |
| 1 Tbsp. butter | 1 Tbsp. black peppercorns, cracked |
| 2 tsp. chopped shallots | 2 tsp. demi-glace (optional) |

1. Trim the filets if necessary, removing all but the central true filet part, as well as the tough silverskin. Season lightly with salt and pepper.

2. Heat a heavy skillet over medium heat. Add the butter and turn the pan to distribute and melt it quickly. Put the steaks into the skillet. Scatter the shallots around the steaks. Cook the steaks for 3–5 minutes per side. The steaks are ready to be turned when they come unstuck from the pan. (That doesn't always happen, but if the steak is really stuck down there, it's probably not ready to be turned yet.) If the steaks are thick, cook them on their sides as well as on their faces. About 6–8 minutes of total cooking time will make for medium rare. (For perfect results, use a meat thermometer and look for a reading of 130–135 degrees for medium rare.) Remove the steaks to a warm platter and keep warm.

3. Add the brandy to the pan and bring to a boil. (Be careful. It may catch fire, which is all right for flavor but potentially dangerous.) With a whisk, dissolve the browned bits of meat in the brandy as it boils. When the brandy is almost boiled away, add the cream and cracked peppercorns (and the demi-glace, if you have it). Bring to a simmer and cook 3–5 minutes, shaking the skillet, until the sauce is reduced by about a third.

4. Place a steak on each of 4 warm plates and spoon on the sauce. SERVES FOUR.

# Carpetbagger Steak

*It's an odd-sounding idea: a steak stuffed with an oyster and served with a sauce of beef essence and more oysters. But the flavors of the two ingredients are most agreeably complementary. The hard part of making this dish is making the demi-glace, the ultimate reduction of an intense stock made from roasted veal bones. Every good cook should try this at least once; if you do it right, it takes two days. If you don't want to go to the trouble, you can buy demi-glace at gourmet food stores or on the Internet. If you're friends with a chef, he might sell or give you some.*

    Four 8-oz. filets mignons
    Salt and freshly ground black pepper
    20 medium-large fresh, shucked oysters
    1 cup Pinot Noir or other dry red wine
    ½ cup demi-glace
    1 stick (8 Tbsp.) unsalted butter
    1 Tbsp. clarified butter (see recipe, page 314)

1. Season the steaks with salt and pepper. With a sharp paring knife, cut a slit in the side of each of the steaks. Stuff an oyster into each steak.

2. Place the remaining oysters into a stainless steel or enamel saucepan or skillet. Pour in the wine and bring to a boil. Cook until the oysters begin to curl. Remove the oysters with a slotted spoon to a bowl and continue to simmer the wine until it's reduced to about ⅓ cup.

3. Stir in the demi-glace and return to a simmer. Reduce the heat to low and add the unsalted butter, a tablespoon at a time and whisking constantly, until the sauce is thick and creamy. Season to taste with salt and pepper. Keep the sauce warm.

4. Cook the steaks in a hot skillet with a little clarified butter, adding more, as necessary, to sear the outside of the steaks. Cook to the desired degree of doneness. Place a steak on each of 4 warm plates. Surround each steak with 4 oysters and spoon the sauce over all. SERVES FOUR.

# Roast Tenderloin of Beef
# with Merlot Sauce

*A few times a year I cook big, festive dinners for people who buy my services at auction for one charity or another. This dish is one I often include in those dinners. My guests seem to be impressed that I turn a whole bottle of wine into about a quarter cup of sauce. That's an easy trick, though.*

1 whole beef tenderloin,
    trimmed of silverskin and fat
Salt and freshly ground black pepper
2 tsp. butter, softened
2 Tbsp. chopped shallots
1 bottle Merlot
    (or other full-bodied red wine)

2 cups rich beef stock (see recipe,
    page 312)
1 tsp. dried tarragon
1 tsp. black peppercorns
1 Tbsp. currant jelly
1 stick (8 Tbsp.) butter, softened

1. Preheat the oven to 350 degrees. Lightly season the tenderloin with salt and pepper. Coat a skillet, large enough to hold the tenderloin, with the butter and heat it over high heat. Add the tenderloin and cook until well browned all over. Transfer the tenderloin to a roasting pan and put it into the center of the oven. Roast until a meat thermometer inserted into the thickest part reads 130–135 degrees (medium rare).

2. While the beef is roasting, add the shallots to the skillet in which you seared the beef. Sauté for about a minute, then add the entire bottle of wine—saving a glassful for yourself to drink. Bring to a boil and hold it there for about a minute. Lower the heat to a fast simmer. Add the beef stock, tarragon, and peppercorns, and reduce to 1 cup of liquid. Strain, then stir in the currant jelly. Remove the sauce from the heat and add the butter, a tablespoon at a time, whisking constantly.

3. When the beef reaches the desired temperature, remove it from the oven and let it rest for 10 minutes. Slice the beef tenderloin into ¾-inch-thick steaks. Spoon the sauce onto the plates and top with the tenderloin. SERVES EIGHT, WITH LOTS OF LEFTOVER STEAK.

# Hot Garlic Filet Mignon

*Really, really spicy, this is a unique dish for times when you want a steak, but not plain old.*

2 heads garlic
1 Tbsp. olive oil
2 jalapeño peppers
2 Anaheim chile peppers
6 medium leaves fresh basil
3 sprigs flat-leaf parsley, leaves only

Salt to taste
4 filets mignons from the big end of
   the loin, about 1½ inches thick
2 Tbsp. butter
3 Tbsp. tequila (or brandy)
½ cup heavy whipping cream

1. Preheat the oven to 300 degrees. Cut off the tops of the garlic heads, taking off enough to cut off the ends of most of the cloves. Pour the oil into a puddle in a small baking pan and set the garlic heads, cut side down, on top of the oil. Bake for 1 hour, or until the cloves are quite soft and browned.

2. Roast the peppers under the broiler (I use my toaster oven for this), turning them until the outside is charred and blistered. Let the peppers cool, then peel away the skin. Open them up and remove the seeds and the membrane inside. Rinse them it hot water and cut into thin strips about an inch long.

3. When the garlic is roasted, remove and peel the cloves. (You can squeeze them out, usually.) Put them into a food processor with the basil, parsley, a pinch of salt, and about 1 tablespoon of the pepper strips. Process into a rough paste. Cut a slit in the side of each filet, making a pocket about 1 inch deep. Using a spoon, stuff with about a tablespoon of the garlic-chile mixture. Season filets on the outside with salt.

4. Melt the butter in a large, heavy skillet over high heat. Add the steaks and pan-broil. They will first stick to the pan, then almost break away; that's the time to turn them (once). Cook to the desired degree of doneness (130–135 degrees for medium rare). Transfer the steaks to a warm platter to let rest.

5. Add the tequila to the skillet in which you cooked the steaks and bring to a boil, whisking to dissolve the browned bits stuck to the bottom of the pan. When the liquid has reduced by two-thirds, add the cream, the remaining strips of jalapeño and Anaheim chile peppers, and salt to taste. Bring to a boil and reduce by one-third, then pour over the steaks on their serving plates. SERVES FOUR.

# Boiled Brisket of Beef

*In New Orleans, the favorite method of cooking brisket is to simmer it for hours. The flavorful meat is served with boiled cabbage, carrots, and potatoes as a classic lunch special in the older restaurants. One of the byproducts of making boiled beef is the ultimate stock for making Brisket and Vegetable Soup (see recipe, page 90).*

| | |
|---|---|
| 8-lb. choice brisket, flat end preferably | ½ tsp. mustard seed |
| 2 medium yellow onions, each cut into 8 pieces | 2 bay leaves, broken in half |
| | 2 cloves (optional) |
| Leafy tops from 1 bunch of celery | 2 Tbsp. salt |
| Stems from 1 bunch of flat-leaf parsley | |
| 4 cloves garlic, crushed | SAUCE |
| 1 tsp. black peppercorns | ½ cup Creole mustard |
| 1 tsp. dried thyme | ½ cup chili sauce (or ketchup) |
| 1 tsp. dried marjoram | ½ cup prepared horseradish |

1. Bring 2 gallons (32 cups) of water to a boil in a large stockpot.

2. Meanwhile, trim any excess fat from the brisket. Cut it in 3 pieces and put it into the water. (No need to wait for it to boil.) Add all of the other ingredients except for the sauce ingredients. Cover the pot and bring to a boil. Reduce the heat to as low a temperature as possible with bubbles still breaking. (The lowest heat setting will usually do the job.) Simmer for 4–5 hours, skimming any foam that rises to the surface.

3. Remove the brisket and set aside. Strain out the vegetables and discard, but save the beef stock for other uses. The stock can be kept in the refrigerator for about a week, or it can be frozen.

4. To make the sauce: Blend the 3 sauce ingredients together in a bowl. Chill in the refrigerator until ready to use.

5. Slice the brisket or serve it in large cubes, but cut against the grain with a sharp, nonserrated knife. The meat will be falling apart and easy to eat. Serve with boiled cabbage, potatoes, carrots, and the chilled sauce. SERVES EIGHT, WITH LEFTOVERS FOR SANDWICHES OR TO ADD TO VEGETABLE SOUP.

# Veal Pannée

*It may be safe to say that there is no known food that tastes bad pannéed, or coated with bread crumbs, New Orleans style. Pannéed veal, which everyone in New Orleans grew up eating, is so easy to prepare that it must have brightened the hearts of chefs and restaurateurs when it became popular in restaurants in the late 1970s. (Before that, strangely, it was almost never seen on a menu.) I personally prefer pannéed pork, but the technique is the same for both types of meat.*

> 8 large slices veal leg, cut across the grain
> ½ cup flour
> 1 tsp. salt
> ¼ tsp. salt-free Creole seasoning
> 2 eggs, beaten
> 1½ cups fresh bread crumbs
> Canola or olive oil
> Chopped flat-leaf parsley, for garnish

1. Pound the veal with a meat pounder between 2 pieces of wax paper until each piece is about twice its original size.

2. Mix the flour, salt, and Creole seasoning together, and lightly dust (don't dredge!) the veal. Pass the veal through the beaten egg. Shake off the excess. Then dredge through the bread crumbs.

3. Heat about ½ inch of oil in a heavy skillet (cast-iron is perfect) over medium-high heat until a pinch of bread crumbs fries vigorously. Cook the veal, as many pieces as will fit without overlapping, for about 1½ minutes per side, or until the exterior is golden brown. Remove and drain on paper towels. Garnish with the parsley and serve alongside pasta Alfredo or Pasta Bordelaise (see recipe, page 230). SERVES FOUR.

# Veal with Oyster Stuffing

*This is a Creole-Italian dish if ever there was one. It is reminiscent of what Italians call "involtini di vitello." (For some reason, New Orleans Italians call the same thing "spiedini," even though it's not skewered with anything more than a toothpick.) But the flavor is distinctly Creole.*

1 stick (8 Tbsp.) plus 2 Tbsp. butter
1 large yellow onion, chopped
1 rib celery, chopped
2 dozen fresh, shucked oysters, drained and oyster liquor reserved
1 Tbsp. lemon juice
One 8-inch-long piece of stale French bread, cut into cubes

Eight 2-oz. veal-leg medallions, cut across the grain
½ cup flour
1 tsp. salt-free Creole seasoning
1 tsp. salt
½ cup dry white wine
2 Tbsp. small capers

1. Melt the stick of butter in a skillet. Add the onion and celery, and sauté until soft. Add the oysters and lemon juice, and cook until the oysters just begin to curl.

2. Pour the oyster liquor into a 1-cup measuring cup and add enough cold water, if necessary, to make 1 cup. Soak the bread cubes in the oyster liquor and add to the skillet. Cook until everything is heated through. Remove from the heat.

3. Pound the veal with a meat pounder between 2 pieces of wax paper until each piece is about twice its original size. Mix the flour, Creole seasoning, and salt together, and lightly dust (don't dredge!) the veal.

4. Spoon one-quarter of the oyster dressing in a line down the center of each piece of veal. Roll the veal around the stuffing and secure with toothpicks.

5. Melt 1 tablespoon of the butter in a large skillet and brown the veal rolls well on all sides. Remove and keep warm in a 200-degree oven.

6. Add the wine to the skillet and bring to a boil, whisking to dissolve the veal juices in the pan. Reduce the wine by about half, then remove from the heat and whisk in the remaining tablespoon of butter. Add the capers and stir to combine. Divide the rolls among 4 plates and spoon sauce over all. SERVES FOUR.

# Veal with White Wine and Vanilla Butter

*Vanilla works with only a narrow range of savory ingredients, but this combination is a winner. I was trying to come up with a new take on veal Marsala, whose sauce is made with an aromatic, slightly sweet red wine. Without Marsala in the kitchen, I remembered how much I liked a veal piccata I'd made using an intensely oaky (and therefore vanilla-scented) Chardonnay. So I took it up to the next level.*

*When you buy veal for this dish, make sure it has been sliced across the grain. I find butchers have an annoying habit of slicing it with the grain, which will make the finished dish tough. As for the vanilla, if you're in New Orleans, look for Ronald Reginald's Melipone vanilla, which has an especially beguiling aroma.*

| | |
|---|---|
| 1 lb. white veal round scallops | ½ stick (4 Tbsp.) butter |
| 1 cup flour | 1 Tbsp. olive oil |
| 1 tsp. salt | ½ cup oak-aged Chardonnay |
| ¼ tsp. ground white pepper | 1 Tbsp. lemon juice, strained |
| ½ tsp. paprika | ¼ tsp. vanilla extract |

1. Pound the veal with a meat pounder between 2 pieces of wax paper until each piece is about twice its original size.

2. Combine the flour, salt, pepper, and paprika in a wide bowl. Dust the veal slices with the seasoned flour to very lightly coat.

3. Heat 2 tablespoons of the butter and all of the olive oil in a skillet over medium heat until it bubbles. Add the veal, without overlapping any of it, and cook it just under 30 seconds on each side. Remove the veal to a plate and place in a warm 200-degree oven until ready to serve.

4. Add the Chardonnay and lemon juice to the pan and simmer for about 2 minutes, scraping the bottom of the skillet to dissolve the browned bits. Reduce the heat to low, stir in the vanilla, then whisk in the remaining 2 tablespoons of butter.

5. Divide the veal among 4 warm plates and spoon on the sauce. SERVES FOUR.

# Liver à l'Orange

*This is my version of a creation of chef Tom Cowman, who came to town to open the kitchen at the fabled Restaurant Jonathan and who later became everybody's favorite chef at the Upperline. The sauce is similar to the one in duck à l'orange, but it goes perfectly with liver. This is a dish for you if you never liked liver before. It may turn you around.*

1 cup flour
1 Tbsp. salt
1 tsp. salt-free Creole seasoning
1½ lb. (approximately) veal liver
Juice of 1 large orange, strained
¼ cup Cointreau or Grand Marnier
¼ cup dry white wine

3 Tbsp. orange marmalade
¼ cup chopped sweet onion
⅛ tsp. dried marjoram
8 slices bacon
2 Tbsp. butter
8 half-moon slices of orange,
   about ¼ inch thick

1. Preheat the broiler. Combine the flour, salt, and Creole seasoning in a wide bowl and set aside. Slice the liver in 8 wide slices, about ¼ inch thick, and set aside.

2. Combine the orange juice, Cointreau, wine, marmalade, onion, and marjoram in a small saucepan and cook, stirring, over medium heat until thick enough to coat a spoon. Keep warm on the lowest heat.

3. Fry the bacon in a skillet until crisp. Allow to cool, then break into small pieces (but not quite crumbled). Pour off the excess bacon fat, but don't wipe the pan. Add the butter and heat over medium-high heat. Pass the liver through the seasoned flour, shaking off the excess. Add the liver to the skillet and sauté for about 2 minutes on each side, leaving some pink in the center.

4. Transfer the liver to a baking sheet, with the slices slightly overlapping. Tuck an orange slice between each slice of liver and spoon some of the sauce over each slice. Broil until the sauce starts bubbling, about a minute.

5. Arrange 2 liver slices and 2 orange slices on each of 4 warm plates and spoon a little sauce around the side. SERVES FOUR.

# Pannéed Pork Chops
# with Fennel Creole Sauce

*Some years ago, the annual March of Dimes Gourmet Gala took the form of a celebrity cooking competition, to which I was invited. My dish was pannéed sweetbreads prepared with the sauce below. I won!*

*As much as I like sweetbreads, I give you this recipe with pork chops because sweetbreads are hard to find and fool with and a lot of people don't like them.*

SAUCE

3 Tbsp. butter

1 medium yellow onion, chopped

1 medium green bell pepper, chopped

1 bulb fresh fennel

1 rib celery, chopped

½ tsp. chopped garlic

One 28-oz. can whole tomatoes

2 large ripe tomatoes, seeds and diced

2 cups chicken stock (see recipe,
   page 312)

½ bunch of green onions, chopped

2 bay leaves

1 sprig fresh thyme

1 tsp. Louisana hot sauce,
   such as Crystal

1 tsp. salt, plus more to taste

½ tsp. ground white pepper,
   plus more to taste

½ tsp. Worcestershire sauce

PORK CHOPS

8 center-cut pork chops, trimmed

½ cup flour

1 tsp. salt

¼ tsp. salt-free Creole seasoning

2 eggs, beaten

1½ cups fresh bread crumbs

Canola or olive oil

Fresh chervil (or parsley), for garnish

1. To make the sauce: Melt the butter in a heavy saucepan. Add the onion, bell pepper, fennel, celery, and garlic, and sauté until just tender but not browned, about 5 minutes.

*(continued)*

2. With your fingers or a food processor, crush the canned tomatoes. Add them, all the juice from the can, and the fresh tomatoes to the pan, along with the chicken stock, and bring to a simmer. Add all of the remaining sauce ingredients and cook over medium heat for 5 minutes.

3. Reduce the heat to a simmer and cook until the sauce has reached a non-runny consistency. Adjust the seasonings with salt and pepper, and keep warm until time to serve. (Makes about 4 cups of sauce. This is a bit more than you'll need, but you'll find that some people can't get enough of the sauce. Refrigerate the rest and keep it on hand for omelets, grilled chicken, or grilled shrimp. It will keep for about a week.)

4. Pound the pork chops with a meat pounder between 2 pieces of wax paper until they're about twice their original size. Mix the flour, salt, and Creole seasoning together, and lightly dust (don't dredge!) the pork chops with the seasoned flour. Pass the pork chops through the beaten eggs, shaking of the excess. Then dredge through the bread crumbs.

5. Heat about ½ inch of oil in a heavy skillet (cast-iron is perfect) over medium-high heat, until a pinch of bread crumbs fries vigorously. Cook the pork chops, one at a time, until golden brown, about 1½ minutes per side. Remove and drain on paper towels.

6. Spoon about ¼ cup of sauce around each chop and serve garnished with chervil or parsley. SERVES FOUR.

# Pepper-Crusted Pork Loin
# with Sweet Heat Sauce

*As the Chinese have known for ages, sweet heat is a wonderful flavor effect. The sweetness in the sauce balances an otherwise over-the-top degree of pepper heat in the dish, resulting in greatly heightened flavor. You can use either pork tenderloin or pork rib loin for this dish. The latter is better if you're cooking on the outdoor grill.*

*I will always associate this dish with Hurricane Katrina. I made it up the weekend before the storm hit. Then, after my family and I were evacuated to the home of our niece Jennifer Donner in Atlanta, I cooked (and perfected) it there.*

### PORK LOIN
1 pork rib loin, 10–12 inches long, trimmed of fat and silverskin,
    or 2 pork tenderloins
¼ cup soy sauce
¼ cup coarsely ground black pepper
Salt

### SAUCE
¼ cup fig preserves
¼ cup orange marmalade (or other kinds of preserves)
½ cup apple juice
2 Tbsp. steak sauce
1 Tbsp. soy sauce
¼ tsp. salt

1. If cooking outside, build a fire with some wood chips or other smoking fuel in the pit. If cooking indoors, preheat the broiler and pan, positioning the pan 6 inches from the heat.

2. If using the rib loin, cut it from end to end into 2 pieces of the same size. (The pork tenderloin is already the perfect size.) Pour the soy sauce over the loins and coat them all over. Sprinkle on the coarse pepper and a bit of salt. The pepper should create a distinct crust.

*(continued)*

3. Place the pork loins right over the fire in the grill and cook, turning every few minutes, until the internal temperature reaches 160 degrees on a meat thermometer. There may still be a blush of pink in the center, but that is well past the safety point for pork. If using the oven, place the loins under the broiler and broil, turning once, for 10 minutes, until the exterior is well browned. Lower the heat to 275 degrees and continue to cook until the interior temperature reaches 160 degrees.

4. Slice the pork loins into ½-inch-thick medallions. If using tenderloin, slice it on the bias.

5. Combine all of the sauce ingredients in a saucepan and heat through. Reduce the sauce a little if you think it's too thin. SERVES EIGHT TO TEN.

# Pork Tenderloin Diane

*Steak Diane is a famous dish from the really old days and persists in only the few restaurants that still perform a lot of tableside preparation. (Brennan's is one.) I thought pork tenderloin might work with the recipe, so I played around with it until I came up with this.*

2 whole pork tenderloins, cut into 1-inch-thick medallions

2 Tbsp. salt-free Creole seasoning

1 tsp. salt

2 Tbsp. butter

2 Tbsp. bourbon

1 Tbsp. lemon juice, strained

3 Tbsp. Worcestershire sauce

2 Tbsp. Tabasco Caribbean Style Steak Sauce or Pickapeppa

1 tsp. Dijon mustard

⅓ cup heavy whipping cream

1 Tbsp. shallots, very finely chopped, for garnish

½ tsp. coarsely cracked black pepper, for garnish

1. Season the pork with the Creole seasoning and salt.

2. Heat the butter in a large skillet over medium heat. Add the pork and cook until browned on each side. Remove and keep warm.

3. Add the bourbon to the skillet and bring to a boil, whisking to dissolve the browned bits. Add the lemon juice, Worcestershire sauce, steak sauce, and mustard, and cook for a minute. Add the cream and reduce heat to a simmer.

4. Return the pork to the pan and heat through while spooning sauce over the medallions.

5. Divide the pork among 6 warm plates. Spoon on the sauce and garnish with a light sprinkle of the shallots and pepper. SERVES SIX.

# Open-Mouth Pork Chop

*This variation on stuffed pork chops is so off-center that I had to call it something else. Do not be distressed that the stuffing wants to fall out; there's no avoiding this other than by using toothpicks to hold the chop together during the cooking.*

2 oz. Parmesan cheese
½ stick (4 Tbsp.) butter
4 cloves garlic, chopped
¼ tsp. crushed red pepper
3 crimini mushrooms or 1 small portobello, sliced
3 firm Italian plum tomatoes, seeded and sliced
6 sprigs flat-leaf parsley, leaves only, chopped
¼ cup bread crumbs
Four 16–20-oz. double pork chops
Salt
Salt-free Creole seasoning

1. Preheat the broiler. Using a vegetable peeler, slice off thin but wide shavings of the Parmesan cheese and set aside.

2. Melt the butter in a medium skillet over medium-low heat until it bubbles. Add the garlic and crushed red pepper, and sauté until the garlic is fragrant. Add the mushrooms and cook until the mushrooms just begin to soften. Add the tomatoes and parsley, and toss to combine. The tomatoes should not get hot. Remove from the heat and sprinkle the bread crumbs evenly over the top.

3. Using a sharp knife, cut a slit in the pork chops all the way to the bones. Open the chops and spoon in some of the mushroom-tomato mixture. Tuck some of the cheese shavings into the pocket and pin the edges of the pork chop (you won't be able to close it) with toothpicks.

4. Season the chops with salt and Creole seasoning. Broil about 4 inches from the heat for about 5 minutes and turn. Broil on the other side until done. Remove the toothpicks and serve. SERVES FOUR.

# Noisettes d'Agneau Maison d'Or

*"Nuggets of lamb in the style of the House of Gold" was for many years the premier lamb dish at Antoine's. It was revised in the late 1970s—a good idea, since the sauce was an impossibly old-fashioned concoction riddled with sweetbreads, turkey chunks, and mushrooms. My recipe is really different from Antoine's dish, but I wanted to keep the name alive because my first golden retriever, Noisette—a wonderful dog—was named after it.*

1 rack of American lamb
Salt and freshly ground black pepper
2 Tbsp. extra-virgin olive oil
2 cloves garlic, crushed

SAUCE
2 Tbsp. red wine
1 Tbsp. fresh orange juice, strained

1 tsp. tarragon vinegar
1 tsp. dried chives
½ cup thinly sliced crimini
   mushrooms
½ tsp. Tabasco Green Pepper Sauce
2 egg yolks
1 stick (8 Tbsp.) butter, softened

1. Preheat the oven to 350 degrees. Trim the lean central part of the rack away from the bones and fat. Season it with salt and pepper. Heat the oil in a large ovenproof skillet over medium-high heat. Add the garlic and cook until the garlic browns a little. Add the lamb and brown it all over. Transfer the skillet to the oven and bake the lamb until it is done to your liking. (For medium-rare, look for a meat-thermometer reading of 130–135 degrees. This should take about 25 minutes.)

2. While the lamb is roasting, make the sauce. Combine all of the sauce ingredients except the egg yolks and butter in a small saucepan. Cook over low heat until almost all the liquid has been absorbed or evaporated. Set aside.

3. Put the egg yolks into a metal bowl and set over a saucepan of gently boiling water. Whisk constantly until the yokes turn a pale yellow color. Add the butter, a little at a time, whisking constantly. When the sauce is fluffy, add the mushroom mixture. Keep warm.

4. Remove the lamb from the oven and let it rest for 10 minutes before carving. Slice the lamb into ¾-inch-thick medallions. Serve 2 medallions per person with the sauce spooned generously over the top. SERVES FOUR.

# Roasted Venison Backstrap with Cherry-Peppercorn Sauce

*I have about a dozen friends who hunt. All of them must be pretty good at it because they seem always to have freezers full of venison that they're eager to give away. I'm pleased to accept it so I can make up dishes like this one. By the way, this is the kind of dish that will turn around those who say they don't like game. Even my kids liked this, and that's saying something.*

4 venison backstraps (loins), about 4–6 lb. total

**MARINADE**
1 cup Cabernet Sauvignon or Merlot
½ cup orange juice
1 Tbsp. black peppercorns
2 bay leaves
1 tsp. dried marjoram
1 tsp. dried thyme

**SAUCE**
Salt and freshly ground black pepper
3 Tbsp. butter
1 Tbsp. chopped shallots
3 Tbsp. black cherry or currant jam
1 Tbsp. Tabasco Steak Sauce

1. A day before cooking, put the venison into food-storage bags with all of the marinade ingredients. Refrigerate until cooking time.

2. Preheat the oven to 350 degrees. Remove the venison from the marinating bag and shake off the excess. Season the loins with salt and pepper. Strain the marinade into a bowl and set aside.

3. Heat 2 tablespoons of the butter in a large, heavy skillet over medium-high heat until it bubbles. Add the venison and brown it all over. Transfer the venison to a roasting rack and bake until the temperature registers 135 degrees on a meat thermometer for medium-rare. Let the venison rest for 15 minutes before carving.

4. Meanwhile, add the shallots to the skillet in which you cooked the venison and sauté for a few seconds. Add the strained marinade to the pan and bring to a boil, whisking it to dislodge the browned meat juices and bits on the pan. Reduce the marinade to about ⅔ cup. Stir in the jam and steak sauce. Continue cooking until the jam is dissolved.

5. Strain the sauce once more into a clean, small saucepan and return to a simmer. Season to taste with salt and pepper. You can also reduce the sauce some more to get a thicker sauce. Remove from the heat and whisk in the remaining tablespoon of butter.

6. Slice the venison into ½-inch-thick medallions and spoon on the sauce. SERVES SIX TO EIGHT.

# Wild Mushroom
# and Rabbit Ragout

*Created by chef Gerard Maras when he was at Mr. B's, this has a bigger flavor than we get out of most rabbit dishes, yet it doesn't lose the character of that tender meat. The main ingredient is rabbit "tenderloins." (These are actually backstraps; the real tenderloin is only as big as a child's little finger.) Sear them fast at first, then let them cook slowly to develop the flavor.*

3 Tbsp. butter
3 Tbsp. flour
3 cups rich veal or chicken stock, hot (see recipe, page 312)
3 whole rabbit tenderloins, cubed
Salt and freshly ground black pepper
2 Tbsp. vegetable oil
¼ cup chopped yellow onion
3 ripe plum tomatoes, chopped
2 sprigs fresh thyme, leaves only (or 1 tsp. dried)
3 cups whole wild mushrooms, or sliced shiitakes or criminis

1. Make a blond roux by melting the butter in a saucepan. Add the flour and cook, stirring constantly, until the mixture barely begins to brown. Whisk in the stock and keep warm on low heat.

2. Season the rabbit with salt and pepper. Heat the oil in a skillet over high heat. Add the rabbit and brown all over. Lower the heat to medium and add the onion, tomatoes, and thyme, and cook until soft. Add the roux-stock mixture and bring to a boil. Lower to a simmer and cook for 20–25 minutes, or until the sauce coats a spoon and the rabbit pieces are tender but not falling apart.

3. Add the mushrooms and cook until they just begin to soften—about 2 minutes. Serve hot by itself or over pasta or rice. SERVES FOUR.

# Rabbit with Apricots and Creole Seasoning

*This savory dish with sweet highlights blends the cooking approaches of Creole and Eastern European cuisines. Use a late-harvest sweet wine, which brings out the flavors of the fruit without making the dish too sweet. When I first made this, I used Chappellet Late-Harvest Chenin Blanc.*

1 rabbit, about 4 lb.,
   cut up into 8–10 pieces
2 Tbsp. flour
2 Tbsp. salt-free Creole seasoning
1 tsp. salt, plus more to taste
½ stick (4 Tbsp.) butter
¼ cup brandy

2 cloves
8 ripe apricots or 3 ripe peaches,
   peeled and pitted
½ cup late-harvest white wine
½ tsp. Tabasco
Freshly ground black pepper to taste
1½ cups cooked rice

1. Rinse and dry the rabbit pieces. Combine the flour, Creole seasoning, and salt in a bowl. Add the rabbit pieces and toss to coat in the mixture.

2. Melt the butter in a large, heavy skillet over medium-high heat. Add the rabbit and brown the pieces all over. Remove from the skillet and set aside.

3. Add the brandy to the skillet in which you cooked the rabbit and bring to a boil while whisking the pan to dissolve the browned bits at the bottom. Careful! The brandy can catch fire, which is okay for flavor but potentially dangerous.

4. When most of the brandy has evaporated, add ½ cup of water to the pan, along with the cloves, apricots or peaches, and the browned rabbit pieces. Lower the heat and simmer, covered, until the rabbit legs are tender, 35–40 minutes.

5. Remove the rabbit pieces and keep warm. Add the wine and Tabasco to the skillet and bring to a boil. Reduce for 5 minutes, then pour the pan contents into a food processor. Puree, then strain into a clean skillet. Return the rabbit to the strained sauce and simmer until everything is hot and combined. Add a little water if the sauce is too thick and season to taste with salt and pepper. Serve with rice. Serves four.

# Sweetbreads Normande

*Veal sweetbreads are the thymus glands of a veal calf. They have the flavor of veal but with an incomparable richness and tenderness. This dish gets added richness from the cream sauce. The most time-consuming part of the recipe is getting the sweetbreads ready for the sauté pan. The fresh product seems almost liquid but firms up when you poach it.*

2 lb. sweetbreads
1 cup flour
1 Tbsp. salt, plus more to taste
1 tsp. ground white pepper, plus
   more to taste
5 Tbsp. butter
½ cup Calvados

¼ cup apple juice
1 Tbsp. Dijon mustard
3 cups sliced mushrooms, preferably
   shiitakes or chanterelles
1½ cups heavy whipping cream
8 oz. orzo pasta, cooked al dente

1. Bring a pot of water to a boil and blanch the sweetbreads for about 5 minutes. Drain and plunge into a bowl of ice water. Peel the membrane from the outside of the sweetbreads. You may have to pull apart the lobes to get the little shreds of membrane out, but don't break the sweetbreads up too much. Drain excess water.

2. Combine the flour, salt, and pepper in a wide bowl. Dust the sweetbreads with the mixture.

3. Melt the butter in a skillet over medium heat until it bubbles. Add the sweetbreads and sauté until lightly browned all over. Remove the sweetbreads from the pan and keep warm.

4. Pour off the excess butter, but don't wipe the pan. Lower the heat to medium-low and add the Calvados. Bring to a boil, whisking the bottom of the pan to dissolve the juices. Be careful; Calvados is highly alcoholic and its fumes may flame.

5. When the Calvados is almost all gone, add the apple juice, mustard, and mushrooms, and cook until the mushrooms are soft, about 3 minutes. Add the cream and bring to a boil, stirring to blend the ingredients. Don't let the cream foam over.

6. Season the sauce to taste with salt and pepper. Return the sweetbreads to the pan and cook until heated through. Serve with orzo pasta. SERVES FOUR.

# Alligator Creole

*This dish takes advantage of the resemblance alligator tail meat has—in texture, color, and weight—to baby white veal. The hardest part of the recipe is finding the alligator meat. (One online source is www.cajuncrawfish.com; see Food Sources, page 327.) If alligator meat is unavailable, you can use veal, pork loin, or even chicken instead. The best side dish for this is buttered stone-ground grits.*

1 lb. alligator tail meat, sliced against the grain into ¼-inch-thick cutlets
Flour
½ tsp. salt, plus more to taste
¼ tsp. ground white pepper, plus more to taste
¼ cup olive oil
1 red bell pepper, chopped
1 rib celery, chopped
½ medium yellow onion, chopped
½ bulb fennel, chopped
One 28-oz. can Italian plum tomatoes, with ½ cup of the juice
¼ cup dry white wine
2 tsp. lemon juice
4 sprigs flat-leaf parsley, chopped
⅛ tsp. cayenne

1. Dust the alligator lightly with the flour and season with the salt and white pepper. Heat the oil in a large skillet until it begins to shimmer. Add the alligator and sauté about a minute on each side. Remove from the skillet and keep warm.

2. Add the bell pepper, celery, onion, and fennel to the skillet in which you just cooked the alligator and sauté until tender. Chop the tomatoes and add them to the skillet, along with the tomato juice, wine, lemon juice, parsley, and cayenne. Bring to a simmer.

3. Return the alligator cutlets to the pan and cook them in the sauce for 2–3 minutes. Adjust the seasonings with salt and pepper. Serve with lots of sauce and hot buttered grits on the side. SERVES FOUR.

# Root Beer–Glazed Ham

*This is without a doubt the most-asked-for recipe in the 17-year history of my radio show. Demand for it rises during the holidays but never goes away completely.*

*The root beer–glazed ham is a fixture on my table on Thanksgiving, Christmas, and Easter. It's in the oven all morning (good thing my turkey is usually out on the grill!), and it makes the whole house smell good. You'll find that lots of your guests will fight over the black crusty parts of the ham (and all the rest of it, too).*

*If you live in New Orleans, I strongly urge you to buy the superb locally produced Chisesi ham for this. It's widely available at supermarkets, usually in the deli department. Otherwise, a top-quality, lean, naturally smoked boneless ham is what you want.*

*I usually make the glaze the night before so I can get the ham right into the oven in the morning. You'll also want to use a disposable pan to bake the ham. The drippings get so crusty that they are very hard to dislodge.*

GLAZE

24 oz. (2 cans) Barq's root beer
4½ tsp. pepper jelly
4½ tsp. Tabasco Caribbean Style Steak Sauce or Pickapeppa
6 cloves
1 stick cinnamon
1 bay leaf
Peel and juice of ½ orange
Peel of ½ lemon

HAM

One 10–14-lb. cured, smoked ham
¾ cup dark brown sugar
½ tsp. dry mustard

1. Combine all of the glaze ingredients in a large saucepan. Bring the mixture to a boil, then lower to a simmer and cook for about 30 minutes. Strain the pan contents and discard the solids. Reduce the liquid to about ½ cup. Refrigerate if you do this in advance.

2. Preheat the oven to 350 degrees.

3. Place the ham on a rack in a disposable aluminum pan. Cut shallow gashes in a crisscross pattern across the top half of the ham. Spoon just enough of the glaze over the ham to completely wet the surface. Combine the brown sugar and mustard together and pat it all over the ham. Pour ½ cup of water into the pan.

4. Bake the ham, spooning some of the remaining glaze over it every 15 minutes until the glaze is all used up. Try to get some glaze on all parts of the ham. Add more water to the pan when it dries up. Continue baking for a total of 3½–4 hours, or until the ham reaches an internal temperature of 160 degrees on a meat thermometer. Remove from the oven and allow to rest for 30 minutes before carving. Serves twenty-five to thirty.

# Corned Beef and Cabbage

*Corned beef is brisket that's been corned with seasonings and then brined for several weeks. Trust me: It is not worth attempting to corn beef yourself. Buy a nice one at the store and just boil it. I do have a trick for you, however: Add crab boil to the mixture. It will not taste like crab or be noticeably spicy—just good.*

*The cabbage component will be better if it's boiled all by itself. Also, you need some salt in the water for the cabbage, but the corned beef will get tough if you cook it with salt.*

*Now, my favorite corned beef story. When the late chef Jamie Shannon was chosen to succeed Emeril Lagasse as executive chef at Commander's Palace, Dick Brennan, Sr.—one of the owners of the restaurant—told him, "Just make sure the corned beef is tender on St. Patrick's Day." Corned beef was served only on that day at Commander's, whose culinary ambitions were quite a bit higher. Jamie shrugged that off as a joke. Later in the day, he encountered Dick's brother, John Brennan. John congratulated Jamie, then added only this advice: "Okay, young fella. Make sure the corned beef is tender on St. Patrick's Day." The Brennans have never been ashamed of being Irish.*

**BRISKET**

1 corned beef brisket, about 4 lb.
1 medium yellow onion, quartered
2 Tbsp. liquid crab boil
1 Tbsp. black peppercorns
1 tsp. dried marjoram
½ tsp. mustard seeds

**CABBAGE**

1 head green cabbage, quartered
2 Tbsp. salt

Creole mustard

1. Wash the seasonings that were in the vacuum-packed bag off the corned beef. Put it in a large pot and cover with cold water. Add the onion, crab boil, peppercorns, marjoram, and mustard seeds, and bring to a boil. Reduce the heat to medium-low and simmer, covered, for 3½ hours.

2. Boil the cabbage separately in about 2 gallons (32 cups) of salted water.

3. When the corned beef is cooked, drain it from the water and let it stand for about 20 minutes. Slice it against the grain, noting that the grain in brisket has a way of changing directions as you slice it. The thinner you slice it, the better. Serve with the boiled cabbage and Creole mustard on the side. SERVES FOUR TO SIX.

# Chicken, Duck, and Other Birds

Since chicken is perceived as ordinary and inexpensive by many people, chefs give disproportionate attention to their chicken dishes in particular and their poultry dishes in general. The chicken dish in a first-class restaurant is usually one of the best eats in the house.

But I'd trade it any time for a well-made stewed chicken, falling off the bone into a plate of brown gravy with dirty rice. Hardly a restaurant cooks that anymore. So we have to make it at home. And let's not even talk about how the fast-food industry has destroyed the reputation of fried chicken.

I'm also put off by the trend in recent years to replace the roasted half-duck with a fanned-out, grilled, undercooked duck breast. It's only occasionally that I find such dishes turn me on. Again, the heart begs for the Cajun smothered duck, tender and awash in a sauce of its own juices.

I give you those dishes and a few others. I love chicken, don't you?

# Roasted Chicken Aline

*If I had to live on just one entrée the rest of my life, this would be it. I love a good roasted chicken, like the one my mother (Aline) used to make every Sunday when I was a kid. After this chicken comes out of the oven, you can add almost any sauce or garnish to it you like, but it's very good as is. Buy a free-range chicken or the smallest chicken you can find at the store.*

*Feel free to vary the array of fruits, vegetables, and herbs that I like to stuff inside the cavity before putting the chicken into the oven.*

One 3–3½-lb. whole chicken,
Stems of 1 bunch of fennel, chopped, or tops from 1 bunch of celery
Stems of 1 bunch of flat-leaf parsley
½ orange, sliced
1 good-sized branch rosemary
10 cloves garlic, crushed
Salt to taste
Salt-free Creole seasoning or freshly ground black pepper to taste
½ tsp. dried tarragon
1 Tbsp. butter

1. Preheat the oven to 500 degrees. If you have a convection oven, set it to convect.

2. Rinse the chicken and remove the giblets. Stuff the cavity with as much of the fennel or celery, parsley, orange, rosemary, and garlic as will fit inside it. Season the outside of the chicken with salt and Creole seasoning or pepper.

3. Put the chicken, breast side down, on a broiler pan with a rack and set it in the center of the oven. Reduce the oven to 350 degrees. Roast for 1 hour and check the temperature of the chicken with a meat thermometer. When it reaches about 170 degrees, turn the oven up to 450 degrees and dot the outside of the chicken with small slivers of butter.

4. Roast the chicken another 5–10 minutes. Check to make sure the juices run clear from the thigh. Remove from the oven and let stand for 15 minutes before serving. SERVES TWO TO FOUR.

# Chicken Bonne Femme

*"Good woman's chicken" and its variations (chicken Clemenceau and chicken Pontalba) are among the best dishes in the Creole cookbook. Although there is little agreement on how chicken bonne femme is prepared, potatoes and garlic are always part of the recipe. This one evolved in my kitchen from the very good version prepared at Antoine's, with inspiration from the super-garlicky, great bonne femme at Tujague's.*

4 slices bacon, cut into 1-inch squares
Two 3½-lb. whole chickens, quartered
Salt and freshly ground black pepper to taste
2 Tbsp. flour
½ cup ham, cut into tiny dice
1 cup chopped green onion tops
1 cup chopped yellow onion
2 cups sliced fresh mushrooms
1 cup dry white wine
1 Tbsp. Worcestershire sauce
¼ tsp. Tabasco
Vegetable oil, for frying
2 lb. white potatoes, peeled and cut into ¾-inch dice
1 stick (8 Tbsp.) butter
8 cloves garlic, chopped

1. Preheat the oven to 400 degrees. Fry the bacon in a large skillet until crisp, then remove with a slotted spoon and reserve, leaving the fat in the skillet. Meanwhile, season the chicken with salt and pepper, then dust lightly with the flour. Cook the chicken in the rendered bacon fat over high heat until browned on all sides. Remove the chicken pieces to an ovenproof platter and keep warm.

2. Add the ham, green onion, and yellow onion to the skillet in which you cooked the chicken and sauté until the onions turn translucent. Add the mushrooms, wine, Worcestershire sauce, and Tabasco, and bring to a boil. After a minute, reduce the heat to maintain a simmer.

3. Pour the oil into a deep skillet to a depth of 1 inch and heat to 375 degrees. Add the potatoes and fry until very lightly browned. Drain them well and add to the skillet with the ham and onions. This is bonne femme garnish.

4. Continue simmering the garnish until all of the liquid is absorbed; lightly stir to distribute the ingredients. Remove from heat.

5. Heat the butter in a small saucepan until it starts bubbling. Lower the heat, skim the foam off, and add the garlic. Cook the garlic in the hot butter for about a minute.

6. Spoon the bonne femme garnish over and between the chicken pieces. Spoon the garlic butter over the garnish and season to taste with salt and pepper. Crumble the reserved bacon over the top.

7. Bake for 7–12 minutes. Turn the chicken pieces, redistribute the garnish, and bake for another 5–7 minutes. If the white meat is cooked, remove it from the pan and keep warm. Continue cooking the leg quarters until the juices run clear when the thigh is pierced. Return the breasts to the mixture and serve with lots of the garnish. SERVES FOUR.

# Stewed Chicken with Brown Gravy

*This is one of New Orleans's favorite lunch specials—one which, unfortunately, is slipping away from us. The old Delmonico used to make the definitive version of this dish. Now Mandina's version is probably best. It's always served with brown gravy over the chicken and rice. The vegetable of choice is peas, preferably with mushrooms in a roux.*

*Stewed chicken is made sort of like chicken gumbo but with bigger pieces of chicken and less broth.*

½ cup vegetable oil
½ cup flour
1 rib celery, chopped
½ yellow onion, chopped
½ green bell pepper, chopped
⅛ tsp. dried thyme leaves

Two 3-lb. whole free-range chickens,
   cut into 8 pieces
¼ cup red wine
½ tsp. salt
¼ tsp. freshly ground black pepper
¼ tsp. Tabasco
Cooked long-grain rice

1. Make a dark roux by heating the oil in a saucepan over medium-high heat. Add the flour and cook, stirring often, until the mixture turns the color of dark chocolate. After the roux has reached the right color, remove from the heat and add the celery, onion, bell pepper, and thyme. Continue to stir for a minute or so until the vegetables get soft and the roux cools.

2. In a large saucepan or Dutch oven, sear the pieces of chicken until browned all over. Remove the chicken. Add the wine and bring it to a boil, scraping the bottom of the pan to dissolve the browned bits in the wine.

3. Add 3 cups of water to the pan and bring to a simmer. Add the roux and whisk until smooth. Return the chicken to the pot.

4. Cover and simmer on very low heat for about 30 minutes. Remove the breasts and wings, and continue to cook 20–30 minutes longer, or until the meat on the chicken legs begins to fall away from the bones. Remove the chicken from the pot and keep warm. Add the salt, pepper, and Tabasco to the gravy pot and cook until the sauce thickens. You can strain it or not, according to your taste. Serve the chicken with rice and spoon the gravy over both. SERVES FOUR.

# Fried Chicken

*Confession: I never make fried chicken the same way twice. It's still a work in progress. The problem with any method of cooking chicken is that the various pieces cook at different rates. This is why, I suspect, the Colonel didn't use the standard breast-wing-thigh-drumstick configuration. The trick is to pull the breastbone and the cartilage in the center of the full breast away from the rib sections, leaving the two tenders still attached to the cartilage.*

*The problem is not entirely solved. Breast meat cooks faster than leg meat of the same size. So consider that as you cook. One more thing: There is no question that the flavor of the chicken gets better after you've fried about six pieces and that it starts deteriorating after you've fried about 16 pieces. So refresh the oil—strain it and add fresh—along the way.*

MARINADE

4 cups buttermilk
¼ cup yellow mustard
2 Tbsp. salt
1 Tbsp. dried tarragon
1 Tbsp. dried dill
1 Tbsp. Tabasco Garlic Pepper Sauce

2 whole chickens, each cut up into breast tenderloin, 2 breasts, 2 thighs,
    2 drumsticks, and 2 wings

COATING

4 cups self-rising (yes!) flour
2 Tbsp. freshly ground black pepper
1 Tbsp. granulated onion
1½ tsp. turmeric
1 tsp. dried marjoram
1 tsp. dried thyme
½ tsp. ground white pepper
¼ tsp. cayenne

2 cups Crisco (preferred) or vegetable oil, plus more for refreshing the oil

*(continued)*

1. Combine the marinade ingredients in a bowl, mixing until the salt is dissolved. Divide the chicken equally among gallon food-storage bags. Add enough marinade to completely soak the chicken. Place the bags in the refrigerator for at least 8 hours or overnight.

2. Remove the chicken from the marinade and shake off any excess. Place the chicken pieces on a rack over a pan. (The racks you use to cool cakes are perfect.) Place the chicken out of the way but in the open air and allow it to warm up for about 30 minutes.

3. When ready to begin cooking, combine the coating ingredients in a bowl. Pour into a large, clean paper bag.

4. Heat the Crisco or vegetable oil in a deep, heavy pot over medium-high heat until its temperature reaches 375 degrees. Put 3–4 pieces of chicken into the bag with the seasonings. Shake to coat uniformly. (The bag method will also shake off excess coating.)

5. Using tongs, put 4–5 pieces of chicken into the hot shortening and fry, without turning, for 8–10 minutes. Turn the chicken pieces over and fry on the other side, again for 8–10 minutes. The color you're looking for is a bit darker than the usual golden brown.

6. As you remove the pieces of chicken from the pot, drain them on paper towels. If nobody grabs it immediately—the recommended way of eating fried chicken—keep it warm in a 150-degree oven until serving. SERVES FOUR TO EIGHT.

# Chicken with Artichoke Sauce and Pasta

*The Red Onion was a great Metairie restaurant that closed in the early 1980s. On its menu was a terrific chicken dish that involved artichokes somehow. It's almost impossible to get recipes from closed restaurants, but I remembered the taste, so I took a shot at recapturing it. I doubt this is how they did it, but it's close enough for me.*

4 chicken breasts, deboned and each cut into 3 pieces
½ cup flour
½ tsp. salt-free Creole seasoning
1 tsp. salt, plus more to taste
⅓ cup olive oil
2 cloves garlic, crushed

6 artichoke hearts, poached and cut into quarters (or use canned or jarred artichoke hearts)
1 Tbsp. lemon juice
2 green onions, finely chopped
Tabasco
½ lb. fettuccine, cooked al dente

1. Pound out the chicken pieces with a meat pounder between 2 pieces of wax paper to about double their original size. Blend the flour, Creole seasoning, and salt, and dust the chicken pieces lightly.

2. Heat 1 tablespoon of the oil in a heavy skillet over medium-high heat until it shimmers. Add the garlic and sauté for a minute. Add the chicken and sauté until browned all over. Remove the pan from the heat. Remove the chicken and keep warm. Discard the garlic cloves.

3. If using canned or jarred artichoke hearts, pour off the water or oil. Chop the artichokes roughly.

4. Return the pan to medium heat. Add the remaining oil, artichokes, lemon juice, and green onions. Cook until the onions wilt, then add 1 cup of water. Whisk to dissolve the pan juices and lower the heat to a simmer. Reduce the pan contents until they thicken a bit. Season to taste with salt and Tabasco.

5. Return the chicken to the pan and heat through, cooking until the sauce soaks into the chicken a bit. Add the pasta to the pan and toss to coat. Adjust seasonings with salt and Tabasco, and divide among 4 warm plates. SERVES FOUR.

# Grilled Marinated Chicken with Hot and Sweet Peppers

*This was a standard dish for years at Brigtsen's, and it's a good example of the robust, painstaking, but essentially simple dishes from that great little Creole bistro. Frank Brigtsen says it was the sort of thing he did a lot when he worked for chef Paul Prudhomme.*

**MARINADE**

1¼ cups balsamic vinegar
¼ tsp. chopped garlic
Leaves of 1 sprig fresh oregano, chopped
2–3 fresh basil leaves, chopped
⅔ cup extra-virgin olive oil

**CHICKEN**

⅛ tsp. chopped fresh thyme
4 boneless chicken legs and thighs
4 boneless chicken breasts, skinned
¼ cup clarified butter (see recipe, page 314)
1 tsp. Chef Paul Prudhomme's Poultry Magic Seasoning (see Food Sources, page 327)

**SAUCE**

2 Tbsp. butter, softened
½ cup diced sweet bell pepper—red, yellow, green, or some of each
½ tsp. chopped fresh jalapeño pepper
¼ tsp. chopped garlic
½ cup rich chicken stock (see recipe, page 312)
½ tsp. honey
¼ tsp. lemon juice

1. Combine all of the marinade ingredients except the oil in a mixing bowl. While whisking, add the oil in a thin stream until fully incorporated. Place the chicken pieces and marinade in food-storage bags and marinate in the refrigerator for 6–8 hours.

2. Remove the chicken from the marinade, shaking off the excess. Lightly brush the chicken with some of the clarified butter and season lightly with the Magic Seasoning. Place the chicken on a very hot grill or in a cast-iron skillet and cook for 3–5 minutes on each side, until done. Cook the legs and thighs, skin side down, first. If using an outdoor barbecue grill, you might want to baste the chicken with the leftover marinade.

3. To make the sauce: Melt 1 tablespoon of the butter in a heavy skillet over medium-high heat. Add the bell pepper, jalapeño, and garlic. Cook for about a minute, stirring constantly. Add the stock and bring to a boil. Add the honey, lemon juice, and remaining tablespoon of butter and cook, stirring, until the butter is melted and fully incorporated. Spoon over the grilled chicken and serve immediately. SERVES FOUR.

# Cornish Hens with Peppercorn Red Wine Sauce

*I found this recipe in a folder deep in my file cabinet. It was written in my hand on radio station stationery and dated 1988. I remembered it only vaguely. So I cooked it and liked it enough to know that it's not an original recipe of mine, but I wish I had thought of it.*

*It's very French in style and turns the chickenlike Cornish hen (which I rather like anyway) into something wonderful. It's worth trying to find the demi-glace this recipe calls for. You can now buy demi-glace in gourmet food stores and gourmet-to-go places. And if you have a good relationship with a fine restaurant, you may be able to buy it there, too.*

2 Tbsp. butter
½ small yellow onion, cut in half and pulled apart
½ tsp. dried marjoram
2 Cornish hens
Salt and freshly ground black pepper to taste
12 oz. duck pâté de campagne
6 thick slices smoky bacon
1 tsp. chopped shallots
1 tsp. chopped garlic
½ cup brandy
2 Tbsp. green peppercorns (the marinated kind, not dried)
1 cup Cabernet Sauvignon or Merlot
½ cup demi-glace

1. Preheat the oven to 375 degrees. Melt the butter in a large, ovenproof skillet over medium-low heat. Add the onion pieces and marjoram, and sauté until the onions become soft. Turn off the heat and with a slotted spoon, remove the onions and allow to cool.

2. Season the hens with salt and pepper. When the onions are cool enough to handle, line the inside of the Cornish hens' cavities with them. Divide the pâté in half and stuff the hens' cavities with it. Tie the legs closed with kitchen twine. Wrap each hen with 3 slices of the bacon, holding them in place with toothpicks.

3. Return the skillet to medium heat. Place the hens in the skillet and sear them until the bacon starts to crisp. Put the skillet into the preheated oven and roast the hens for 35 minutes.

4. Remove the pan from the oven and the Cornish hens from the pan. Leave the oven on. Pour off excess fat from the pan, but don't wipe. Place the shallots and garlic in the skillet and sauté over medium heat for about a minute. Add the brandy and peppercorns. (Be careful—the brandy might flame briefly.) Bring the brandy to a boil for about 30 seconds, then add the wine and demi-glace. Bring to a light boil and reduce until the sauce thickens enough to coat a spoon, 5–6 minutes. Season to taste with salt and pepper.

5. Remove toothpicks and strings from the hens. Cut each hen in half from front to back and place each half on a plate. Pour the sauce around the hens and put the plates into the oven for 2–3 minutes to warm everything back up. Serve with wild rice. SERVES FOUR.

# Cajun Smothered Duck

*This old-fashioned Cajun way of preparing wild fowl—another of my mother's recipes, although she would never call it (or herself) Cajun—is so full of flavor as to be almost rich, but the spice level is moderate. It's great with Dirty Rice (see recipe, page 216) and yams.*

2 farm-raised ducklings or
    4 wild ducks, cleaned
2 Tbsp. salt-free Creole seasoning, plus
    more to taste
1 cup flour
½ cup vegetable oil
2 yellow onions, chopped
2 large green bell peppers, chopped

1 celery rib, chopped
1 cup water or chicken stock (see
    recipe, page 312)
1 bay leaf
1 cup chopped green onion
½ cup chopped flat-leaf parsley
Salt and freshly ground black pepper
    to taste

1. Preheat the oven to 300 degrees. Wash the ducks and pat dry. Season inside and out with the Creole seasoning, then dust the outside lightly with the flour.

2. Heat the oil in a roasting pan or large, heavy pot over medium-high heat. Brown the ducks in the oil, turning frequently, until the skin begins to crisp on all sides. Remove and keep warm. Pour off all but about 1 tablespoon of the oil from the pan. Add the yellow onions, bell peppers, and celery, and cook over medium-low heat until soft, about 2 minutes.

3. Return the ducks to the roasting pan. Add the water or chicken stock and bay leaf. Cover the pan, place it in the preheated oven, and bake for about 2 hours. Every half-hour turn the ducks over. Add a little water if the pan juices begin to dry out. The ducks are cooked when the meat begins to fall from the leg bones.

4. Remove the ducks from the pan and keep warm. Let the pan contents stand for a few minutes; the fat will rise to the top. Skim and discard the fat. Bring the remaining pan contents to a very light simmer and reduce until it thickens to a gravy consistency. Add the green onion, parsley, and more Creole seasoning or salt and pepper to taste.

5. With a large knife, cut the ducks in half from end to end. Remove and discard the backbone and rib cage, and serve the rest with the sauce. SERVES FOUR TO SIX.

# Duck Confit

*There's really only one challenge in making duck confit: getting enough duck fat. Restaurants have no problem with this. They break down the ducks for duck breast dishes, which gives them lots of skin and fat for making a confit of the legs. So, in other words, if you're going to try this, be prepared to eat other duck dishes. One other piece of bad news: You need to start this recipe days ahead. Good news: It can be a week or two ahead.*

2 whole ducks
Salt

1. Preheat the oven to 250 degrees. Thaw the ducks if necessary. Cut them into quarters. Reserve the breasts for another dish, but remove all of the skin except the part right over the breast and on the leg quarters.

2. Render the fat from all of the duck skin in a skillet over medium-low heat. Coat the leg quarters generously with salt and transfer to the rendered fat in the skillet. Place the skillet in the oven and roast slowly for 2 hours, or until the meat begins to fall away from the bones.

3. After 2 hours, transfer the duck legs to a deep dish and pour the fat over it. You may need additional fat to completely cover the duck legs. Cover the dish and refrigerate for at least 3 days. It will hold for days or even weeks in the refrigerator.

4. When ready to serve, preheat the oven to 450 degrees. Arrange the duck legs on a broiling pan and top them with all the fat you can. Bake until the skin sizzles audibly. Serve immediately, with a small salad of something sharp (like arugula with raspberry vinaigrette). SERVES FOUR.

# Pat Gallagher's Smothered Quail

*I'm not nuts about quail. As cute as the little birds are, I find their flavor not sufficiently interesting to justify the amount of work involved in eating them. So it's saying something when I tell you that I would never turn away from any quail dish prepared by Pat Gallagher. Gallagher had a number of restaurants over the years on the North Shore, and quail was always a great specialty. None were pretentious dishes. Just fresh, prepared simply and very, very well. Now that quails are relatively easy to buy fresh, consider trying this one night.*

*It's better to buy the quails with the bones in—the quality is better than boned quail. The only bones you need to remove for cooking are the backbone and rib cages. Use kitchen shears to cut down the backbone. Spread the quail open and pull out the backbone and the ribs. This takes a little patience, but you'll get the hang of it quickly.*

*An excellent accompaniment for this dish is Dirty Rice (see recipe, page 216). Not-so-dirty rice would work, too.*

8 quails, partially deboned and split
Salt and freshly ground black pepper
  or Creole seasoning to taste
2 sticks (16 Tbsp.) butter
1 medium yellow onion, sliced
4 cloves garlic, chopped

8 large mushrooms, sliced
¼ cup brandy
2 cups chicken stock (see recipe,
  page 312)
½ cup dry red wine
½ tsp. dried thyme

1. Season the quails front and back with salt and pepper or Creole seasoning.

2. Melt the butter in a large skillet over medium heat and bring it to bubbling. Add the quails and sauté for about 2 minutes. Add the onion, garlic, and mushrooms, and cook until the onion turns translucent. Carefully pour on the brandy and touch a flame to it. (Skip this if you have even a shred of doubt about safety and just let the brandy simmer for a few minutes to let the alcohol cook off.)

3. When the flames die out, add the stock, wine, and thyme, and bring to a boil. Cover the pan and cook over medium-low heat until the quails are tender, 7–10 minutes.

4. Serve 2 quails per person with plenty of the sauce. SERVES FOUR.

# Outdoor Grill

There is no outdoor-grilling season in New Orleans. Outdoor grilling goes on all year round. My charcoal grill is as likely to be fired up on Mardi Gras as on the Fourth of July. I can assure you it will contain a fire on Thanksgiving, along with a couple of turkeys.

Outdoor grills, especially those fired with wood or charcoal, offer a pair of advantages beyond the special flavors they give. The first is that you can achieve much higher temperatures than you can indoors, making possible styles of cooking that would be impossible or quite dangerous in the home kitchen. Second, you can use techniques that create a great deal of smoke without polluting the air in your living space.

In addition to the grillwork you find in this chapter, two other outdoor-cooking routines are popular in South Louisiana. You'll find the recipe for one of them—boiled crawfish—in the Casual Food section. The other is fried turkey, the omission of which was entirely intentional.

# Drago's Char-Broiled Oysters

*Drago Cvitanovich has been the oyster king of New Orleans for four decades—and that's saying something. Like most other people in the oyster business, he's a Croatian immigrant. When he opened his restaurant in the 1970s, he kept his ties with his countrymen down the river and, as a result, always had the best oysters available.*

*Drago's son Tommy, who now runs the restaurant, created this dish in the early 1990s. It became wildly popular, and restaurants all over town now copy it. The dish is simple enough to prepare. The only tough part is obtaining oysters of Drago's quality and then opening them. Don't attempt this recipe without freshly shucked oysters and an outdoor grill.*

*This is the perfect dish for those who want to enjoy oysters in their unadorned form but can't, or won't, eat them raw. Once you start eating these, you won't be able to stop. My personal best is four and a half dozen.*

8 sticks (2 lb.) butter, softened
½ cup finely chopped garlic
1 Tbsp. freshly ground black pepper
1 tsp. dried oregano
6 dozen oysters on the half shell
1 cup grated Parmesan and Romano cheeses, mixed
3 Tbsp. chopped flat-leaf parsley

1. Mix the butter, garlic, pepper, and oregano together in a bowl.

2. Heat a gas or charcoal grill and put oysters on the half shell right over the hottest part. Spoon enough of the seasoned butter over the oysters so that some of it will overflow into the fire and flame up a bit.

3. The oysters are ready when they puff up and get curly on the edges. Sprinkle the grated Parmesan-and-Romano mixture and parsley on top. Serve on the shells immediately with hot French bread. SERVES EIGHT TO TWELVE NORMAL PEOPLE, OR TWO SERIOUS OYSTER FANATICS.

# Fish on the Half Shell

*If you cut big fillets from a redfish or drum and leave the skin and scales on, you can grill it over a hot fire without having to turn it. The skin and scales get black, but the fish stays moist because it's steaming in its own juices. You absolutely must do this outdoors because the smell of the burning scales in the beginning is not the nicest thing you will ever sniff. (Don't worry—it won't affect the flavor of the fish.)*

¼ cup dry white wine
¼ cup olive oil
1 Tbsp. soy sauce
1 Tbsp. lemon juice
4 large fillets of drum, redfish, or sea bream (sheepshead), skin and scales on
6 Tbsp. butter
2 Tbsp. finely chopped garlic
2 Tbsp. chopped fresh oregano
4 sprigs flat-leaf parsley, leaves only, chopped
Salt and cracked black pepper to taste
1 lemon, cut into wedges

1. Mix the wine, oil, soy sauce, and lemon juice together in a wide bowl big enough to fit the fish. Marinate the fish for about a minute, skin side up.

2. Place the fish, skin side down, on a very hot grill. Mix the garlic, oregano, parsley, salt and pepper into the butter and spread it on top of the fish.

3. Grill the fish without turning, until the very top of the fish is distinctly warm to the touch. It's best when some of the butter falls into the flames and smokes up over the fish. The scales will char.

4. Serve with lemon wedges. Tell your guests to beware of bones as they cut into the fillets. SERVES FOUR.

# Grilled Lemonfish

*Lemonfish is a large, much admired Gulf fish that also goes by the names cobia and ling. It is as good a grilling fish as I've ever encountered. During a campout when my son was a Boy Scout, we grilled a 10-pound slab of lemonfish over an open fire. Coated only with Creole seasoning, the fish was unforgettable—tender, flavorful, and moist. For an elegant touch, serve grilled lemonfish with a beurre blanc sauce (see Seared Scallops with Artichokes, page 55, but omit the garlic and substitute lemon juice for the vinegar in that recipe's garlic beurre blanc).*

1 large lemonfish fillet, up to about 10 lb.
2 lemons, quartered
Salt-free Creole Seafood Seasoning (see recipe, page 309)
Salt

1. Wash the fish fillet and make sure all the bones are out. Rub the fish all over with the cut lemons.

2. Cover the fish with a liberal coating of 2 parts Creole seasoning to 1 part salt. Put on as much as will stick to the fish. Let the fish sit with the seasoning in place while you prepare the grill.

3. Heat a charcoal or wood grill (or gas, if you must) until very hot, with the heat source about 5 inches from the grill surface.

4. Place the fish on the grill and cook for about 4 minutes. Turn and continue to grill, turning every 4 minutes or so. The exterior will get very dark, but it will not burn. The fish is done when you poke a kitchen fork into the center and it comes out warm to the touch of your lips. This will take 20–30 minutes, depending on the size of the fish.

5. After removing the fish from the grill, let it sit on the cutting board for about 3 minutes before cutting serving-size portions across the fillet. SERVES TWO TO THREE PEOPLE PER POUND OF FISH.

# Cold-Smoked Pompano or Amberjack

*All the fish in the jack family (the most familiar around here are pompano and amberjack) have a higher-than-average oil content and so are perfect for smoking. Cold smoking also works well for salmon, mackerel, or tuna. The fish picks up a terrific smoke flavor throughout, without getting a barbecued taste.*

*I learned how to make this from chef Roland Huet, the original chef at Christian's, who developed the method for that restaurant's excellent house-smoked salmon. He went through four different smokers before finding that the barrel-shaped kind with the water pan in the center works best. I ignored that discovery and use a standard rectangular barbecue pit. I put the fish on a rack over a pan on one side of the grill. The fire requires a minimum amount of wood on the other side, with a pan of water over it. At best, the fish never gets warm to the touch. The technique works best in the winter.*

3 large pompano or 2 small (2-lb.) amberjacks
1 lb. salt
⅓ cup brown sugar
1 tsp. dried basil
½ tsp. freshly ground black pepper
Extra-virgin olive oil
Fresh dill
Cracked black peppercorns

1. Fillet and skin the fish. If using amberjack, remove the big blood line that runs through the center.

2. Dissolve all the other ingredients in 1 gallon (16 cups) of cold water. Marinate the fish in the brine for 12 hours, refrigerated.

3. Using a fruit wood (cherry, apple, or grapevine), cold-smoke the fish at 75–90 degrees for 2 hours.

4. Slice the fish at a very narrow bias into slices as thick as a coin. Serve dressed with extra-virgin olive oil, dill, and cracked black peppercorns. SERVES TWELVE AS AN APPETIZER.

# Cane-Smoked Turkey

*I cook my turkey in a big barbecue pit. It gets hotter than a smoker, but because I keep the turkey away from direct heat, it cooks slowly and absorbs a lot of smoky flavor. The skin comes out crisp, with a beautiful orange-bronze color, and the meat retains more moisture than it would if cooked any other way. The sugarcane that I use with the charcoal comes from a friend's plantation. It's worth the trip upriver to St. James Parish to get it. If you can't get sugarcane, standard smoking woods like pecan, oak, hickory, or mesquite will do the job.*

One 12–15-lb. turkey
Salt and freshly ground black pepper
2 ribs celery, chopped
1 yellow onion, chopped
1 orange, cut into eighths
1 lemon, cut into quarters
1 shake of dried tarragon
1 stem of fresh rosemary

1. Thaw the turkey if frozen. This takes at least 4 days and should be done in the refrigerator. Put the turkey into the pan you'll roast it in to catch any leaks. After it thaws, remove the metal or plastic tie holding the legs together. (A pair of pliers is essential, I find.) Remove the giblets and neck from the cavity and clip off the wing tips. (You can use these parts for making stock for the gravy.)

2. The day before, marinate the turkey in a brine. The standard proportion is 1 cup of salt to 1 gallon (16 cups) of water. Make enough of this to completely cover the turkey in an ice chest with an unopened (so as not to dilute the brine) bag of ice to keep everything cold. The brining process takes 12–18 hours for a 15-pound turkey. Another method is to put the turkey and the brine solution inside a leak-proof plastic bag and put it into the refrigerator.

3. The morning of the day you want to serve the turkey, dump the brine and rinse the bird very well inside and out with cold water. Season it with salt (yes!) and pepper. Stuff the cavity with all the other ingredients and tie the legs just tightly enough to keep everything inside.

*(continued)*

4. Fire up the grill with charcoal. Add pieces of smoking wood, soaked in water and then shaken dry. Stack 6 or so foot-long pieces of sugarcane on the grill directly over the fire. Put the turkey into an aluminum pan with a loose tent of foil over the top. Place the turkey as far from the fire as possible and hang a curtain of foil down to ward off direct heat. Any heat that gets to the turkey should arrive in smoke.

5. Close the cover. Add coals and cane at intervals to maintain a temperature of 200–250 degrees inside the pit. It takes 6–7 hours for the internal temperature of the turkey to reach about 180 degrees. Use a meat thermometer to check; the useless pop-up plastic indicator will pop only when the turkey is overcooked.

6. Take the turkey out and put it on the table to rest and cool before carving. Although it may be tempting, don't use the drippings for the gravy. They reduce so much during the long cooking time that they become impossibly salty. SERVES EIGHT TO TWELVE.

# Smoked Duck Breast with Jalapeño Glaze

*Although you can use an outdoor smoker, the first time I prepared this recipe I used a stove-top smoker—essentially a big pan with a rack inside and a cover. You put very fine wood chips (almost sawdust) in the bottom of the pan, put the duck (or whatever) on the rack, cover, and place the whole shooting match atop a burner. Amazingly, it does the job in just about 10 minutes. (This is essentially the technique Chinese cooks use to smoke duck in tea leaves.) This makes a good appetizer for meals with seafood as the main course.*

1 cup salt
1 cup sugar
1 gallon (16 cups) water
4 duck breasts, skin on
2 Tbsp. orange marmalade
½ cup highly reduced chicken or duck stock (see recipe, page 312)

1 Tbsp. Tabasco Green Pepper Sauce
¼ cup Cointreau, Grand Marnier, or triple sec liqueur
½ cup orange juice, strained
⅛ tsp. salt, plus more to taste
Freshly ground black pepper, plus more to taste

1. Dissolve the salt and sugar in the water in a large bowl. Add the duck and brine it in the refrigerator for 4–8 hours.

2. Using an outdoor cold smoker at about 80 degrees, smoke the duck breasts for 30–45 minutes. Or use a stovetop smoker as outlined in the headnote. In either case, fruitwoods (apple, cherry, or peach) are recommended.

3. Preheat the oven to 450 degrees. Meanwhile, combine all of the remaining ingredients except the duck breast in a small saucepan over medium-low heat. Bring to a boil, reduce the heat, and simmer until the sauce is thick enough to coat an upside-down spoon for a second or two.

4. Brush the duck breast lightly with the sauce. Season with a little salt and pepper. Roast in the oven for 15–20 minutes until just a blush of pink remains at the center.

5. Spoon some of the sauce on the plate. When the duck breast is ready, carve it on the bias into ¼-inch-thick slices. Fan out the slices on the sauce. SERVES FOUR AS AN APPETIZER.

# Pulled Barbecued Pork Shoulder

*The cut you want for this is pork shoulder—also known as Boston butt—preferably bone-in. Pork shoulder tastes terrible if you try to cook it quickly but responds with a wonderful texture and flavor if it's smoked slowly. The expression "pulled" means that the meat is not sliced but torn from the bone. In the case of pork shoulder, it comes off in lovely long morsels, perfect for sandwiches, but not at all bad for a platter either. Tongs are the usual tool for pulling the meat from the bone, but you can sometimes do it with a fork. On the other hand, even in Memphis—where this is the primary barbecue meat—there are lots of famous places that chop it.*

1 whole pork shoulder

MARINADE
2 cloves garlic, pureed
¼ cup Worcestershire sauce
2 Tbsp. honey
½ tsp. Tabasco Chipotle Pepper Sauce
⅓ cup Barbecue Dry Rub, brown sugar version
   (see recipe, page 310)
2 cups Cool Water Ranch Barbecue Sauce (see recipe, page 324)
   or bottled barbecue sauce

1. A few hours before you start cooking (or the night before), cut the skin (if any) off the pork shoulder. Don't trim any more fat than what comes off with the skin. Blend the marinade ingredients. Brush the outside of the pork with the marinade.

2. Start a charcoal fire in your pit, with all the charcoal on one side of the grate. If you're using wood chips (which you'll have to if using gas), wrap them in heavy aluminum foil and punch a few holes in the resulting packet. (There's no need to soak the chips.)

3. Brush the shoulder with the marinade once more, then cover with a thick coating of dry rub. If using a grill, place the pork as far away from the fire as you can and drape a sheet of aluminum foil down to prevent direct heat from hitting the meat. Top the fire with the smoking wood and close the cover.

4. Maintain a temperature of about 175–200 degrees, adding fuel and wood as needed. After 4 hours, check the internal temperature by inserting a meat thermometer (without touching bone). You eventually want to see a reading of 170 degrees, but it probably won't be there yet. This is good: The longer the meat is in there, the better. Smoking time is usually about 8 hours, but it can go even longer than that.

5. When the pork reaches the desired temperature, allow it to cool for about 15 minutes, then pull the meat from the bone with tongs. Or cut away and chop. Serve with barbecue sauce on the side. SERVES FOUR TO EIGHT.

# Barbecue Brisket

*The meat most closely identified with the Texas style of barbecue is brisket, which is more commonly found around New Orleans in its boiled form. Brisket needs to be cooked very slowly for its goodness to emerge, and that's why it's such a natural for barbecue.*

*I've always done my briskets on a large barbecue pit instead of a smoker. I got this idea from my Texas-born buddy Oliver Kluna. Astonishingly, he uses no wood: just charcoal smoke. I usually add oak wood picked up in the woods around my home, the Cool Water Ranch.*

One 4–8-lb. beef brisket, preferably flat end
Salt-free Creole seasoning
Salt

1. Start a natural-wood charcoal fire in your pit, with all the charcoal on one side of the grate. If you're using wood chips (which you'll have to if using gas), wrap them in heavy aluminum foil and punch a few holes in the resulting packet. (No need to soak them.)

2. Trim off the brisket's really thick slabs of fat, but don't be too aggressive—you should never cut into the lean. Don't worry about the fat in the middle, if any.

3. Mix 2 parts Creole seasoning with 1 part salt. (For a big brisket, mix ¼ cup seasoning with 2 tablespoons salt.) Coat the brisket liberally with the seasoning.

4. Place the meat on the grill, fatty side up, with the thicker end facing the fire, as far away from the heat source as possible. To keep direct heat from the fire from hitting the meat, hang a curtain of aluminum foil between the two. Close the lid and maintain a temperature of 225–250 degrees inside, adding coals and wood now and then. There is no need to turn the brisket, but you might move it around on the grill so the bottom is more evenly smoked.

5. The brisket is done when the internal temperature, measured with a meat thermometer, hits 165 degrees. This takes 3–5 hours, depending on the size of the brisket and the heat in your grill. Let the brisket rest for about 20 minutes. Remove any remaining fat before slicing. Slice against the grain for easy, tender eating. Note that the direction of the grain changes as you cut; change with it. Serve with warm barbecue sauce and cole slaw. SERVES TWO PEOPLE PER POUND.

# Red Beans, Rice, Vegetables, and Pasta

It's lucky that we have the tradition of eating red beans every Monday in New Orleans. Loaded with soluble fiber, red beans are thought to counter the effects of the fats we have a habit of overusing in our local diet. (The sausage that traditionally comes with the beans, for example.) Beans of all colors are a big deal in New Orleans, especially at lunch, and they are the center of the meal, not just a side dish.

Rice is important, too. New Orleanians eat more rice than any other Americans except those of Asian descent. Most of us prefer it to potatoes. Even dishes like beef stew are served over rice here, and every family has two or three unique side dishes made with rice.

When I began writing about restaurants, side dishes were the weakest part of menus everywhere in New Orleans. Even in the best restaurants, vegetables were an afterthought. That changed in the 1980s. A generation of young chefs demanded and got better-quality vegetables from the markets. Still, a love for the old long-cooked dishes lives on. Here's a bit of all of that, both old and new.

# Red Beans and Rice

*Red beans and rice is the official Monday dish in New Orleans, on special menus in all kinds of restaurants all over town. Although most people agree on the recipe, the trend in recent years—especially in restaurants—has been to make the sauce matrix much thicker than what I remember from my youth. This version is the old (and, I think, better) style, with a looser sauce. The way my mother made it for us every Monday throughout my childhood.*

*I have, however, added two wrinkles. One came from a radio listener, who advised that beans improve greatly when you add much more celery than the standard recipe calls for. The other is adding the herb summer savory. Both provide pleasant flavor complements.*

*Red beans are classically served with smoked sausage, but they're also great with Fried Chicken (see recipe, page 187), Oysters en Brochette (see recipe, page 46), or grilled ham. But the ultimate is chaurice—Creole hot sausage—grilled to order and placed, along with all the dripping fat, atop the beans.*

1 lb. dried red beans
½ lb. bacon or fat from a fresh or smoked ham, salt pork, or pork belly
4 cloves garlic, minced
3 ribs celery, chopped
1 green bell pepper, chopped
1 small yellow onion, chopped
1 bay leaf
1 tsp. dried summer savory
½ tsp. freshly ground black pepper
1 tsp. Tabasco, plus more to taste
Salt
6 cups cooked long-grain rice
1 Tbsp. chopped green onion tops, for garnish
2 Tbsp. chopped flat-leaf parsley, for garnish

*(continued)*

1. Sort through the beans and pick out any bad or misshapen ones. Soak the beans in cold water overnight. When ready to cook, pour off the soaking water.

2. Fry the bacon or ham fat in a large, heavy pot or Dutch oven until crisp. Remove the bacon or ham fat and set aside for garnish (or a snack while you cook).

3. In the hot fat, sauté the garlic, celery, bell pepper, and onion until the vegetables just begin to brown. Add the beans and 1 gallon (16 cups) of water. Bring to a light boil, then lower to a simmer. Add the bay leaf, savory, black pepper, and Tabasco.

4. Simmer the beans for about 2 hours, stirring occasionally. After about 1½ hours, fish out about ½ cup of beans and mash them. Return the mashed beans to the pot. Smash more of them if you like your beans extra creamy. Add a little water if the sauce gets too thick. Add salt and more Tabasco to taste. Serve the beans over rice cooked firm. Garnish with chopped green onion and parsley. SERVES SIX TO EIGHT.

THE ULTIMATE: Fry skinless hot sausage and deposit it, along with as much of the fat as you can permit yourself, atop the beans. Red beans seem to have a limitless tolerance for added fat.

HEALTHY ALTERNATIVE: Leave the pork and ham out of the recipe completely and begin by sautéing all of the vegetables other than the beans in ¼ cup olive oil. At the table, pour extra-virgin olive oil over the beans. This may sound and look a bit odd, but the taste is terrific and everything on the plate—beans, rice, and olive oil—is a proven cholesterol-lowerer.

# Field Peas

*When the wonderful old West Bank café Berdou's was still around, one of its lunch specials was field peas and rice. Mr. Berdou told me he didn't sell many orders of it. "But I like them, so we cook them almost every week," he said. I'd never given field peas a second thought before, but they were so good that I added them to my regular bean rotation at home.*

*Field peas are a lot like crowder peas but smaller. They're a light brown, bigger than lentils, but shaped like red beans. They have a unique savory flavor that I find makes a great side dish. This version steers away from the bacon-fat, salt-pork kind of thing we do for red beans. If anything, it's inspired by the way they cook beans in Italy. So I suggest serving them with orzo pasta instead of rice.*

⅓ cup extra-virgin olive oil
1 medium yellow onion, chopped
1 medium bulb fennel, chopped
1 lb. field peas, sorted, rinsed, and
   soaked for a few hours or overnight
1 bay leaf
1 tsp. dried summer savory
¼ tsp. dried thyme

Pinch of nutmeg
4½ tsp. salt
1 Tbsp. Louisana-style hot sauce,
   such as Crystal
8 oz. orzo pasta, cooked and drained
6 sprigs flat-leaf parsley,
   leaves only, chopped, for garnish

1. Heat the olive oil in a large pot over medium-high heat until it shimmers. Add the onion and fennel, and cook until soft.

2. Drain the field peas and add them to the pot. Add 6 cups of fresh cold water, the bay leaf, savory, thyme, nutmeg, salt, and hot sauce. Bring to a boil, then lower to a simmer. Cover and cook for 1 hour. Check after an hour to see that the peas have not absorbed all the water. If they have, add more. The peas should still have a soupy texture.

3. Continue to cook until the peas are completely soft but not falling apart, another 30–45 minutes. Remove the bay leaf. Taste for seasoning and adjust. There should still be enough liquid so that the beans have a stewlike texture.

4. Add the orzo to the pot and gently stir into the beans. Serve garnished with chopped parsley. SERVES ABOUT SIX.

# Peas in a Roux

*This is an old, nearly extinct local dish that intrigues me, especially after Arnaud's revived it for a while. After failing a couple of times to get it right, I came up with this, which I now serve at Thanksgiving in place of plain old peas.*

1 stick (8 Tbsp.) butter
½ cup flour
½ cup sliced mushrooms
1 green onion, sliced
1½ cups chicken stock (see recipe, page 312)
1 tsp. Worcestershire sauce
½ tsp. Tabasco Garlic Pepper Sauce
3 cups large peas, frozen
Salt and freshly ground black pepper to taste

1. Make a blond roux by melting the butter in a saucepan over medium heat. Add the flour and cook, stirring constantly, until the mixture just barely begins to brown. Lower the heat to almost nothing. Add the mushrooms and green onion, and stir lightly to blend into the roux. The heat of the roux will cook the mushrooms and onion, and the vegetables will bring down the heat of the roux so it won't brown any further.

2. Add the stock, Worcestershire sauce, and Tabasco, and whisk to blend into a smooth sauce. Add the peas and raise the heat a little. Cook until the peas are heated through, stirring while they're still frozen to blend them into the sauce. The sauce should have the texture of gumbo. If it's too thick, add a little more stock or water. Season to taste with salt and pepper. SERVES EIGHT TO TWELVE.

# Baked Black-eyed Peas

*Black-eyed peas have a much more assertive taste than most beans. For this reason, I really think that you have to cook them differently from the way you cook red beans. This method heads off in the direction of barbecue beans, without the sauce. It helps to boil the beans the night before, then bake them all morning long. This is actually my wife's recipe, and we serve it at most of our casual barbecues.*

1 lb. dried black-eyed peas
¼ lb. lean bacon, cut into squares
½ cup chopped yellow onion
⅔ cup Steen's cane syrup
½ cup dark brown sugar
2 Tbsp. Pickapeppa or Tabasco New Orleans Steak Sauce
2 Tbsp. Creole mustard
1 tsp. salt
½ tsp. dried summer savory

1. Sort through the beans to remove bad ones and dirt, then rinse well. Put them into a pot with 3 quarts of water and bring to a light boil. Boil for 1 hour.

2. Preheat the oven to 275 degrees. Bring 4 cups of water to a boil. Meanwhile, drain the parboiled beans well and transfer to a baking dish. Add all of the remaining ingredients and mix well.

3. Top the beans with just enough boiling water to just barely cover them. Bake for 5 hours. Check it every hour, stirring the pot and adding a little more water if the beans seem to be getting dry. MAKES EIGHT TO TWELVE SIDE PORTIONS.

# Dirty Rice

*Dirty rice is jambalaya's less complex brother, yet in its way, it's every bit as delicious. Unlike jambalaya, which can be served as a main course, dirty rice is a side dish. It's also a way to use all the stuff you pull out of the cavity of a whole chicken. While you can use the heart, I usually leave it out because it's tough, even chopped up. If the liver component of the giblets is about 50 percent, that's perfect.*

½ lb. chicken giblets (heart removed)
1 large yellow onion, quartered
1 green bell pepper, stemmed and seeded
1 rib celery, halved
½ lb. ground pork (or better yet, substitute ⅓ of this with pork liver)
2 Tbsp. butter
2 tsp. salt-free Creole seasoning

2 tsp. salt, plus more to taste
1 tsp. Worcestershire sauce
½ tsp. crushed red pepper
½ tsp. marjoram
2½ cups chicken stock (see recipe, page 312)
1½ cups Uncle Ben's or other parboiled rice
Freshly ground black pepper to taste

1. Preheat the oven to 300 degrees. Working in 2–3 batches, finely chop the giblets, onion, bell pepper, and celery in a food processor. Set aside. Sauté the ground pork in a skillet until all the pink is gone. Drain the excess fat and set aside.

2. Melt the butter in a large, heavy saucepan. Add the giblet-vegetable mixture and sauté until the onion is clear. Add the Creole seasoning, the 2 teaspoons of salt, Worcestershire sauce, crushed red pepper, and marjoram, and stir to combine. Cover the pot, lower the heat, and let simmer while you prepare the rice.

3. Put the stock, rice, and salt to taste into another saucepan. Bring the stock to a boil, lower to a simmer, cover, and cook 25 minutes, or until all the liquid has been absorbed.

4. When the rice is cooked, fluff it with a kitchen fork and add it to the pan with the chicken-vegetable mixture. Add the ground pork and stir to distribute all the ingredients. Season to taste with salt and pepper.

5. Place the rice loosely in a casserole dish and bake for 5 minutes, or longer if the rice is very damp. It should be a little dry but not hard. **MAKES EIGHT SIDE PORTIONS.**

# Lyonnaise Potatoes

*The classic potato side dish in New Orleans–style steak houses, this is a simple combination of potatoes and onions.*

3 lb. white potatoes, peeled
1 stick (8 Tbsp.) butter
1 large yellow onion, coarsely chopped
1 green onion, finely chopped
Salt and freshly ground black pepper to taste

1. Boil the potatoes for about 10 minutes, or until a kitchen fork jabbed into the biggest potato slips out when you lift the potato out of the water. Rinse the potatoes in cool water to stop further cooking. Slice the potatoes first from end to end, then into half-disks about ½ inch thick.

2. Melt 4 tablespoons of the butter in a large skillet over medium-high heat until it bubbles. Add the yellow onion and sauté until it just begins to brown at the edges. Add the potatoes, green onion, and the remaining 4 tablespoons of butter to the pan and cook, without stirring, until the potatoes have browned on the bottom. Turn the potatoes over and brown the other side. Season to taste with salt and pepper. SERVES SIX.

# Gratin Dauphinois

*This is potatoes au gratin with class. I am no fan of the melted-Cheddar-topped potato gratins that steak houses serve, popular though they may be. This French classic gets all the same things accomplished with much better flavor.*

4 large white potatoes (about 3 lb.), peeled and sliced ¼ inch thick
3 cloves garlic, crushed
Salt and ground white pepper
8 oz. Gruyère cheese, shredded
1¾ cups grated Parmesan cheese
2 cups heavy whipping cream
2 egg yolks, beaten
½ cup bread crumbs

1. Preheat the oven to 400 degrees. Bring a pot of water to a boil. Add the potatoes and cook for 5 minutes. Drain and cool.

2. Rub the inside of a 12 x 8-inch glass baking dish with the garlic. Discard what's left of the garlic. Layer the potato slices all the way across the bottom of the dish, seasoning each layer with salt and pepper and a sprinkling of Gruyère and Parmesan. (Reserve ¼ cup of the Parmesan for the topping.)

3. Whisk the cream and egg yolks together and pour over the potatoes. It should come up about two-thirds of the way to the top. Cover with aluminum foil and bake in the oven for an hour.

4. Remove the foil. Combine the bread crumbs and the reserved ¼ cup of Parmesan cheese, and sprinkle in a thin layer over the top of the potatoes. Return, uncovered, to the oven and continue baking until the crust browns. (If you have a convection oven, set it to convect.)

5. Remove from the oven and allow to rest and cool for at least 15 minutes before serving. MAKES ABOUT TWELVE SIDE PORTIONS.

# Mashed Potatoes

*My daughter, Mary Leigh, loves my mashed potatoes and won't allow my wife to make them. I'm pleased to have such a hold on her affection. I, too, like creamy, lumpy, buttery, peppery mashed potatoes, without the other flavorings that have become the vogue in recent times.*

*The variety of potato matters. When the red creamers look good, I get those. Yukon Golds are excellent, too. But white russet potatoes with no trace of green in the skin also come out nice. I boil the potatoes with the skins on and peel them later. That does burn the fingers a little, but if you do it in the sink under a thin stream of cold water, it's not too bad and you get a better flavor.*

4 lb. potatoes
1½ sticks (12 Tbsp.) butter, cut into pats
1 cup whole milk
1 tsp. salt
¼ tsp. freshly ground black pepper

1. Boil the potatoes until a kitchen fork jabbed into the biggest one slips out when you lift the potato out of the water. Drain and peel the potatoes as soon as they're barely cool enough to handle. (I usually do this under a little running water.)

2. Put the potatoes in a large non-metallic bowl. (Metal promotes cooling, and you want the potatoes to stay hot.) Add the butter, and using a large, heavy wire whisk or a potato masher, mash the potatoes into pieces about the size of your little finger.

3. Heat the milk in the microwave until steaming. Add it and the salt to the potatoes and continue mashing. They will seem very wet at first, but as you continue to mash, they will become creamy. Add a little more milk, if necessary, to achieve a lighter texture.

4. Add the pepper and mix well. Ignore the small lumps that will inevitably be in there. They lend authenticity. These obviously did not come from a box! SERVES FOUR TO EIGHT.

# Brabant Potatoes

*In most restaurants, these are nothing more than cube-shaped french fries. But there is much more to the dish than that. Brabant potatoes can be a surprisingly delicious side dish if you use this two-step preparation.*

   2 large white potatoes, very starchy (no green)
   2–3 cups vegetable oil (preferably canola or peanut oil)
   ½ stick (4 Tbsp.) butter
   1 Tbsp. olive oil
   1 clove garlic, minced
   1 sprig flat-leaf parsley, minced

1. Preheat the oven to 350 degrees. Scrub the outsides of the potatoes under cold running water, or peel if you don't like potato skins. Cut into ½-inch dice, wash again to remove excess starch, and drain well. Allow 5-10 minutes for the potatoes to dry.

2. Meanwhile, in a large saucepan or deep skillet, heat the vegetable oil to 375 degrees. Put the potatoes in and fry until they are very lightly browned. Remove them from the oil with a skimmer and drain on paper towels. Once drained, arrange the potatoes in a single layer on a baking sheet or dish and set aside.

3. Heat the butter and olive oil in a skillet over medium-low heat. Add the garlic and parsley, and cook just until the garlic is fragrant. Spoon the garlic-parsley mixture over the potatoes and bake until their edges become crisp and medium-dark brown, 7–10 minutes. Serve with a little extra garlic butter if you have any left. SERVES FOUR.

# French Fries Soufflées

*Almost all french fries in restaurants are terrible, made with frozen potatoes and rarely to order. We put up with that because fries made with fresh potatoes at home are such a pain in the neck to prepare. Our kids love them so much, however, that we're constantly finding ourselves going through the ordeal—and then enjoying the results very much.*

*Start with large, starchy potatoes (such as russets). Blanch them briefly in boiling water. Then fry them twice. The second frying is not essential, as the people who crowd in grabbing fries after the first frying will prove. But it adds a magical crunch to the fries.*

*If you want to go to the outer limits of excellence in french fries, use rendered beef fat to fry them in. But few of us have the heart to do that.*

5 lb. starchy potatoes
Canola oil
Salt and freshly ground black pepper to taste

1. Bring a large pot of water to a boil while you're peeling the potatoes (if you want them peeled). After peeling, slice the potatoes as thick as you like in whatever shape you like, but put them into a bowl of cold water while they're waiting for the next step.

2. Boil the sliced potatoes for about a minute. This will not only begin their cooking but will also prevent the sugars from oxidizing and turning the raw potatoes brown. Drain and collect them in a colander.

3. Bring at least 2 quarts (8 cups) of oil to a temperature of 375 degrees in another large pot. Use a fat thermometer to monitor this. The oil should not fill more than half the pot.

4. It's safest to use a fry basket. Put a handful of the cut, blanched fries into the basket and lower it into the hot oil. Be prepared to lift the basket should the oil foam up to near the top. Fry the potatoes until they're just light brown. Remove and drain. Let the temperature of the oil return to 375 degrees before lowering the next batch.

*(continued)*

5. If you can keep from eating them at this point, let the french fries cool a bit. When ready to serve, heat the oil back up to about 400 degrees. I warn you that we are in grease-fire territory here—be very careful and have a dry-chemical fire extinguisher handy. Place a handful of the once-fried fries back into the basket and lower it into the hot oil. Fry for about 15 seconds; they will brown very quickly and may even puff up. Drain, season with salt and pepper, and serve immediately. For a distinctly New Orleans way of eating fries (the Belgians also like this), serve with a dish of Spicy Garlic Mayonnaise (see recipe, page 317). SERVES EIGHT.

# Creole Eggplant Gratin Delmonico

*Here's another extinct restaurant dish. It was the favorite side dish at the old Delmonico, before chef Emeril bought and modernized it. Especially right after it comes out of the oven, it's delicious—even if you don't like eggplant.*

*I had this dish for the last time at Delmonico two days before the old regime closed down. It was the night of the Babylon parade, which passed right in front of the restaurant on St. Charles Avenue. We had most of our dinner, went out to watch the parade, and came back in for dessert with Angie Brown and Rose Dietrich, the sisters who owned Delmonico. The combination of that Mardi Gras experience with one of the best meals I ever had there (the old place was good to the last) is forever engraved in my memory.*

2 eggplants, peeled and
    cut into large dice
2 Tbsp. butter
1 medium yellow onion, chopped
2 ribs celery, chopped
1 cup small (25–30 count) peeled
    shrimp
½ lb. claw crabmeat

1 fresh ripe tomato, chopped
¼ tsp. Tabasco
¼ tsp. Worcestershire sauce
¼ tsp. dried marjoram
3 sprigs flat-leaf parsley, leaves chopped
½ tsp. lemon juice
½ tsp. salt
¼ cup bread crumbs

1. Preheat the oven to 350 degrees. Bring a large pot of water to a rolling boil and drop the eggplant in for about 2 minutes. Drain and set aside.

2. Melt the butter in a large skillet. Add the onion, celery, and shrimp, and cook until the shrimp turn pink. Add all of the remaining ingredients except the bread crumbs and cook, stirring very lightly, until everything is heated through.

3. Load the mixture into a baking dish and top with the bread crumbs. Bake until the bread crumbs are toasty, about 15 minutes. **SERVES FOUR TO EIGHT.**

# Savory Bread Pudding
# with Mushrooms

*In New Orleans, bread pudding is usually a dessert. But not this one. Out come the sweet ingredients, replaced by mushrooms, onions, and cheese. It's my wife Mary Ann's idea, and we often use it as side dish, especially for Thanksgiving. The dish is at its best with meaty, wild-tasting mushrooms: portobellos, criminis, shiitakes, chanterelles, porcinis, etc. The best cheeses are the ones that melt well and have an interesting tang: Gruyère, fontina, Swiss, provolone, mozzarella. (If you use the last two, add a little Parmesan, as well.)*

3 cups half-and-half
4 eggs, beaten
1 tsp. Worcestershire sauce
¼ tsp. Tabasco
¼ tsp. salt
1 Tbsp. butter
18 inches of a loaf of stale poor boy
    bread or French bread, cut into
    ¼-inch-thick slices

1½ cups shredded Gruyère, fontina,
    or other easy-melting white cheese
1½ cups sliced meaty mushrooms,
    such as portobellos, shiitakes,
    criminis
¾ cup finely chopped green onion

1. Preheat the oven to 300 degrees. Whisk the half-and-half, eggs, Worcestershire sauce, Tabasco, and salt together in a bowl and set aside.

2. Grease a 9 x 5 x 4-inch baking dish or casserole with the butter. Place a layer of bread along the bottom of the dish. Sprinkle a third each of the cheese, mushrooms, and green onion over the bread. Pour about a quarter of the milk-egg mixture over this, enough to soak it well. Push down gently until the bread is soaked. Repeat the layers in the same order as above, topping each tier with a dousing of liquid. Finish with a layer of bread and the last of the liquid.

3. Set the baking dish into a second larger baking pan and pour in enough hot water to come halfway up the side of the baking dish. Bake for an hour and 15 minutes. Let it cool for at least 30 minutes before serving. The bread pudding can be sliced, but it's perfectly fine to spoon it right out of the dish at the table. SERVES EIGHT.

# Broiled Asparagus Parmigiano

*This is my favorite recipe for asparagus as a side dish. It takes a few minutes longer than just boiling them, but the result is superb.*

2 lb. fresh medium asparagus
2 Tbsp. extra-virgin olive oil
¼ tsp. crushed red pepper
1 Tbsp. lemon juice
½ cup finely grated Parmesan cheese

1. Preheat the broiler. Place water in a wide skillet and bring to a rolling boil. Meanwhile, trim the tough bottom inch or so off the asparagus spears. Blanch the asparagus for 2 minutes (or steam them for 90 seconds), then remove. Rinse with cold water until they're no longer hot.

2. Arrange the asparagus on a baking sheet, parallel to one another and almost touching. Pour a ribbon of olive oil back and forth across the asparagus, but not so much that it collects on the baking sheet. Sprinkle lightly with the crushed red pepper and lemon juice. Then top with enough of the Parmesan cheese to form a lacy layer.

3. Put the pan under the broiler, about 4 inches from the heat, cooking until the cheese melts and just begins to brown. Remove from the oven and allow to cool enough for the cheese to set. Then, using a metal spatula, transfer 4–6 asparagus spears per portion, still held together by the cheese, to individual plates. SERVES SIX TO EIGHT.

# Spinach à la Wohl

*In my bachelor days, I was a regular guest at the large Thanksgiving gatherings hosted by my good friends Kit and Billy Wohl. (Kit is the author of* Arnaud's Cookbook.*) We'd divide the kitchen down the middle: cooks and burners on one side, talkers and wine drinkers on the other. I was usually recruited to wash and chop spinach (on the talker side—we usually had actual chefs in attendance) for an ever evolving creamed spinach recipe that was always part of the dinner, although it never tasted the same twice. Here's a recipe based on a particularly good batch.*

Four 10-oz. bags of fresh spinach, picked of stems and washed well
½ cup half-and-half, heavy whipping cream, or milk
½ cup grated Cheddar cheese
½ stick (4 Tbsp.) butter or margarine, melted
One 5.2-oz. package Boursin Garlic & Fine Herbs Gournay Cheese
One 8-oz. package cream cheese
2 Tbsp. grated Parmesan cheese
Pinch of nutmeg
½ cup sour cream
Salt and freshly ground black pepper to taste

1. Place the spinach in a large saucepan over low heat with just the water that clings to it after washing and cook until completely wilted. Squeeze out any excess water.

2. Put the spinach in a food processor and process for 10 seconds. Add all of the remaining ingredients, except the sour cream, salt, and pepper, and puree. Add a little more half-and-half (or cream or milk) if a looser texture is desired.

3. Transfer the spinach mixture to a butter-coated saucepan and cook over medium-low heat until just heated through. Remove from the heat and fold in the sour cream until it is evenly blended. Season to taste with salt and pepper. If you want to be fancy and have the oven space, reheat the dish in the oven with a grated Cheddar cheese topping. MAKES ABOUT TWELVE SIDE PORTIONS.

# Gratin of Pumpkin

*This dish is a variation on the French classic Gratin Dauphinois (see recipe, page 218). I originally served it at one of my Thanksgiving dinners, in another effort to use the meat of the jack-o'-lantern–style pumpkins that are so plentiful and cheap that time of year. I've made it often since.*

1 medium jack-o'-lantern–type pumpkin, 4–6 lb.
5 cloves garlic, 2 of them chopped
2 lb. carrots, peeled and cut on the bias into ¼-inch-thick coins
1 cup finely grated Parmesan cheese

1 cup grated Gruyère cheese
Ground white pepper to taste
2 cups half-and-half
2 egg yolks
Pinch of nutmeg
1 cup bread crumbs

1. Preheat the oven to 350 degrees. If you have a convection oven, set it on convect.

2. Cut open the pumpkin from top to bottom. Scrape out all the seeds and fibers. Cut the pumpkin into eighths. Carve the meat out in pieces as large as you can, leaving ½-inch-thick shells. Cut the meat into ⅛-inch-thick slices.

3. Crush the 3 whole garlic cloves and use them to wipe the inside of a 12 x 8-inch glass baking dish. Discard what's left of the crushed cloves. Shingle half of the pumpkin and half of the carrots along the bottom of the dish. Sprinkle on half of the chopped garlic, one-third of each of the cheeses, and white pepper to taste. Repeat the process with the remaining ingredients, finishing with a generous layer of the cheeses.

4. Beat the half-and-half, egg yolks, and nutmeg together, then pour over the casserole. Wrap a relatively tight seal of aluminum foil over the top of the dish. Bake for 1 hour and 10 minutes.

5. Raise the oven temperature to 400 degrees. Remove the foil, sprinkle bread crumbs in a thin layer over the top, and return to the oven. Continue baking, uncovered, until the crust browns.

6. Remove from the oven and allow to rest and cool for at least 15 minutes before serving. MAKES ABOUT TWELVE SIDE PORTIONS.

# Stuffed Onions Florentine

*This dish was in my very first cookbook, a little tome published in 1982, now out of print. One day not long ago, someone called me on the radio and said she'd made it and loved it. I cooked it again and found out why.*

ONIONS
6 medium yellow onions, peeled
6 slices bacon
Two 10-oz. bags of fresh spinach, cooked and chopped
2 crimini mushrooms, chopped
½ cup chicken stock (see recipe, page 312)
1 Tbsp. red wine vinegar

1 tsp. brown sugar
¼ tsp. salt-free Creole seasoning
¼ tsp. salt
1 tsp. Herbsaint or Pernod (optional)
Dash of Worcestershire sauce

TOPPING
¼ cup bread crumbs
2 Tbsp. Parmesan cheese

1. Preheat the oven to 400 degrees. If you have a convection oven, set it on convect. Cut off the root ends of each onion, about one-fourth the way down. Scoop out the centers of the onions, leaving ¼-inch-thick onion shells. Chop the onion centers.

2. Cook the bacon in a skillet until crisp. Remove and crumble the bacon and set aside. Pour off the fat, but don't wipe the pan. Cook the chopped onion in the remaining fat until tender.

3. Lower the heat to medium-low and stir in all of the remaining ingredients, along with the bacon. Cook until all of the moisture has been absorbed and the mixture begins to dry out.

4. Fill the onion shells loosely with the spinach mixture. Blend the topping ingredients together and sprinkle generously on top of the onions. Arrange the stuffed onions in a shallow baking dish, cover with foil, and bake for 20 minutes, then remove the foil and bake until the topping browns. SERVES SIX.

# Stuffed Artichokes

*Stuffed artichokes, Italian style, are an old New Orleans favorite. They're at their best in springtime, when the new crop of artichokes appears. The stuffing is mostly bread crumbs and garlic. Not everybody likes (or understands) stuffed artichokes. My wife does; I don't. This recipe came from the old Toney's on Bourbon Street, which sold them by the hundreds.*

4 fresh medium artichokes
Salt
¼ cup olive oil
3 Tbsp. chopped garlic
4 anchovy fillets, chopped
2 cups bread crumbs

¼ cup grated Romano cheese
3 Tbsp. chopped flat-leaf parsley
1 tsp. dried oregano
⅛ tsp. sugar
⅛ tsp. freshly ground black pepper
1 large lemon

1. Thoroughly wash the artichokes. Carefully trim the top inch or so off each. Trim the stem so that the artichokes will sit straight up. With scissors, trim off points of leaves. Soak artichokes 30 minutes in ½ gallon (8 cups) of water with 2 teaspoons of salt dissolved.

2. Meanwhile, heat the oil in a large skillet. Add the garlic and sauté until fragrant. Add all of the remaining ingredients except the lemon and continue cooking, stirring frequently, over low heat until everything is well blended.

3. To stuff the artichokes, spread the outer leaves and spoon in the stuffing, starting from the top and going around to the bottom. Form foil cups around the bottom half of each artichoke.

4. Arrange the stuffed artichokes in a large kettle or Dutch oven with an inch of water in the bottom. Squeeze lemon juice liberally over all. Cook, covered, over medium heat for 30–40 minutes. Do not boil dry. Artichokes are done when the inner leaves can be pulled out easily. If you can lift the artichoke by its inner leaves, it's not done.

5. Allow the artichokes to cool until you can touch them, then dig in. Also good cold as a late-night snack—in moderation, and only if your mate eats them with you. SERVES FOUR.

# Pasta Bordelaise

*The Italians call this pasta aglio olio. In New Orleans, it's pasta bordelaise, even though there's not a drop of red Bordeaux in it. We eat it as a side dish to all sorts of things, from Deviled Crab (see recipe, page 34) to Veal Pannée (see recipe, page 161).*

Salt
1 lb. angel hair pasta
⅓ cup extra-virgin olive oil
4–8 cloves garlic, chopped
6 sprigs flat-leaf parsley, leaves only, chopped
¼ tsp. crushed red pepper
¼ tsp. dried oregano
Parmesan cheese

1. Bring a large pot of water to a rolling boil with a tablespoon of salt dissolved in it. Cook the pasta for about 4 minutes, leaving it al dente—firm to the tooth. Drain the pasta, but save about ¼ cup of the pasta cooking water.

2. In a large skillet, heat the olive oil until it shimmers. Add all of the remaining ingredients except the pasta and cook until the garlic smells good. Add 3 tablespoons of the reserved pasta cooking water and whisk to blend.

3. Turn the heat off and add the pasta, tossing it with a fork to coat with the sauce. Divide among the plates and serve with grated Parmigiano Reggiano or Grana Padano cheese. SERVES FOUR AS A MAIN COURSE OR EIGHT AS A SIDE DISH.

# Oyster and Pecan Stuffing

*Here is a different approach to oyster dressing for the holidays. This recipe should be made a day ahead of time so that the flavors of the ingredients will merge together. (If you do, refrigerate it and take it out of the refrigerator an hour before baking it.) Although you might want to stuff this into a bird, it's probably better baked separately.*

¼ cup dry vermouth
24 fresh, shucked oysters, with
   their liquor
3 cups stale French bread,
   cut into cubes
1 stick (8 Tbsp.) butter
1 medium yellow onion, chopped
3 green onions, chopped

2 cloves garlic, chopped
Pinch of dried thyme
Pinch of cayenne
1 bay leaf
½ cup chopped flat-leaf parsley leaves
1 cup chopped pecans
½ cup bread crumbs

1. Warm the vermouth in a large saucepan over medium heat. Add the oysters and gently poach until the oysters curl at the edges, about 8 minutes. Turn off the heat. Chop the oysters coarsely and set aside. Add the bread cubes to the poaching liquid and mash them a bit with a wire whisk. Set aside.

2. Melt the butter in a skillet over medium heat. Add the yellow and green onions, garlic, thyme, cayenne, and bay leaf, and sauté until the onions turn translucent. Add the poached oysters, oyster liquor, and parsley, and simmer for 3–5 minutes. Remove from heat and discard the bay leaf. Stir pan contents into bread mixture.

3. Add the chopped pecans. Toss to evenly distribute them in the mixture, which should be fairly loose and wet. Stir in the bread crumbs to stiffen the mixture and transfer it to a baking dish. Refrigerate, covered, overnight if you like. Take the baking dish out of the refrigerator about an hour before baking.

4. Preheat the oven to 350 degrees. Bake the stuffing, covered, until warmed all the way through. Then bake another few minutes, uncovered, to get a bit of a crust on top. Serves six to eight.

# Hush Puppies

*Hush puppies are essential to Fried Catfish (see recipe, page 123), and they're good with any other seafood platter, too. You make them especially good by keeping the texture light and including flavors other than that of the cornmeal. Fry them in the same oil that you used to fry fish or (even better) chicken.*

*Although the original idea for hush puppies is to use the same stuff you used to coat the fish, better results come from making a batter specifically for hush puppies. I like white self-rising cornmeal.*

Vegetable oil, for frying, preferably oil previously used for frying fish or chicken
1½ cups white self-rising cornmeal
1½ cups self-rising flour
1 tsp. salt
½ tsp. salt-free Creole seasoning
½ tsp. sugar

1 cup canned corn, drained
2 green onions, finely chopped
1 small jalapeño pepper, seeded and membrane removed, chopped
2 sprigs flat-leaf parsley, chopped
1¾ cups milk
1 egg, beaten

1. Pour the oil into a heavy saucepan to a depth of 1 inch. Heat over medium-high heat until the temperature reaches 350 degrees.

2. Whisk the cornmeal, flour, salt, Creole seasoning, and sugar together in a small bowl. Add the corn, green onions, jalapeño, and parsley, and stir to blend well.

3. In a second, larger bowl, beat the milk, egg, and ¼ cup of water together. Add the cornmeal–green onion mixture to the wet ingredients and mix with a whisk until no dry flour is visible. (Add a little more milk to the mixture if necessary. The mixture should be sticky but not runny or grainy.)

4. With a tablespoon, make balls of batter. Fry 4–6 at a time until they're medium brown; they should float on the oil when they're ready. Remove and drain, and allow the oil temperature to recover before adding more hush puppies.

5. Serve as an appetizer with a mixture of equal parts mayonnaise, horseradish, and sour cream, or tartar sauce. Or alongside fried seafood or chicken. MAKES ABOUT EIGHTEEN HUSH PUPPIES.

# Salads

Sometime in late May or early June in New Orleans, a day will begin hot and will just keep getting hotter. It's the first of many such days, and by September, it seems as if they will never end. This has a definite effect on our dining habits. Suddenly the idea of replacing a plate of red beans and rice or a bowl of gumbo with a refreshing salad sounds very good, indeed.

Even at those times, Orleanians remain suspicious of salads. It wasn't until recent memory that local greens were good enough to hold up their end of the flavor bargain. Even expensive restaurants kept throwing jejune stacks of iceberg lettuce at us until the 1990s. Fortunately, we've managed to move past that, and both stores and restaurants provide Orleanians with interesting greens and vegetables for the salad bowl.

The most popular big salads in New Orleans are those made by tossing some of those leaves with our big boiled shrimp, lump crabmeat, or both. Fried oysters or crawfish tails also become salad garnishes, functioning like the most interesting croutons you can imagine. Such salads are easy enough to figure out. Here are a few more complicated salads for the end of summer, when you've worn out all of the obvious ideas. Many of them can do duty not just as salads, but as cold appetizers or even light, fresh summer entrées.

# Chicken Tenders with Pepper Jelly and Spinach Salad

*This dish will help you get rid of some of that pepper jelly you're always getting as gifts (or the pepper jelly you made yourself that you can't seem to unload). Maybe the stuff would be in greater demand if it came with a recipe like this one.*

1 cup pepper jelly
2 Tbsp. orange juice
2 cups flour
1 Tbsp. salt-free Creole seasoning
2 Tbsp. salt
2 lb. chicken tenders, or chicken breasts cut into thirds
1 stick (8 Tbsp.) butter
8 oz. crumbled blue cheese
Two 10-oz. bags of fresh spinach leaves, well washed and dried
1 cup Creole Mustard Vinaigrette (see recipe, page 245)

1. Preheat the broiler with the broiler pan about 4 inches from the heat.

2. Whisk the pepper jelly and orange juice together and set aside. Combine the flour, Creole seasoning, and salt in a wide bowl. Dust (don't dredge!) the chicken tenders with the seasoned flour.

3. Melt 2 tablespoons of the butter in a large (preferably stainless steel) skillet over medium heat. Working in batches, cook the chicken, turning occasionally, until lightly browned, about 5 minutes. (They will not be cooked all the way through at this point.) Add more butter, as necessary, to cook all the chicken.

4. Generously coat the chicken with the pepper-jelly mixture and place the pieces on the preheated broiler pan. Broil the chicken pieces until they are fully cooked and browned on top. Allow them to cool for 5 minutes, then cut them on the bias into ¾-inch-thick slices.

5. Toss the chicken slices and spinach with the Creole mustard vinaigrette and serve. Makes eight entree salads.

# Cobb Salad, New Orleans Style

*What makes this Cobb salad different is that the chicken is seasoned with Creole seasoning and grilled. The dressing also includes a few local favorites among its ingredients. The result is a classic Cobb with a bit more bite. The choice of greens is critical. Use at least two varieties: one mild (such as Boston, iceberg, or romaine), the other sharper (such as escarole, frisée, or arugula). Ratio: about two parts mild to one part sharp.*

CHICKEN
2 chicken breasts
Blackening Seasoning (see recipe, page 311)
3 Tbsp. butter, melted

DRESSING
1 Tbsp. Creole mustard
3 dashes of Worcestershire sauce
3 Tbsp. tarragon vinegar
¼ tsp. salt
5 dashes of Tabasco Garlic Pepper Sauce
1 Tbsp. paprika
½ cup olive oil

SALAD
Enough mixed greens to make 4 salads (about 2 standard bags)
1 green onion, tender parts only, thinly sliced
1 hard-boiled egg, finely diced or crumbled
2 ripe but not soft avocados, cut into medium dice
2 ripe tomatoes, cut into medium dice
1 red radish, chopped
6 slices thick bacon, fried crisp
½ cup crumbled blue cheese

1. Generously season the chicken with the blackening seasoning. Brush with the butter and either grill or broil until cooked through and crusty. Let cool, then chop into medium dice.

2. To make the dressing: Combine all the ingredients except the oil in a bowl. Add 1 tablespoon of water. Add the oil a little at a time, whisking constantly, until emulsified.

3. The greens are best torn into small pieces, not chopped. Either way, prepare them right before serving. In a bowl, combine the chicken and all the remaining salad ingredients, except the greens, and toss with three-quarters of the dressing. Add the greens and toss gently until all the leaves are coated. Add more dressing if necessary. SERVES FOUR.

# Watercress and Spinach Salad with Pecans

*This is one of my favorite salads. I love the way the softness and pepperiness of the watercress plays against the crisp nuttiness of the pecans. And it doesn't have ambitions to become an entrée. Don't even try it unless the watercress is very fresh. Any yellow at all is bad news.*

SALAD

1 bag of spinach, picked and washed
1 bunch of watercress, trimmed and washed
1½ cups sliced white mushrooms

DRESSING

¼ cup chopped toasted pecans
½ cup walnut oil
1 Tbsp. lemon juice
2 Tbsp. red wine vinegar
2 grinds fresh black pepper
Generous pinch of salt
½ tsp. fresh dill, finely chopped
2 sprigs flat-leaf parsley, finely chopped

1. Tear the larger spinach leaves into pieces. Toss the spinach with the watercress and mushrooms in a salad bowl.

2. Put the dressing ingredients into a food processor or blender and process until emulsified. Add the dressing to the greens and toss until the leaves are well coated. SERVES FOUR.

# Pasta Salad Allegro

*This pasta salad has a distinctly Creole flavor, along with a clear Italian accent. It was created by chef Ron Wilemon, who's turned up in a number of great restaurants over the years, including one of his own—the Allegro Bistro.*

 2 lb. cheese tortellini, preferably tri-color
 2 Tbsp. Creole mustard
 ½ cup red wine vinegar
 1 cup olive oil
 1 lb. andouille (see page 326) or other smoked sausage, cut into small slivers
 2 large, ripe tomatoes, cubed
 16 sun-dried tomatoes, soaked a few minutes in warm water,
  sliced into julienne strips
 3 cans artichoke hearts packed in water, drained, rinsed, and quartered
 20–30 leaves fresh basil, chopped
 1 each red, yellow, and green bell peppers, thinly sliced
 1 green onion, thinly sliced
 ½ cup finely shredded Parmesan cheese
 2 tsp. dried oregano

1. Cook the tortellini in rapidly boiling water until it's still firm to the bite. Drain and refrigerate.

2. Whisk the mustard and the vinegar together in a large bowl. Add about a third of the oil, whisking until smooth. Add 2 tablespoons of cold water, then gradually add the rest of the oil while whisking constantly.

3. Add the remaining ingredients, along with the tortellini, and toss carefully (avoid breaking the pasta) to distribute the ingredients evenly. Let it sit for about 15 minutes before serving. SERVES EIGHT TO TWELVE.

# Squid with Spicy Creole Vinaigrette

*One of the best ways to serve squid is as a salad. This is sort of that, although it's really more akin to Shrimp Rémoulade with Two Sauces (see recipe, page 13) and Crabmeat Ravigote (see recipe, page 31). The best squid to use are the small ones, about three to four inches long.*

2 lb. small squid
¼ cup red wine vinegar
¼ cup dry white wine
¼ tsp. crushed red pepper
¼ tsp. cracked black peppercorns
1 sprig fresh thyme
⅓ cup extra-virgin olive oil
4½ tsp. Creole mustard

4½ tsp. lemon juice
¼ tsp. salt
½ cup thinly sliced white onion
½ cup chopped flat-leaf parsley,
   leaves and stems
1 rib celery, chopped
½ tsp. chopped garlic
1 tsp. chopped fresh oregano

1. The only difficulty with squid is cleaning it, and even that task is easy if you remember that the undesirable parts are where the tentacles meet the body. Cut out the ¼-inch section that includes the beak and the eyes. Then carefully remove the ink sac and the cartilage pen from the body and rub off the dark, thin skin. On the tentacle part, make sure there is a clear ring you can see through and remove any thin skin that may be there. Then slice the body into rings about ½ inch thick.

2. Put 2 tablespoons of the vinegar, 2 tablespoons of the wine, the crushed red pepper, black peppercorns, thyme, and ⅓ cup water into a saucepan. Add the cleaned squid and bring to a simmer. Cook for about 3 minutes, then remove from the heat and allow to cool for about 2 minutes more. Drain.

3. Meanwhile, whisk the olive oil, mustard, lemon juice, salt, remaining vinegar, and 2 tablespoons of water together in a large bowl. Add the squid and all the other ingredients, and toss to combine.

4. Let the squid marinate, refrigerated, for about 4 hours. Remove from the refrigerator and bring to room temperature before serving. SERVES FOUR.

# Guacamole

*This is a little more complicated than most guacamole recipes and probably not authentic, but it sure tastes good. If you have fresh chile peppers available, chop about two tablespoons' worth and substitute it for some or all of the Tabasco Green Pepper Sauce. To keep the avocados from browning, don't cut them until everything else is chopped and combined. At this point, I'd like to apologize for the green ketchup. But blind tasting doesn't lie: The ketchup adds a nice little something, and the green makes it greener.*

1 medium white onion
10 sprigs cilantro, leaves only
Juice of 1 small lime
1 Tbsp. olive oil
1 large clove garlic
3 Tbsp. Tabasco Green Pepper Sauce, plus more to taste
3 large, very ripe tomatoes, seeds and pulp removed
½ tsp. salt, plus more to taste
1 Tbsp. ketchup (preferably green ketchup)
4–6 ripe Hass avocados (depending on size)

1. Put the onion, cilantro, lime juice, olive oil, garlic, and green pepper sauce into a food processor and chop finely, but don't let it become a slush. Transfer to a bowl.

2. Chop the tomatoes coarsely and add to the bowl. Add the salt and ketchup.

3. Cut the avocados in half. Remove the pits. With a spoon, scoop out the flesh into the bowl, avoiding any discolored or stringy parts. Using a large wire whisk, mash and mix everything together. The guacamole should be on the chunky side, not a puree. Add more green pepper sauce and salt to taste. Serve with tortilla chips. SERVES TEN TO FIFTEEN.

# Cole Slaw

*Cole slaw is an essential part of my barbecue menu. My wife, who is not given to spewing unwarranted praise and who is a cole slaw fan, says this is the ultimate. And you know she's never wrong. This makes quite a bit—enough for 20 or 30 portions.*

**VEGETABLES**

1 head green cabbage, finely shredded or finely chopped
1 head red cabbage, finely shredded or finely chopped
2 bunches of green onions, finely chopped
1 lb. carrots, peeled and finely shredded

**DRESSING**

1 quart mayonnaise
1¼ cups cider vinegar
2 Tbsp. yellow mustard
¼ cup sugar
2 Tbsp. celery seed
1½ tsp. dried dill
¼ tsp. dried tarragon
¼ tsp. ground white pepper
1 tsp. salt
¼ tsp. Tabasco Green Pepper Sauce
1 cup buttermilk

1. Toss all of the vegetables together in a large bowl and set aside

2. Whisk all of the dressing ingredients together in a bowl. Pour about half the dressing over the vegetables and toss until well coated. Add more dressing to coat but not to make a puddle of dressing in the bottom of the bowl. SERVES TWENTY TO THIRTY.

# Deviled Eggs Rémoulade

*Deviled eggs are not thought of as a particularly brilliant appetizer, but I say that's because most people have never eaten them with New Orleans–style red rémoulade sauce. That combination was a specialty at the historic, lost Creole cafe called Maylie's. Arnaud's revived the idea some years ago with its superb rémoulade sauce, and it still holds up. Add some sliced ripe avocado, lettuce, and tomatoes to the plate, and you have a fine little salad. For an extra touch, garnish each serving with a couple of boiled, peeled shrimp.*

8 hard-boiled eggs, peeled and halved
1 Tbsp. chopped yellow onion
1 Tbsp. chopped celery
½ tsp. small capers
¼ cup mayonnaise
2 Tbsp. yellow mustard
⅛ tsp. salt
4 dashes of Tabasco
4 small ripe but not soft Hass avocados, halved, pitted, and peeled
2 large ripe tomatoes (Creoles or beefsteak), cut crosswise into ¼-inch-thick
   slices, then into half-moons
One 8–10-oz. bag of baby lettuces or spring mix
½ cup red rémoulade sauce (see Shrimp Rémoulade with Two Sauces, page 13)

1. Scoop the yolks out into a bowl. Reserve the egg-white halves.

2. Add the onion, celery, capers, mayonnaise, mustard, salt, and Tabasco to the yolks and mix well with a whisk. (You can even beat it to fluffiness.)

3. Load the mixture into a pastry bag and pipe it into the centers of the egg-white halves.

4. Cut the avocado halves into ¼-inch-thick slices. Fan out each sliced avocado half on one side of an individual plate, with the slices overlapping. Place an egg half in the avocado's pit indentation. Put 2 tomato half-moons and another egg half on the other side of the plate. Surround all with lettuce leaves. Drizzle the rémoulade sauce generously over each salad and serve chilled. SERVES EIGHT.

# Creole French Vinaigrette

*Have you ever wondered why French dressing is orange in America but nowhere else? No? Well, the orange element is paprika, and originally the dressing included enough paprika to make it spicy. The French eventually cut back on the paprika, but in America—where the paprika rarely had much spice—it was left in. I have gone back to using the spicy paprika, and I enjoy the effect it has on an otherwise straightforward vinaigrette.*

1 Tbsp. Dijon mustard
¼ cup red wine vinegar
1 cup olive oil
2 Tbsp. Hungarian spicy paprika
3 Tbsp. finely grated Parmesan cheese
⅛ tsp. salt
Pinch of ground white pepper

1. Whisk the mustard, vinegar, and 2 tablespoons of water together in a bowl. Add the olive oil in a slow stream, whisking constantly, until the dressing takes on a smooth, almost opaque quality.

2. Whisk in the paprika, cheese, salt, and pepper. Store in a tightly closed bottle in the refrigerator until ready to use. This dressing can be stored, refrigerated and covered, for 2 weeks. MAKES ABOUT A CUP AND A HALF OF DRESSING.

# Lemon Vinaigrette Dressing

*Here's a tart, refreshing salad dressing that's especially good on bitter greens like arugula, radicchio, endive, or frisée.*

  1 tsp. Dijon mustard
  2 Tbsp. lemon juice
  1 Tbsp. balsamic vinegar
  ⅓ cup olive oil
  ¼ tsp. salt
  ⅛ tsp. ground white pepper

Combine the mustard, lemon juice, vinegar, and 2 tablespoons of cold water together in a bowl with a wire whisk. Add the oil in a slow stream, whisking constantly, until incorporated fully. Add the salt and pepper, and toss with salad greens. This dressing can be stored, refrigerated and covered, for 2 weeks. MAKES ABOUT A HALF CUP.

# Creole Mustard Vinaigrette

*Whoever came up with idea of making a vinaigrette with our pungent Creole mustard instead of the standard Dijon mustard was really onto something. It's the dressing I most often make at home, and it's good on all sorts of salads, from simple greens to seafood salad to even pasta salads.*

2 Tbsp. Creole mustard
¼ cup red wine vinegar
1 cup olive oil
⅛ tsp. ground white pepper

1. Whisk the mustard, vinegar, 1 tablespoon of cold water, and a third of the oil together in a bowl. Add the remaining oil in a slow stream, whisking constantly, until emulsified.

2. Add the white pepper and whisk. You can also do this in a shaker bottle, but whisking gives a much better, creamier consistency. This dressing can be stored, refrigerated and covered, for 2 weeks. MAKES ABOUT A CUP AND A HALF OF DRESSING.

# Roasted Onion (or Garlic) Vinaigrette

*Onions give this great dressing a touch of sweetness. You can also get more or less the same result with a head of garlic.*

½ medium yellow onion, diced, or 1 head garlic, peeled and chopped
½ tsp. salt-free Creole seasoning
¾ cup olive oil
¼ cup red wine vinegar
Salt and freshly ground black pepper

1. Combine the onion (or garlic, if using), Creole seasoning, and 2 tablespoons of the oil in an ovenproof pan with a lid. Cover and bake in a 225-degree oven for 2 hours. Cool to room temperature.

2. Whisk in the vinegar, remaining oil, and salt and pepper to taste. This dressing can be stored, refrigerated and covered, for 2 weeks. MAKES ABOUT A CUP OF DRESSING.

# Avocado Ranch Salad Dressing

*Every time I look at this recipe, the image of an avocado ranch comes to mind. Rounding them up . . . branding them . . . Okay, enough. As is the case with any dish using avocados, the challenge here is to make it during the half-hour or so when the avocados you have on hand are perfectly ripe. Also, make only enough of this dressing for one use, as it does not hold up well, even refrigerated.*

½ cup mayonnaise
¼ cup buttermilk
¼ cup cider vinegar
¼ tsp. salt
¼ tsp. dried tarragon
½ tsp. dried dill
1 tsp. celery seed
2 Tbsp. Tabasco Green Pepper Sauce
Dash of Worcestershire sauce
2 medium ripe Hass avocados, halved and pitted

1. Whisk all of the ingredients, except the avocados, together in a bowl. Let this sit for about an hour before moving on.

2. Scoop the avocado out of the skin with a spoon. Avoid any stringy parts at the stem end. Add the avocado to the other ingredients and mash it in with the whisk. Add ¼ cup of cold water and whisk until smooth. Add a little more water to thin the texture, as desired.

3. Right before serving, toss the greens (red and green leaf, romaine, or Boston lettuces recommended; watercress makes a nice accent) with the dressing. Garnish individual salads with thin slices of avocado and tomato. MAKES ABOUT A CUP AND A HALF OF DRESSING.

# Blue Cheese Dressing

*For a long time, this meant that thick, gluey stuff made with mayonnaise and so heavy it's a wonder any salad survived it. Lately many of us are going back to the original blue cheese salad, which was essentially a green salad dressed with vinaigrette and sprinkled with blue cheese. This recipe puts the cheese in the dressing, but it's still pretty light. It also works very well with feta cheese.*

¼ cup red wine vinegar
1 Tbsp. Dijon mustard
1 cup olive oil
½ tsp. dried dill
¼ tsp. Tabasco
4 oz. blue cheese (Roquefort, Stilton, Gorgonzola, or domestic) or feta

1. Whisk the vinegar, mustard, and 2 tablespoons of water together in a bowl. Add the olive oil in a slow stream, whisking constantly, until the dressing takes on a smooth, almost opaque quality.

2. Add the dill and Tabasco, and crumble the cheese into the dressing. Stir well with a fork. This dressing can be stored, refrigerated and covered, for up to a week. MAKES ABOUT A CUP AND A QUARTER OF DRESSING.

# Casual Food

Many of the essentials in a well-rounded New Orleans eating regimen are the most informal of dishes. The best demonstration of this is provided at the annual New Orleans Jazz and Heritage Festival, where vendors sell more than 100 different dishes that are best eaten without tables, and sometimes even without plates or utensils.

The most celebrated of these dishes is boiled seafood, particularly boiled crawfish. The advent of live crawfish by the sack in the spring triggers a wave of crawfish boils all across South Louisiana. Everybody who boils crawfish has his own special way of doing it. I offer my version for first-timers.

The poor boy sandwich was invented in the mid-1920s during a streetcar strike. Bennie and Clovis Martin, owners of a busy restaurant in the Faubourg Marigny, served the poor boys on the picket lines a sandwich of roast beef gravy with just bits of beef on French bread for a nickel. After the strike, they added sliced beef to the gravy, and their baker, John Gendusa, devised an extra-long French loaf to put it on. The poor-boy sandwich soon became the official sandwich of New Orleans, filled with anything the maker thought might work (which is just about anything).

Rivaling the poor boy in local popularity is the muffuletta. The word is obsolete Sicilian dialect for the round bread loaf it's made with. The muffuletta made its first appearance in New Orleans shortly after the first wave of Italian immigrants arrived in the city in the late 1800s.

Jambalaya is a distant descendant of Spanish paella but much more rustic. The best versions are made in giant pots outside, stirred with boat oars. Jambalaya is served in gigantic piles, almost always on a paper plate.

Here's my pick of the best of these casual New Orleans favorites.

# Boiled Crawfish

*A crawfish boil is the great casual party food in South Louisiana, especially in Cajun country. It's also a celebration of springtime, when the crawfish are available in abundance.*

*The peeling process goes like this: You break the crawfish where the thorax meets the tail. After removing a segment or two of the tail's carapace, you can squeeze the meat out by applying pressure just above the tail fin. There is also some good crawfish fat inside the head, which you need to suck out—but that is not for beginners.*

*It's traditional to boil potatoes, corn, heads of garlic, and other things in the pot with the crawfish and eat them as side dishes. It sounds better than it is, as everything winds up tasting the same. I say—knowing this is heresy—cook at least the corn separately.*

2 cups salt
20 lb. live crawfish
8 large lemons, quartered
6 yellow onions, quartered
1 bunch of celery, with leaves,
    cut into eighths
1 bunch of green onions, chopped
1 bulb of garlic, halved
1 bunch of flat-leaf parsley
Four 3-oz. bags of crab boil (see Food
    Sources, page 327)
4–6 bay leaves
1 Tbsp. cayenne
3 lb. whole new potatoes

1. Fill a bucket or your kitchen sink with 2–3 gallons of cold water. Add about ½ cup of the salt and the crawfish; the salted water will purge the crawfish. Repeat the process with new, unsalted water 2–3 times until the water is only slightly dirty.

2. In a large stockpot, bring 5 gallons of water to a boil. Add the remaining 1½ cups of salt and all the ingredients except the crawfish and potatoes, and return to a boil. Let cook for 10 minutes.

3. Add the crawfish and potatoes, return to a boil, and continue boiling for 15 minutes. Make sure there's enough water to completely cover the crawfish. Remove a crawfish after 15 minutes and see if it's cooked through. If it is, turn off the heat and let the crawfish steep until the potatoes are tender.

4. Now the peeling and eating process begins. Serve the potatoes on the side. SERVES EIGHT NORMAL EATERS OR TWO SERIOUS CRAWFISH FANATICS.

# Creole-Cajun Jambalaya

*As with many Louisiana dishes, jambalaya has distinctive Creole and Cajun versions. Creole jambalaya is reddish, a color it gets from tomatoes. Cajun jambalaya never includes tomatoes and is brown. Creole jambalaya almost always contains shrimp. Cajun jambalaya always has smoked sausage or tasso. Instead of stepping into the endless "which jambalaya is better" debate, I present here my favorite version. It has elements of both styles, with oysters providing a unique flavor. I don't include tomatoes—but if you add a 16-ounce can of crushed tomatoes with the vegetables, that would be perfectly okay and quite authentic.*

¼ cup vegetable oil

4 lb. chicken-leg quarters,
  each cut into 4 pieces, bone in

2 lb. andouille (see page 326) or other
  smoked sausage, cut into ¼-inch-
  thick slices

2 large yellow onions, coarsely chopped

2 green bell peppers, coarsely chopped

2 ribs celery, coarsely chopped

2 cloves garlic, chopped

2 cups oyster liquor or chicken stock
  (see recipe, page 312)

2 Tbsp. Worcestershire sauce

1 Tbsp. Tabasco

1 Tbsp. salt-free Creole seasoning

1 Tbsp. salt

1 bay leaf

1 tsp. dried thyme

½ tsp. dried marjoram

4 cups (uncooked) Uncle Ben's rice,
  or similar parboiled rice

2 green onions, chopped

3 sprigs flat-leaf parsley, chopped

4 dozen large fresh, shucked oysters

1. Heat the oil in a heavy kettle or Dutch oven. Add the chicken and sausage, and brown the chicken all over. Add the onions, peppers, celery, and garlic, and sauté until they wilt. Add the oyster liquor or stock and 5 cups of water. Bring to a simmer, stirring to dissolve the browned bits in the pot.

2. Add the Worcestershire sauce, Tabasco, Creole seasoning, salt, bay leaf, thyme, and marjoram. Bring to a boil, reduce the heat, and simmer for 30 minutes. Remove the chicken and set aside. Stir the rice into the pot. Cover and simmer for 30 minutes.

3. Meanwhile, remove the chicken meat from the bones and set aside. When the rice is cooked, stir in the chicken meat, green onions, parsley, and oysters. Continue to cook, uncovered, gently stirring occasionally, until the rice just starts to dry out. Adjust the seasonings as needed. SERVES TWELVE TO EIGHTEEN.

# Oyster Boat

*Lakeview Seafood was a joint on the road to the old lakefront fishing-camp community of Little Woods. Its owner, a former Marine Corps baker, had an interesting idea. Instead of serving the traditional oyster loaf on French bread, he baked a standard loaf of white bread, cut off the top, hollowed it out, buttered the inside, and filled it with fried seafood. He called these boats, and they were a big hit. Oysters are a natural for this great oversized sandwich, but you can also use fried shrimp, catfish, or even small soft-shell crabs. Serve with lemon wedges, hot sauce, and french fries on the side.*

1 loaf unsliced white bread (sold at supermarkets with in-house bakeries)
1 stick (8 Tbsp.) butter, softened
2 Tbsp. chopped garlic
1 Tbsp. chopped flat-leaf parsley
½ tsp. lemon juice

3 dozen medium fresh, shucked oysters
½ cup corn flour (Fish-Fri)
½ cup yellow cornmeal
1 Tbsp. salt-free Creole seasoning
1 Tbsp. salt
Peanut oil, for frying

1. Preheat the oven to 300 degrees. Cut the loaf horizontally into 2 halves; set the top half aside. Make a vertical cut about 2 inches deep all around the top of the lower half of the loaf, about ½ inch from the sides. Push down the bread within the cut perimeter to form a pocket in the center of the loaf.

2. Melt 1 tablespoon of the butter in a saucepan. Add the garlic and parsley, and cook until fragrant, then add the lemon juice and remove from the heat. Put the remaining butter in a bowl and stir in the garlic-parsley-butter mixture. Coat the inside of both halves of the loaf with the garlic butter. Toast the bread in the preheated oven until the inside surfaces of both halves just start to brown.

3. Pour the oil into a cast-iron pot or deep skillet to a depth of 1 inch. Heat the oil over medium-high heat until the temperature reaches 375 degrees.

4. Meanwhile, combine the Fish-Fri, cornmeal, Creole seasoning, and salt in a large bowl. Toss the still-wet oysters, 6 at a time, in the Fish-Fri mix. Fry the oysters in batches until golden brown and crisp, then load them into the pocket half of the loaf. Place the top of the loaf over the oysters and serve with lemon wedges, hot sauce, and french fries. MAKES ONE OYSTER BOAT—ENOUGH FOR TWO PEOPLE.

# Roast Beef Poor Boys

*The poor-boy sandwich is one of the essential flavors of New Orleans, and roast beef is king of the poor boys. (For a bit of poor boy history, see page 250.) Making roast beef for poor boys is more about making gravy than roasting beef. Inside round seems to taste best, but some cooks like eye of round or even rib-eyes. It's best to cook the beef the day before because it will throw off lots of good juices for the gravy and the cold beef will be easier to slice. You can keep the gravy in a well-sealed container in the refrigerator for a few weeks or freeze it for even longer storage.*

*The most critical step in making a roast beef poor boy is to put the whole, assembled sandwich into a hot oven for two or three minutes before serving it. The flavor and aroma of the toasted French bread double the goodness.*

ROAST BEEF AND GRAVY
4–6-lb. inside round of beef, trimmed
Salt and freshly ground black pepper
4 ribs celery, coarsely chopped
2 medium carrots, coarsely chopped
1 large yellow onion, quartered
1 whole garlic bulb, outer papery skin
    removed and bulb cut in half
2 bay leaves
½ tsp. dried thyme
½ tsp. dried marjoram
¼ tsp. black peppercorns
1–3 Tbsp. flour
1 Tbsp. Worcestershire sauce

SANDWICH
3 loaves poor-boy bread or 6 French
    baguettes, cut lengthwise and into
    sections 6–8 inches long

GARNISH
1 head lettuce, shredded coarsely
8 tomatoes, thinly sliced
Mayonnaise
Dill pickle slices

1. Preheat the oven to 350 degrees. Season the beef with salt and pepper. Put it in a Dutch oven or kettle filled about a third of the way up with water. Add the celery, carrots, onion, garlic, bay leaves, thyme, marjoram, and black peppercorns. Roast, uncovered, for 4–6 hours, turning the roast and adding water every hour or so. The water level should slowly drop, but don't let it get less than about 2 inches deep. The beef is ready when a meat thermometer inserted into the center reads 160 degrees.

2. Remove the roast from the pot and place in a pan that will catch all the juices that come out as it cools. If you're cooking a day ahead (recommended), wrap the beef and refrigerate it as soon as it's cooled to room temperature. If making it the same day, wait at least an hour before slicing.

3. Skim off fat from the stock in the pot. Use a coarse sieve to strain the stock into a bowl, then return the stock to the pot. Add any juices that come out of the roast as it rests. Bring the stock to a simmer. Skim off any fat that rises to the surface. Cook to a thin gravy consistency. (This also benefits from being made a day ahead and cooling in the refrigerator.)

4. When you're ready to make sandwiches, preheat the oven to 400 degrees. Bring the gravy to a simmer and whisk in the flour (but only if the gravy appears to need thickening). Add the Worcestershire sauce and season to taste with salt and pepper. (It's a common practice in New Orleans to add Kitchen Bouquet to darken the sauce, but I never do.)

5. Slice the roast beef as thin as possible. Collect all the crumbs and slivers that fall off as you do this (the debris) and add them to the gravy. Stack as much sliced roast beef as you want on a length of French bread. Garnish with lettuce, tomatoes, mayonnaise, and dill pickles. Spoon on as much gravy as the sandwich can hold. Bake the assembled sandwich for about a minute to toast the bread. MAKES TWELVE TO EIGHTEEN POOR BOYS.

# Muffuletta

*Muffulettas are right up there with poor boys in popularity and goodness among local sandwiches. What makes them special is the dressing. It's called olive salad, and it's something like antipasto, made by marinating not only olives but also a host of other vegetables in olive oil, a little vinegar, and a lot of garlic and herbs. This recipe starts from scratch, but you can use prepared Italian giardiniera in place of the non-olive vegetables.*

*The muffuletta is filled with as many as three meats and three cheeses, all sliced very thin. Ham and Genoa salami are essential; mortadella is optional but desirable. Mozzarella, provolone, and Swiss cheese can be used in any combination. The best bread to use is the muffuletta loaf made by the United Bakery, an old, small company whose limited output never satisfies the demand. Any crusty round loaf with a medium-light texture will do.*

*The great controversy concerning muffulettas is whether they should be heated or not. The current vogue is to do so until the cheeses melt. My take is that this throws off the flavors and textures of everything and that a room-temperature muffuletta is superior.*

OLIVE SALAD

2 medium carrots, sliced into
　¼-inch-thick rounds
1 cup cauliflower florets
1 small red bell pepper
16 large green olives, pitted
2 cups medium green olives, pitted
1 cup brine-cured black olives, pitted
1½ cups extra-virgin olive oil
¼ cup red wine vinegar
¼ cup brining juice from the olive jar
6 large cloves garlic, chopped
4 ribs celery, chopped
¼ cup (a small jar) capers
10 sprigs flat-leaf parsley, chopped
2 tsp. dried oregano
1 tsp. dried basil
½ tsp. crushed red pepper flakes

SANDWICH

1 lb. lean, smoked ham (I recommend
　the local Chisesi ham), thinly sliced
1 lb. Genoa salami, thinly sliced
½ lb. mortadella (optional),
　thinly sliced
2 lb. total of at least 2 of these cheeses:
　mozzarella, provolone, or Swiss,
　thinly sliced
3 loaves muffuletta bread, or other
　medium-texture loaf, 8 inches
　in diameter

1. Bring a small pot of water to a boil. Boil the carrots and cauliflower until crisp-tender, about 5 minutes. Rinse with cold water, drain, and set aside.

2. Roast the bell pepper under a broiler until the skin turns black and blistered in spots. Keep turning until the entire exterior is that way. Remove, cool, peel, and remove stem and seeds. Cut into ½ x 1-inch pieces and set aside.

3. With a knife (not a food processor), coarsely chop the olives. It's okay if some of the olives are cut into just 2 pieces or not at all. Transfer the olives to a large non-metallic bowl. Add all of the remaining olive salad ingredients and mix well. Cover and refrigerate for at least a day; a week is better (stored in jars).

4. To make the sandwich: Cut each loaf in half crosswise and spoon olive salad with a lot of the marinating oil onto both halves. Put 3–4 slices (or more) of each of the meats and cheeses onto the bottom half. Cover with the top half of the loaf and cut each sandwich into quarters. Figure 1–2 quarters per person, but know that it is hard to stop eating muffulettas, even if you're full. SERVES SIX TO TEN.

# Grilled Pizza

*When we have a pizza party, we often make it an outdoor event and bake the pizzas on the grill. This works better than you can possibly imagine. You don't even have to put the top down on the grill, unless it's a windy, cold day. Any pizza topping works, except one: pepperoni, which needs heat from above, just sits there getting flaccid and unpleasant. Spinach and other vegetable pizzas are particularly good done on the grill.*

*The best way to make pizza dough is in a big, strong mixer (like a KitchenAid) with the dough-hook attachment. You can also do it, in batches, in a large food processor, or you can make the dough manually. I have instructions for both mixer and manual methods.*

*This pizza crust can also be baked in the oven. It's especially good using a thick pizza stone, heated for a half-hour in the oven before the first pizza goes on.*

1 package active dry yeast
1 tsp. sugar
3½ cups bread flour
1 Tbsp. extra-virgin olive oil
½ tsp. salt
1½ cups Fresh Pizza Sauce (see recipe, page 321)
2 lb. mozzarella cheese, grated
Your choice of pizza toppings

1. In a small bowl, stir the yeast and sugar into 1 cup of warm water. Allow the yeast to come alive for 5 minutes.

2. Mixer method: Combine the flour, oil, and salt in the bowl of a standing mixer fitted with the dough-hook attachment. Add the yeast-water mixture and mix on the low speed until the dough pulls away from the sides of the mixer bowl. If necessary, add more water, a little at a time, to get a smooth, but not sticky, dough.

Hand method: Pile the flour on a clean work surface. Make a depression in the center and add the oil and salt. Add the yeast-water mixture, a little at a time, and mix to form a dough. Knead the dough on a lightly floured surface until dough is smooth but not sticky, about 15 minutes. Roll dough ball away from you while, with the same motion, tearing it in half. Put it back together and repeat a few times.

3. Place the dough on an oiled baking sheet or pizza pan, cover it with a damp, clean towel, and let it rise for 1½ hours in a warm, moist place. (The inside of an oven, turned on for 1 minute, then turned off, works well.) When the dough is double its original size, punch it down and divide it into 6 balls. Flatten each slightly, sprinkle with some flour, and return them to the oiled pan, well apart. Let them rise again, covered, for about 30 minutes.

4. Fire up the grill to get a medium-high heat. Roll each piece of dough out to a 12-inch round. Place the dough on the grill and let it bake for 1–2 minutes, or until lightly browned on the bottom. (It may balloon; this is okay.) Turn the crust over and top with some of the sauce, cheese, and other toppings of your choice. Continue to grill the pizza for 3–5 minutes until the cheese melts. You do not need to close the top of the grill. Slice and serve immediately. MAKES SIX 12-INCH PIZZAS.

# Hot Bacon Shrimp

*Near as I can tell, this dish infiltrated New Orleans from the West Coast and caught on in a wide variety of restaurants. It's a great party dish: big shrimp butterflied and stuffed with a mixture of mozzarella cheese and jalapeño, wrapped in bacon, and broiled until crispy. Its goodness owes much to the quality of the shrimp we have in New Orleans. Make a million of these: Once people start eating them, they won't be able to stop.*

24 large (16–20 count) shrimp, peeled, with tail shell intact, and deveined
8 oz. mozzarella cheese
12 slices bacon, cooked until lightly browned but not crisp
2 Tbsp. chopped jalapeño pepper

1. Preheat the broiler. Wash the shrimp and pat dry. Butterfly the shrimp. Cut the cheese into pieces a little smaller than the shrimp. Cut each piece of bacon in half.

2. Fill the center of each shrimp with about ¼ teaspoon chopped jalapeño, top each with a piece of cheese, and wrap a piece of bacon around all. Secure the bacon with a toothpick.

3. Place the shrimp on a baking sheet and broil until they turn pink. Turn the shrimp and return to the broiler until the cheese begins to melt. Serve immediately. MAKES TWENTY-FOUR.

# Mary Ann's Spinach and Mushroom Dip

*My wife, Mary Ann, loves to improvise dips. This is the best one she's ever made.*

3 Tbsp. butter
1 bunch of green onions, chopped
8 oz. small button mushrooms, sliced
One 10-oz. bag of fresh spinach, picked and washed
⅓ cup heavy whipping cream
12 oz. cream cheese, at room temperature
Salt and freshly ground black pepper to taste
Dash of Tabasco Green Pepper Sauce

1. Melt the butter in a skillet over medium-high heat. Add the green onions and sauté until soft. Add the mushrooms, spinach, and ¼ cup of water, and cook until the liquid is evaporated. Transfer the mixture to a cutting board and chop.

2. Return the mushroom-spinach mixture to the skillet. Add the cream and simmer over medium heat, stirring occasionally, for about 3 minutes. Turn off the heat.

3. Cut the cream cheese into pieces and stir into the pan contents. Season to taste with salt and pepper, and Tabasco. Serve with croutons, pita crisps, or other dippable food. MAKES THREE CUPS.

# Tom's Hamburger Sauce

*This is what I slather all over the hamburgers I make at home. Aficionados of Bud's Broiler, an old local chain of charcoal-broiled hamburger joints around New Orleans, may note that this is a bit similar to the sauce on Bud's Number One.*

½ cup mayonnaise
3 Tbsp. dill relish, well drained
2 Tbsp. smoke-flavored barbecue sauce
1 tsp. Tabasco Chipotle Pepper Sauce

Mix all of the ingredients together in a bowl. Refrigerate what you don't use immediately. MAKES ABOUT A HALF CUP.

# Breakfast

**W**hen Brennan's invented its grand all-morning breakfast, it started an entirely new tradition of eating in New Orleans and elsewhere. Any chef attempting to make his breakfast or brunch menu distinctive felt compelled to invent his share of poached egg dishes with something interesting underneath them and a convincing (usually rich) sauce overhead. There must be hundreds of them now.

Before that vogue came along, however, New Orleans already had its fair share of unique breakfast dishes. Calas, Creole cream cheese, and grillades and grits go back a long way. They were on the road to extinction when chefs, looking for bits of authentic heritage to incorporate into their menus, revived them. These traditional breakfast dishes struck a chord with those of us who remember our parents eating them but never took up the Creole cream cheese or grillades habit ourselves. It was eye-opening to discover why our forebears liked those Creole breakfast items so much: they're simply delicious.

And you can't talk about breakfast in New Orleans without beignets, the partner to our café au lait for a century and a half now. When the Morning Call and the Café du Monde began making beignets again a few weeks after Hurricane Katrina, it made news nationwide. Some things are indispensable.

# Beignets

*Beignets are a distinctive part of the New Orleans breakfast, although they're enjoyed even more as a late-night snack. Our beignet is a square of straightforward dough, fried until it puffs up and becomes golden brown. It's covered with confectioners' sugar, placed on a plate with two more of its kind, and sent to the table or counter, where the person who ordered it is already sipping café au lait.*

*The best beignets have two qualities that rarely come together: They're doughy enough that there's more than just air inside but they're not so heavy that they sink to the bottom of the fryer. The beignets in the French Market are made with a yeast dough, which is fine for a large operation but too involved for home use. I prefer something similar to a biscuit dough.*

2 cups self-rising flour
3 Tbsp. Crisco
1 Tbsp. sugar
Vegetable oil, for frying
1 cup confectioners' sugar, sifted

1. Combine the flour and Crisco in a bowl with a wire whisk until the mixture resembles coarse cornmeal, with perhaps a few lumps here and there.

2. Warm ¾ cup of water in the microwave oven until barely warm to the touch. Pour the water into a large bowl, add the sugar, and stir until dissolved. Add the flour mixture and blend it with kitchen fork. Work the dough as little as possible.

3. Turn the dough out on a clean counter and dust with a little flour. Roll it out to a uniform thickness of about ¼ inch. Cut into rectangles about 2 x 4 inches. Let sit for a couple of minutes while you heat the oil.

4. Pour oil to a depth of 1 inch in a large, deep skillet and heat to about 325 degrees. When the beignet dough squares have softened and puffed up a little, drop 4–6 at a time into the hot oil and fry until light brown. Turn once and fry the other side. Drain on paper towels. It's all right to fry the misshapen dough pieces from the edge of the dough sheet.

5. Dust with confectioners' sugar and serve hot. MAKES TWELVE TO FIFTEEN BEIGNETS.

# Calas

*In a time prior to the emergence of my consciousness, horse-drawn carts plying the streets of New Orleans sold these wonderful, aromatic rice cakes. They were so popular in the early part of the last century that one of my oldest aunts was nicknamed Cala. They have never been widely available in restaurants; the Old Coffee Pot on St. Peter Street has kept their memory alive almost single-handedly. Calas make a great breakfast or snack. Here's a recipe derived from one that a radio listener, who thinks it came from his grandmother, sent me.*

1 package active dry yeast
1½ cups cooked, cooled rice, preferably short-grain
3 eggs, beaten
1¼ cups rice flour
½ cup light brown sugar
½ tsp. salt
1 tsp. cinnamon
⅛ tsp. nutmeg
Vegetable oil, for frying
Confectioners' sugar, or maple or cane syrup

1. The night before you plan to make these, dissolve the yeast into ¼ cup of warm water. Mix with the rice in a bowl. Cover and let stand in a warm place overnight.

2. The next morning, blend the eggs, rice flour, brown sugar, salt, cinnamon, and nutmeg into the rice-yeast mixture. Add just enough water, a little at a time, to incorporate all of the dry ingredients. (You may not need any.)

3. Pour oil to a depth of 1 inch in a large, deep skillet and heat the oil to 375 degrees. Working in batches, use a spoon to scoop the rice mixture into Ping-Pong–size balls. Drop them into the hot oil and fry until darkish brown, about 3 minutes. Drain on paper towels.

4. Serve hot, sprinkled with confectioners' sugar. You can also serve calas with syrup. MAKES TWO OR THREE DOZEN.

# Grillades and Grits

*This is the most distinctive of Creole breakfast dishes. Despite its name, the meat in this dish is almost never grilled. Restaurants tend to simplify and sanitize grillades and grits. What I'm giving you here is the old, bothersome, incomparably delicious version, simmered to tenderness for a long time. You don't even need to use veal—calf or baby beef is fine.*

2 lb. veal or calf round
½ cup flour
1½ tsp. salt-free Creole seasoning
½ tsp. salt, plus more to taste
¼ cup vegetable oil
1 large yellow onion, chopped
1 very ripe green bell pepper, seeded and coarsely chopped
2 ribs celery, coarsely chopped

2 cloves garlic, chopped
One 28-oz. can whole tomatoes, juice reserved
1 Tbsp. Worcestershire sauce
2 cups veal stock (see recipe, page 312)
¼ tsp. dried thyme
Freshly ground black pepper to taste
¾ cup (uncooked) stone-ground grits
2 Tbsp. butter

1. Cut the meat into 1 x 2-inch rectangles, each about ½ inch thick. Combine the flour, Creole seasoning, and the ½ teaspoon of salt in a bowl. Dust the veal cubes with the seasoned flour. Reserve the remainder of the flour. Heat 1 tablespoon of the oil in a large, heavy pot over high heat. Add the veal and sear until well browned. Remove the veal and reserve.

2. Make a medium-dark roux by adding the remaining oil to the pot. Add the reserved seasoned flour and cook, stirring constantly, until the mixture turns the color of an old penny. Reduce the heat to low and quickly add the onion, bell pepper, celery, and garlic, and cook, stirring constantly, until the onion turns translucent.

3. Crush the tomatoes with your fingers. Add them to the pot, along with ½ cup of juice from the can and the Worcestershire sauce. Bring to a light boil. Return the veal to the pot, add the stock and thyme, and simmer slowly until the sauce is thick enough to coat a spoon. Taste the sauce and add salt and pepper, as necessary.

4. Cook the grits according to package directions. Add the butter when the grits are near desired thickness. Serve grillades with lots of sauce and grits on the side. SERVES FOUR.

# Lost Bread

Pain perdu, *as the Old Creoles like my mother called it, got its name from the day-old stale French bread used to make it. Lost for most purposes to which French bread is usually put, these crusts are soaked in eggs and milk, fried or grilled, and served for breakfast. It is, you've noticed, quite like French toast but a good deal richer.*

*This is another one of those dishes for which my mother's version remains definitive for me. She soaked the bread in the custard until it was almost falling apart and then (hold your breath) deep-fried it. The most outstanding characteristic of this stuff is its oozy richness. It is not oily in any way.*

4 eggs
½ cup half-and-half
2 Tbsp. sugar
1 Tbsp. vanilla extract
1 tsp. cinnamon
2 dashes of nutmeg
18 slices stale French bread, about ¾ inch thick
1 cup vegetable oil, for frying
Confectioners' sugar

1. Whisk the eggs, half-and-half, sugar, vanilla, cinnamon, and nutmeg together in a wide bowl. Add the bread and soak the slices while you heat the oil.

2. Heat the oil in a large cast-iron skillet to about 350 degrees.

3. Lower 2 pieces of bread at a time into the oil and fry about 2 minutes on each side. Let the bread cook to a darker brown than your instincts might tell you.

4. Remove the lost bread as it's cooked and drain it on paper towels. Use another towel to blot the excess oil from the top. Keep the bread pieces warm in a 200-degree oven. Continue cooking the rest of the bread in small batches, allowing the temperature of the oil to recover between batches.

5. Serve immediately with confectioners' sugar. Warn your guests about the lavalike heat on the inside! SERVES SIX TO EIGHT.

# Mary Leigh's Buttermilk Biscuits

*Homemade buttermilk biscuits are our favorite breakfast at the Cool Water Ranch. For years we've made them almost every weekend. When my daughter Mary Leigh was still very small, she started helping me. Now she's completely taken over the job. The recipe is not revolutionary. There are only three ingredients: self-rising flour (White Lily is by far the best), buttermilk, and butter. (We used to use Crisco, but what we now know about trans fats made me convert to butter as the shortening.)*

    6 Tbsp. unsalted butter, softened
    3 cups self-rising flour
    1½ cups buttermilk

1. Preheat the oven to 475 degrees. Cut the butter into the flour with a wire whisk until the mixture resembles coarse cornmeal. A few small lumps are okay.

2. Blend in the buttermilk with light strokes of a kitchen fork. Continue lightly blending until the dough pulls away from the sides of the bowl. Add a little more milk, if necessary, to work all the dry flour at the bottom into a sticky, thoroughly damp dough.

3. Lightly grease a baking sheet or pizza pan with butter or shortening. Spoon out the dough with a large spoon into lumps about 3 inches high and 3–4 inches in diameter and drop them about 1 inch apart on the prepared baking sheet or pizza pan. Dip your fingers in water and mound the dough up a bit if necessary.

4. Bake until the little peaks on the biscuits start to brown, 10–14 minutes. Don't aim for a dark overall brown; that indicates overbaking. MAKES SIX TO TEN BISCUITS.

# Creole Cream Cheese

*Creole cream cheese was once a widely eaten favorite, served most often for breakfast with half-and-half and sugar or fancied up with fresh fruit—strawberries being the classic. It was available in every store, sometimes from several sources. Then it came close to disappearing completely. In the last few years, some small dairies on the North Shore—Mauthe's and Smith's—have begun making it again.*

*Creole cream cheese is clabber—the solid part of milk that has turned and separated. That's it! All you have to do is control the separation, and you're there. Here's how to do it—but I will add that you're probably better off buying the ready-made Creole cream cheese if you can find it.*

    1 gallon low-fat milk
    1 cup buttermilk
    ¼ tablet or 6–8 drops rennet (available at natural foods stores)

1. Combine the milk and buttermilk in a large bowl and add the rennet. (If using rennet tablet, dissolve it in about a tablespoon of warm water before adding it to the milk.) Cover the bowl with plastic wrap and allow to stand at cool room temperature for 24 hours.

2. The next day, the milk should have separated. Place a large sieve over a wide bowl. The bottom of the sieve should be at least 2 inches above the bottom of the bowl. Pour the clabbered milk into the sieve. Wrap the whole thing with plastic wrap and let it drain for another day.

3. On the third day, pour off the liquid from the bowl and set the sieve and its contents on a clean bowl or pan. (There won't be as much liquid now, so the bowl doesn't have to be as large as the first one.) Cover again and store in the refrigerator for one more day.

4. On the fourth day, the Creole cream cheese is ready to be eaten or packaged in plastic containers. It can also be frozen. The classic way to eat it is doused with half-and-half and sugar to taste. MAKES ABOUT A QUART.

# Belgian Waffles

*The distinguishing feature of a Belgian waffle is that its batter is lightened with foamed egg whites. This gives it a wonderful, airy quality that's best appreciated when the waffle iron has big squares. To make a waffle come out crisp, put a substantial amount of butter into the batter. That increases the temperature at the point where the batter meets the iron.*

1 cup self-rising flour
3 Tbsp. sugar
Generous pinch of cinnamon
2 eggs, separated
1 cup milk, lukewarm
½ stick (4 Tbsp.) butter, melted
1 tsp. vanilla extract
Pinch of cream of tartar
Maple syrup

1. Heat a waffle iron and let it get very hot.

2. Use a fork to mix the flour, sugar, and cinnamon together in a medium bowl.

3. In a second, larger bowl, beat the egg yolks. Add the milk, whisk in the melted butter, then add the vanilla.

4. Pour the dry ingredients into the wet ingredients and whisk until the batter is almost blended but still has some lumps. The batter should be very thick, but if it's so thick that it won't pour at all, add a little water.

5. In a clean bowl and using a clean whisk or beater, whip the egg whites with the cream of tartar until soft peaks form. Spoon the egg whites into the batter and, with a wooden spoon, fold them in carefully, without overblending.

6. Pour some of the batter into the waffle iron and cook until crisp. Serve with pure maple syrup. MAKES FOUR TO SIX WAFFLES.

# Shirred Eggs with Crabmeat Remick

*The biggest hit we've ever had at our Sunday brunches is this recipe, which turns a classic crabmeat appetizer into a terrific egg dish. You don't see shirred eggs very often, even in restaurants, but I love the style. The technique is to cook the eggs with powerful heat from above after setting them on something savory.*

SAUCE
½ cup mayonnaise
¼ cup bottled chili sauce
1 Tbsp. Creole mustard
1 Tbsp. tarragon vinegar
½ tsp. Tabasco
½ tsp. salt-free Creole seasoning
¼ tsp. salt

CRABMEAT AND EGGS
6 thick slices smoky bacon
1 lb. jumbo lump crabmeat
1 Tbsp. lemon juice
12 eggs

1. Preheat the oven to 350 degrees. Whisk together the sauce ingredients in a bowl and set aside.

2. Cut the bacon into squares and fry until crisp. Drain very well and set aside.

3. Divide the crabmeat among 6 small, shallow gratin dishes. Sprinkle with the lemon juice and bake until heated through, about 5 minutes.

4. Top each baking dish with an equal portion of crumbled bacon. Spoon in enough of the sauce to cover the bacon and the crab. Then carefully break 2 eggs onto each dish, keeping the yolks whole.

5. Turn the oven up to broil. Put the baking dishes in the broiler and cook until the eggs have set. Serve immediately with a warning that the dish is mouth-searingly hot. SERVES SIX.

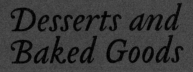

# Desserts and Baked Goods

One of the few things the New Orleans palate has in common with that of the rest of the South is a too-well-developed taste for sweets. We tend to use sugar as liberally in our desserts as we use salt and pepper in our savory dishes.

We also have a taste for variations on custards. Without doubt, the most popular of all New Orleans desserts is bread pudding. It's found on almost every restaurant's dessert menu, from the grubbiest neighborhood hangout to the grandest gourmet establishment. (It's interesting that the best versions are distributed uniformly throughout that whole spectrum.) Unlike the spartan bread puddings served elsewhere, the New Orleans version is rich and glorious.

In a time when flaming desserts are outmoded in most places, the enduring popularity of one great local original—bananas Foster—assures us that the fires will be burning at meal's end for many more years to come.

Pralines have been much loved in New Orleans for as long as sugar has been grown in the area (centuries). The many makers of pralines around town sell a much better product than you would be able to make at home. The same is true of king cake, a sweet yeast bread decorated with purple, green, and gold sugar. It's a lot of work to make yourself, but it's widely and cheaply available during the Carnival season as sliced bread.

I omit yet another difficult recipe: New Orleans–style French bread, a uniquely light loaf made with unusual yeasts and specialty ovens. It's almost impossible to reproduce at home. But I did include a few breads and muffins that my readers and radio listeners have liked a lot over the years.

# Bread Pudding Alaska

*Bread pudding is generally thought of as a poor person's dessert. But the rich New Orleans version is a thing apart, served in even the most expensive restaurants in town. This is an adaptation of my mother's bread pudding. She topped hers with meringue. I surround mine with it, like a baked Alaska. I also like making individual puddings in muffin tins. I unmold them onto baking dishes before adding the meringue and toasting it until browned.*

BREAD PUDDING
5 Tbsp. butter, softened
¾ cup sugar
4 cups half-and-half, warmed
4 Tbsp. vanilla extract
2 Tbsp. cinnamon
5 eggs, separated
1 loaf French bread, torn into chunks
½ cup white raisins

MERINGUE
5 egg whites (reserved from first step)
¼ tsp. cream of tartar
⅓ cup sugar
1 Tbsp. vanilla extract

1. Preheat the oven to 300 degrees. Beat 4 tablespoons of the butter and the sugar together until well creamed. Add the half-and-half, vanilla, cinnamon, and egg yolks (reserve the whites for the meringue), and mix until the custard is well combined. Add just enough bread so that the mixture remains very juicy. Stir in the raisins.

2. Grease 12 pockets in a muffin tin with the remaining butter. Spoon the pudding mixture into the greased pockets, filling each just barely to the top. Set the muffin tin in a baking pan and add enough warm water to come halfway up the sides of the tin. Bake for 45 minutes. Remove and cool.

3. In a clean, grease-free bowl, beat the egg whites and cream of tartar at high speed until peaks begin to form. Slowly add the sugar, then the vanilla, until well blended.

4. After the bread pudding has cooled for 15 minutes, raise the oven temperature to 350 degrees. Carefully lift each pudding out of the tin and place one on each of 12 individual baking dishes. Using a rubber spatula, cover the puddings with a thick layer of meringue. Little swirls and peaks are desirable. Bake until the meringue is browned, about 5 minutes. Serve immediately. SERVES TWELVE.

# Bourbon Whiskey Sauce
# for Bread Pudding

*The best sauces for bread pudding are those that are in essence a combination of after-dinner drink and dessert. This sauce is the kind you'd find in restaurants, but it's not often made at home. You can substitute rum or brandy for the whiskey if you like, or perhaps even vanilla if you'd prefer it to be nonalcoholic (although most vanilla does contain alcohol).*

1 stick (8 Tbsp.) unsalted butter
1 cup sugar
1 Tbsp. orange juice, strained
1 egg
¼ cup (or more to taste) bourbon, or 1 tsp. vanilla extract

1. Melt the butter in a saucepan over medium-low heat. Add the sugar, orange juice, and ¼ cup of water, and cook until the sugar is completely dissolved. Remove from heat.

2. Beat the egg well in a bowl. Add the butter-sugar mixture, about a tablespoon at a time, whisking constantly. (You can pick up the pace after half of the butter-sugar is added.) Add the bourbon or vanilla and whisk until smooth. MAKES ABOUT ONE AND HALF CUPS.

# Pumpkin and Pecan Bread Pudding

*Even by New Orleans standards, this is no ordinary bread pudding. Rich with the fall flavors of pumpkin and pecan, this version of bread pudding is best served not scooped into bowls, but sliced like a cake and elegantly presented on plates.*

¾ cup sugar
3 whole eggs
3 egg yolks
4 cups half-and-half
2 cups heavy whipping cream
2 Tbsp. vanilla extract
1 can solid-pack canned pumpkin
  (the fresh jack-o'-lantern pumpkins
  won't work)

2 Tbsp. cinnamon
¼ tsp. nutmeg
2 Tbsp. butter
1 loaf stale French bread,
  cut into ½-inch-thick slices
1 cup pecan pieces

1. Preheat the oven to 250 degrees. Whisk the sugar, whole eggs and yolks, half-and-half, cream, and vanilla in a large bowl to make a smooth custard. Combine the pumpkin, cinnamon, nutmeg, and ½ cup of the custard mixture in another bowl.

2. Generously grease the insides of two 10-inch cake pans with the butter. Line the perimeters of each pan with the smallest slices of bread, then cover the bottom of each with an overlapping bread layer. Pour one-sixth of the custard mixture over the bread to soak it. Spread one-fourth of the pumpkin over the bread in each pan, then sprinkle about one-fourth of the pecans over the pumpkin. Repeat the process in the same order, ending with a layer of bread, pecans, and a final soaking with the custard.

3. Bake for about 1½ hours. The pudding will rise a great deal, but it will fall again when you take it out of the oven. Remove and cool. Cut into pie-style slices and serve either warm or cold. SERVES TWELVE.

# Crème Anglaise

*Crème Anglaise, or custard sauce, is served with many kinds of desserts, but I like it best with bread pudding and intense chocolate tortes—particularly those with raspberries. You can add a little rum or brandy to this at the end to spike it up a little. But do this strictly to taste—don't guess.*

1 cup heavy whipping cream
3 Tbsp. sugar
4 egg yolks
¼ tsp. vanilla extract

1. Combine the cream and 1 tablespoon of the sugar in a saucepan and bring to a simmer, stirring until the sugar dissolves. Keep warm on low heat.

2. Use an electric mixer to beat the egg yolks with the remaining sugar until thick and pale yellow. Whisk about half of the hot cream into the eggs and continue whisking until smooth.

3. Return the egg mixture to the saucepan. Add the vanilla and cook over medium-low heat, whisking frequently, until the sauce has a medium-thick consistency. MAKES ABOUT A CUP AND A HALF OF SAUCE.

# Crème Caramel

*In this clasic caramel custard, the custard part is easy. The caramel sauce is only a little harder. The most important matter of all is to bake the custards gently, in a water bath, so as not to overbake them.*

CARAMEL
1 cup sugar
3 Tbsp. water

CUSTARD
12 eggs (omit whites from
  4 of them)
4 cups whole milk
1¼ cups sugar
2 Tbsp. vanilla extract

1. Preheat the oven to 325 degrees.

2. To make the caramel: Cook the sugar and water together in a *white* enamel saucepan over medium-high heat until you see the first bit of browning. Brush any sugar crystals off the sides of the pan with a wet brush to prevent regranulation. The sugar is now extremely hot—about 350 degrees—so be careful. It can burn very quickly. Reduce the heat to medium and continue to cook, carefully swirling it around until the center of the pan is light brown. Remove it from the heat immediately. The caramel will continue to cook a bit darker from its own heat. Divide the caramel among eight 6-ounce custard cups and swirl the cups around to coat the sides.

3. To make the custard: Whisk all of the custard ingredients together in a bowl until smooth. Strain the mixture into a clean saucepan. Cook the custard over medium-low heat, stirring constantly, until it feels barely warm to the touch. Pour the custard into the custard cups over the caramel sauce. Arrange the custard cups, 1 inch apart in a baking pan, and add enough hot water to come halfway up the sides of the cups. Bake until the custard has just set and the tops are lightly browned, about 30 minutes.

4. Remove the cups from the water bath and allow to cool at room temperature for about 15 minutes, then refrigerate until well chilled. Unmold onto dessert plates, along with all of the caramel sauce. SERVES EIGHT.

# Crème Brûlée

*Crème brûlée appeared in New Orleans in the early 1980s (Arnaud's served the first one), and over the years, it supplanted the once universal caramel custard. It's now on almost every non-Asian menu in the city. The difference between crème brûlée and crème caramel is that the former is made with cream and has the sugar crusted on top; the latter is made with milk and has sugar caramelized into a syrup at the bottom of the baking cup.*

*Crème brûlée must be baked very carefully and slowly, or it will not reach its proper semiflowing state. You can't do it in standard custard cups; much better are shallow (an inch or so deep) glass or ceramic ramekins or gratin dishes.*

*It is also essential to insulate the bottoms of the dishes from the pan they're sitting on. Those air-insulated baking pans work well. If you don't have one, you can get the same effect by setting a wet dish towel in the bottom.*

½ cup light brown sugar
4 cups heavy whipping cream
9 egg yolks
⅔ cup sugar
4½ tsp. vanilla extract

1. Preheat the oven to 325 degrees.

2. The first step is not essential but does give an extra measure of elegance. Spread the brown sugar out, breaking all the lumps, on a big plate. Put it into the microwave for 10 minutes at 10 percent power, then let it cool for 30 minutes. This will remove the excess moisture from the brown sugar and keep it from turning to syrup when you blast it later.

3. Combine ¼ cup of the cream and the egg yolks in a metal bowl and whisk to blend well. Stir in the sugar until nearly dissolved and set aside.

4. Put the remaining cream into a small saucepan and heat it over medium heat until wisps of steam start appearing. (Don't boil even a little.) Stir in the vanilla. Slowly add the warm cream to the bowl with the egg-cream mixture, whisking constantly to prevent curdling. Strain the custard through a fine sieve into a large measuring cup. Pour the custard into the 8 baking dishes. Place the dishes in an air-insulated baking pan or on a wet towel set inside the pan.

5. Pour in enough hot water to come halfway up the sides of the baking dishes. Bake for 30 minutes. Depending on the type of dishes you're using, the custards may have to continue baking for as long as 15 minutes more. The custard should not flow when you tip the baking cup, but it should not be solid, either. Remove the dishes from the pan and set out to cool for 30 minutes, then refrigerate for at least 3 hours, or as long as a day.

6. When ready to serve, preheat the broiler. (Or the broil feature of your toaster oven, which works better for this than you might imagine.) Sprinkle enough brown sugar on top of each custard to completely cover and run them under the broiler until the sugar melts and caramelizes, about 30 seconds. You might want to turn the dishes so that this happens uniformly. SERVES EIGHT.

# Orange Cheesecake

*I learned the basic recipe for this great cheesecake—one that I am forced to make and bring to every family function—from the late Lonnie Knisley. One of the best pastry chefs who ever worked in New Orleans, Lonnie made all the desserts at Andrea's for years. The orange aspect is my wrinkle on it; I have a personal passion for that flavor, and I think it's especially good in this.*

*The most time-consuming part of making a cheesecake is cooling it. This must be done slowly and gently, or you'll have cracks in the top.*

CRUST

2 packages (out of the 3 in a standard box)
    cinnamon graham crackers
¼ cup sugar
1 stick (8 Tbsp.) butter, melted

FILLING

Four 8-oz. packages cream cheese, at room temperature
1 cup sugar
1 cup sour cream
4 eggs
1 cup heavy whipping cream
1 Tbsp. vanilla extract
¼ cup orange juice
1 tsp. lemon juice
Zest of 1 orange

1. Preheat the oven to 275 degrees. Line the bottom of a 10-inch springform pan with parchment paper.

2. To make the crust: Grind the graham crackers into small crumbs in a food processor. Add the sugar and the butter, and process until the butter has soaked into the crumbs. Dump the crust mixture into the prepared pan and press the crust into the bottom and up the sides of the pan. It is not necessary for the crust to come all the way to the top of the pan. Set aside.

3. To make the filling: Put the cream cheese and sugar into the bowl of a mixer and blend on medium-slow speed until completely blended and fluffy, about 10 minutes. Add the sour cream and mix, scraping down the sides of the bowl until combined. Add the eggs, one at a time, allowing them to blend in completely before adding the next one. (Break each egg into a cup first to make sure it's okay before you add it.) Add the heavy cream, vanilla, the juices, and zest, and mix for another 5 minutes or so, occasionally scraping down the sides of the bowl.

4. Pour the filling into the crust. Set the springform pan into a larger pan (I usually use a pizza pan) and place it in the center of the oven. Pour warm water into the bottom pan. You don't need much—¼ inch deep is fine. Bake until you see the cheesecake has just a hint of brown on top, about 90 minutes.

5. Turn the oven off, but leave the cheesecake inside. After an hour, open the door a crack and let the cheesecake cool in the oven another 30 minutes. Remove the cheesecake and let it finish cooling on a counter. After another hour, remove the sides of the springform pan and put the cheesecake into the refrigerator. Chill at least 3 hours before serving. SERVES TWELVE TO SIXTEEN.

# Pear Clafoutis

*A clafoutis uses a runny version of Belgian waffle batter as a matrix for fruit—classically, cherries—but you can make it with anything sweet. Few fruits would be more appealing in this than ripe pears. When making this recipe, use more pear than you think you'll need. And while the pan will seem to contain too much batter, go with it—it won't run over.*

1 Tbsp. butter, softened
4 eggs, separated
⅔ cup sugar
1 cup buttermilk
1 Tbsp. vanilla extract
1 tsp. almond extract

¼ tsp. cinnamon
¾ cup self-rising flour
Pinch of cream of tartar
3–4 ripe pears, peeled, cored,
   and cut into small chunks

1. Preheat the oven to 400 degrees. Generously butter a 10-inch cake pan and set aside.

2. Use an electric mixer to beat the egg yolks and sugar together until thick and pale yellow. Add the buttermilk, vanilla and almond extracts, and cinnamon, and beat until well mixed.

3. Add the flour and stir with a kitchen fork, leaving small lumps in the batter.

4. In a clean bowl with clean beaters, beat the egg whites and the cream of tartar until soft peaks form. Fold the beaten whites into the batter. Do not overmix—streaks are okay.

5. Scatter the pears into the prepared pan and pour in the batter. Bake for 8 minutes, then lower the oven to 325 degrees and continue baking for another 20 minutes. The clafoutis is ready when barely browned on the top. (It can also be refrigerated for a great breakfast.) SERVES EIGHT.

# Orange Icebox Pie

*Lemon is the standard flavor for this type of pie and it's quite wonderful, but I like to surprise people with this variation. Oranges, however, lack the necessary tartness to make it on their own. The solution is to add lemon juice and cut back on the sugar. I make this when I get a batch of oranges that seem unusually sour.*

*I include a recipe here for making your own pie shell, but you can buy a prebaked one if you prefer.*

CRUST
¾ cup flour
¼ cup sugar
5 Tbsp. butter, softened
1 egg, beaten
1 tsp. vanilla extract
⅛ tsp. salt

FILLING
½ cup sweetened condensed milk
½ cup heavy whipping cream
5 eggs, separated
½ cup freshly squeezed orange juice, strained
¼ cup lemon juice, strained
Zest of 3 oranges
Zest of 1 lemon
¼ tsp. cream of tartar
7½ tsp. sugar
½ tsp. orange flower water, or ¼ tsp. orange extract (optional)

1. Preheat the oven to 350 degrees.

2. To make the crust: Combine the flour and sugar in a bowl. Cut the butter into the dry ingredients with a wire whisk until the mixture resembles coarse cornmeal. A few small lumps are okay. Whisk the egg, vanilla, and salt together, and add to the dry ingredients. Gently knead the mixture in the bowl until a dough comes together. Roll the dough out on a lightly floured surface to a 12-inch circle and carefully tuck the crust into a 10-inch pie pan.

*(continued)*

3. Line the crust dough with aluminum foil and fill it with dry beans. Blind-bake the crust for 10 minutes. (This step keeps the sides from caving in and the bottom from bubbling up.) Remove the foil and beans, and bake, uncovered, for another 5 minutes. Remove and cool the crust. Reduce the oven heat to 325 degrees.

4. To make the filling: With an electric mixer, beat the condensed milk, heavy cream, and 5 egg yolks together. Add the orange and lemon juices and half of the orange and lemon zest. Pour this mixture into the pie shell and bake for 20 minutes. Remove and cool.

5. When the pie has cooled to room temperature, beat the 5 egg whites in a grease-free bowl with the cream of tartar until peaks begin to form. Add the sugar, a little at a time, until completely blended. Add the orange flower water or orange extract and continue to beat until stiff but not dry peaks form. Fold in the remaining zest with a rubber spatula to distribute evenly. Spread the meringue on top of the cooled pie.

6. Bake the pie at 350 degrees until the top is lightly browned, about 5 minutes. Chill for several hours before serving. SERVES EIGHT.

# Pecan Pie

*Here is my current recipe for pecan pie, arrived at after dozens of changes I've made over the years to an old restaurant recipe. As time has gone on, I've reduced the amount of sugar, lowered the baking temperature, and toasted the pecans. One more thing you need to know: If you decide to warm a piece of this in the microwave, do so for only about 15 seconds. For some reason, the pie superheats and splatters after about 45 seconds.*

2 cups coarsely broken pecans
½ cup light Karo syrup
¼ cup dark Karo syrup
1 cup light brown sugar
4 eggs, beaten (reserve 1 egg white)
1 Tbsp. lemon juice
1 Tbsp. vanilla extract
1 tsp. flour
Pinch of salt
1 stick (8 Tbsp.) butter, melted
One 10-inch pie shell, unbaked (see Orange Icebox Pie, page 285)

1. Preheat the oven to 325 degrees. Spread the pecans out on a baking sheet and bake on the top shelf of the oven until they just begin to brown. Set the pecans aside.

2. In a microwave-safe bowl, combine the syrups, sugar, eggs (minus 1 egg white), lemon juice, vanilla, flour, and salt. Add the butter and microwave the bowl at 20 percent power for about 15 seconds. Stir again and repeat this process until the mixture feels slightly warm to the touch and begins to get thick.

3. Brush the unbaked pie-shell bottom with the reserved egg white. This keeps the crust from getting soggy. Pour the filling into the pie shell. Top with the pecans, pushing them down with a spoon, if necessary, so that all the pecans are at least touching the filling. Bake for 10 minutes, then lower the temperature to 275 degrees and continue to bake for 30–40 minutes more. Cool to room temperature. SERVES EIGHT TO TWELVE.

# Strawberry Shortcakes

*A true shortcake is not the sponge cake that's typically used for this famous old dessert, but something a lot like a drop biscuit. We make these all the time, and it's an essential for our Easter parties.*

SHORTCAKES
4 cups self-rising flour
¾ cup sugar
1 stick (8 Tbsp.) butter, softened
1¾ cups half-and-half

FILLING
2 cups heavy whipping cream
⅓ cup sugar
2 pints fresh strawberries,
  hulled and thinly sliced

1. Preheat the oven to 475 degrees. Grease a cookie sheet and set aside.

2. To make the shortcakes: Whisk the flour and sugar together in a large bowl. Cut butter into the flour mixture with a wire whisk until the mixture resembles coarse cornmeal. A few small lumps are okay.

3. Add the half-and-half with light strokes of a kitchen fork. Continue lightly blending until the dough leaves the sides of the bowl. Add a little more milk, if necessary, to work all of the dry ingredients into a sticky, thoroughly damp dough.

4. Spoon out the dough with a large spoon into lumps about 4 inches in diameter and 2 inches high and drop them about 1 inch apart on the prepared cookie sheet. Bake for 10–14 minutes, or until light brown on top. Don't look for a dark brown; that indicates overbaking.

5. To make the filling: Whip the cream in a chilled metal bowl until soft peaks form. Add the sugar and continue whipping until no grittiness remains.

6. Slice the shortcakes in half. Spoon some whipped cream on the bottom half. Add sliced strawberries until they fall off the sides and a little more whipped cream. SERVES TWELVE.

# Bananas Foster

*This creation of Brennan's is not only widely served around New Orleans—I've seen it almost everywhere in the world I've traveled. It was developed because the Brennans had close friends in the banana business. They asked the restaurant's first chef, Paul Blangé, to come up with something. Boy, did he ever! Although the dessert is classically prepared and flamed at the table, there's no reason it can't be done without the show.*

1 cup light brown sugar
½ stick (4 Tbsp.) butter
4 ripe bananas
2 Tbsp. banana liqueur (optional)
1 tsp. cinnamon
½ cup dark rum (80 proof maximum)
4 large scoops vanilla ice cream

1. Melt the sugar and butter together in a large, flat skillet over medium heat, stirring frequently.

2. Peel the bananas and slice them in quarters—first lengthwise, then across. When the sugar and butter have melted together and begun to bubble, add the bananas and sauté until tender. Add banana liqueur, if using, and sprinkle with cinnamon.

3. Add the rum and ignite in the pan (if you like, and if you're prepared for the possibility of a flare-up). Carefully spoon the sauce over the bananas until the flame burns out. Serve immediately over ice cream with lots of sauce. SERVES FOUR.

# Riz au Lait

*Rice pudding is a popular dessert throughout Latin America and the Caribbean, as well as in New Orleans (where it's known by the French name* riz au lait). *It's always better than you think it's going to be. I recommend using short-grain rice, which will absorb more of the sweet liquid and attain a more puddinglike texture. This stuff is pretty good for breakfast, too, especially with some berries on top.*

¾ cup short-grain rice
4 cups whole milk (or half-and-half for a very rich pudding)
⅔ cup sugar
⅓ cup golden raisins
2 Tbsp. honey
1 tsp. vanilla extract
⅛ tsp. salt
¼ tsp. cinnamon
Pinch of nutmeg

1. Rinse the rice well, then put it in a heavy saucepan with the milk, sugar, raisins, honey, vanilla, salt, and cinnamon. Bring the mixture to a boil. Reduce the heat and simmer for 25–30 minutes, stirring often, until thickened into a pudding consistency.

2. Allow to cool at room temperature or even refrigerate. Sprinkle with a little nutmeg before serving. SERVES EIGHT.

# Chocolate and Café au Lait Mousse

*I've long been fascinated by the cocoalike flavors in my morning cup of coffee and chicory. It occurred to me that it would be interesting to make chocolate mousse flavored with a jolt of intense New Orleans–style coffee, and indeed it was. Chocolate mousse is best right after being made because the frothy texture disappears after it's refrigerated.*

1 lb. Baker's semisweet chocolate

6 eggs, separated

⅓ cup warm, brewed very dark coffee, preferably coffee and chicory blend

¼ cup warm milk

½ cup sugar

2 tsp. vanilla extract

1½ cups heavy whipping cream

1. Melt the chocolate in a bowl in a microwave oven in 30-second bursts, stirring between each burst until the chocolate is completely melted and smooth. (This can also be done in a bowl over a pan of boiling water.)

2. In another bowl, whip the egg yolks until they become distinctly lighter in color. Combine the coffee and milk, and add it slowly to the yolks, whisking as you go. Add the chocolate slowly to the egg-and-coffee mixture and whisk well until the mixture is just barely warm and well blended.

3. Beat the egg whites until soft peaks form, then add the sugar and vanilla. Continue beating until stiff. With a rubber spatula, fold the egg whites into the chocolate mixture. Do this gently; don't worry about achieving an absolutely uniform mixture.

4. Whip the heavy cream in a metal bowl. Remember that cream whips best when cold and that if you overwhip, it will break up into butter and buttermilk.

5. If the chocolate mixture is still warm, let it continue to cool to room temperature. Then fold in the whipped cream with the rubber spatula or wooden spoon. Do this gently and keep at it until you have a uniform texture.

6. Spoon the mousse into serving dishes or pipe it in with a pastry bag for a more elegant presentation. If you like, top it with shaved chocolate or a strawberry. SERVES SIX TO EIGHT.

# Heavenly Hash, New Orleans Style

*The words heavenly hash mean only one thing in New Orleans: a chocolate-and-marshmallow candy, studded with almonds, sold in big chunks in the old department stores. (And still, in a more mainstream form, by the local Elmer's Candy Company.) There's really not much to it, as you'll see here.*

24 oz. semisweet chocolate
1 cup whole pecans, almonds, walnuts, or a combination
1 overflowing cup miniature marshmallows

1. Melt the chocolate in a bowl in a microwave oven in 30-second bursts, stirring between each burst until the chocolate is completely melted and smooth. (This can also be done in a bowl over a pan of boiling water.)

2. Pour about half of the chocolate into a pan or baking dish lined with wax paper. Sprinkle the nuts and marshmallows over the chocolate. Cover it all with the rest of the chocolate. Let it cool and harden. To serve, just break into pieces. MAKES ENOUGH TO FILL A LARGE CANDY BOWL.

# Oat Bran and Apple Muffins

*Remember oat bran muffins? Remember how they were supposed to bring your cholesterol down, so everybody was eating them? Remember the cartoon about the man who stood in front of the three-story oat bran muffin he had to eat to make up for everything he'd eaten before? Well, I fell for that stuff, too, and for a couple of years, I made a batch of oat bran muffins every two or three weeks and ate one every day. It was not unpleasant, actually. These are great with a cup of coffee and chicory with hot milk.*

**DRY INGREDIENTS**
2½ cups oat bran
1 cup self-rising flour
1 tsp. cinnamon
Dash of nutmeg
½ cup grated carrots
½ cup pecan pieces
2 medium apples or pears, peeled,
  cored, and chopped
¼ tsp. salt

**WET INGREDIENTS**
1¼ cups buttermilk
6 Tbsp. canola oil
½ cup Steen's cane syrup or molasses
1 Tbsp. honey
1 Tbsp. vanilla extract
2 egg whites
1 egg yolk

1. Preheat the oven to 400 degrees. Grease 15–18 pockets in muffin tins with non-stick cooking spray.

2. Combine the oat bran, flour, cinnamon, and nutmeg in a bowl and mix well. Add all of the remaining dry ingredients and stir until well mixed.

3. Mix all the wet ingredients in a larger bowl. (Measure the syrup after the oil, so that the syrup doesn't stick to the measuring cup.)

4. Pour the dry ingredients into the wet ingredients and, with a minimum of stirring, combine them, making sure the dry ingredients at the bottom get saturated. The batter should be quite wet.

5. Spoon the batter into the prepared tins, filling each pocket three-quarters full. Bang the muffin tins down on a countertop to settle and even out the batter. Bake for 25–30 minutes. Remove from the oven and cool. Freeze the muffins you don't plan on eating right away. MAKES FIFTEEN TO EIGHTEEN MUFFINS.

# Banana–Peanut Butter Bread

*This was the first hit recipe on my radio show, back in 1988. I remember sending out dozens of copies of it every week for a while. Then the interest faded, just the way it does for hit records on a music station. That doesn't make it any less good. It's a terrific loaf of bread that can be eaten during a meal, as dessert, for breakfast, or for a snack.*

5 Tbsp. butter, softened
4 medium, extra-ripe bananas, peeled
⅓ cup chunky peanut butter
2 eggs
2 cups flour
½ cup sugar
1 tsp. baking soda
¼ tsp. salt

1. Preheat the oven to 350 degrees. Grease a 9 x 5-inch loaf pan with 1 tablespoon of the butter.

2. Slice bananas into a blender. Puree until smooth and set aside.

3. Put the peanut butter and the remaining butter in a bowl and beat with an electric mixer until smooth. Beat in the eggs until completely blended. Then beat in the pureed bananas.

4. Combine the sugar, baking soda, and salt in a bowl. Add to the banana mixture a little at a time, beating until completely blended. Pour the batter into the prepared pan. Bake until a skewer inserted into the center comes out clean, about 50 minutes.

5. Cool 10 minutes in the pan, then turn onto a wire rack to finish cooling. MAKES ONE LOAF.

# Ham and Goat Cheese Bread

*This is good not only in a basket of breads for the dinner table but also as a tangy breakfast item. You can bake the entire amount of dough in a loaf pan and make one big bread, but I prefer the small muffin-size version. If you can get it, use the New Orleans–made Chisesi ham, which has the perfect taste and texture for this.*

1 Tbsp. butter, softened

8 oz. fresh (not aged or feta) goat cheese

4 oz. cream cheese

3 eggs

1¼ cups buttermilk

1 tsp. Creole mustard

¼ tsp. salt

Generous pinch of cayenne

½ lb. smoked ham, finely chopped

3 cups unsifted self-rising flour

1. Preheat the oven to 400 degrees. Grease 12 muffin-tin pockets or a 9 x 5 x 3-inch loaf pan with the butter.

2. Combine the goat cheese and cream cheese in the bowl of a mixer and mix until fluffy. Add the eggs, one at a time, while the mixer is running. Wait until the mixture is smooth before adding the next egg. Scrape down the sides of the bowl as you go. Gradually add the buttermilk, mustard, salt, and cayenne, and mix until completely blended.

3. Remove the bowl from the mixer. Fold in the ham, and then stir in the flour using a wooden spoon. The batter will be very wet. Spoon it into the prepared muffin tin(s), filling each pocket to just below the top, or into the prepared loaf pan.

4. Bake the muffins for 30 minutes, or until puffed and brown. If making a loaf, lower the heat to 350 degrees and bake for 1 hour. Let the loaf cool completely before attempting to slice. Refrigerate or freeze any unused part of the loaf. MAKES TWELVE MUFFINS OR ONE LOAF.

# Jalapeño-Cheese Cornbread

*Chef Paul Prudhomme made this cornbread popular in the early 1980s, although it probably originated in Texas long before then. You can leave out the cheese and the jalapeños and substitute other things, like corn kernels, bacon, or green onion. Or add ⅓ cup of sugar to make it sweet.*

*I prefer self-rising flour for this recipe. I find it to be more convenient, and it gives a superior result, especially with the acidity in the buttermilk to kick it off.*

2 cups self-rising yellow cornmeal
1 cup self-rising flour
1 tsp. salt
4 eggs, beaten
1½ cups buttermilk
1½ cups roughly grated sharp Cheddar cheese
2–3 fresh jalapeños, seeded, membranes removed, and chopped
2 Tbsp. vegetable oil

1. Preheat the oven to 400 degrees. If you have a convection oven, set it on convect.

2. Blend the cornmeal, flour, and salt in a bowl. Combine all of the remaining ingredients, except the oil, in a second bowl. Dump the dry ingredients into the wet ingredients and mix completely. If it looks a little stiff, add a little water.

3. Heat the oil in a large cast-iron skillet, tilting the skillet around to coat the entire inner surface. Add the batter to the pan and bang it down on a towel on the countertop. (This evens out the top of the batter.) Place the pan in the oven and bake for about 30 minutes. Check its progress at that point and continue baking until the top is light brown.

4. Allow the cornbread to cool for 5 minutes, then cut into squares. This recipe can also be made as muffins or in those cute little molds that look like ears of corn. SERVES EIGHT TO TEN.

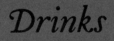

# Drinks

Richard Collin, the city's first restaurant critic and a former history professor of mine, said, "If someone dies in New Orleans of cirrhosis of the liver, it's considered natural causes." That certainly has a ring of truth. Consider this: The only business in New Orleans that never closed during or after Hurricane Katrina was a bar.

New Orleans has a wide array of distinctive beverages, alcoholic and not. We begin with coffee. Long before gourmet coffee swept across America, New Orleans coffee was in a class by itself. It still is. The classic version is a blend of very dark roast coffee and chicory, brewed so intense that when you swirl it, the sides of the cup stay brown for a few seconds. It's cut with an equal amount of hot milk for café au lait. Chicory is the root of a variety of endive, roasted and ground. It doesn't really taste like coffee, but the flavor it adds is complementary. The use of chicory in coffee dates back to a coffee shortage in France during the Napoleonic era. The practice spread to New Orleans, where it remained in vogue long after it died out in France.

New Orleans is also the birthplace of the cocktail. Its inventor, a druggist named Antoine Peychaud, formulated the original bitters (still made under his name and much liked around New Orleans) and added it to Cognac from Sazerac, France, along with a little sugar and absinthe. At his drugstore on Royal Street, Peychaud served up this concoction (for alleged health benefits) in a *coquetier*—a French name for an egg cup, whose mispronunciation resulted in the word cocktail. Peychaud's original drink, now called a Sazerac, is made with rye whiskey these days and is still quite popular. A recipe for one of its offshoots, the old-fashioned, is included here.

# Café au Lait

*The two cups of café au lait I have every morning are a wonderful addiction. I make them with Union coffee and chicory, brewed so dark that it leaves the side of the cup deep brown for a moment when I swirl it. I mix that with an equal amount of milk, and the pleasure begins.*

*Serious purists insist that great coffee and chicory can only be brewed in an enamel coffee biggin (an old-fashioned pot that requires one to slowly drip small amounts of water through the grounds manually). However, I find that a good drip coffeemaker—especially the kind with cone-shaped filters—does just as fine a job as long as you use enough coffee. Err on the side of too much ground coffee and step it back if it's too strong.*

*Union coffee and chicory, in its distinctive soft green bag, can be hard to find even in New Orleans. Other good brands include CDM, French Market, and the widely distributed but relatively light Community New Orleans Blend.*

½ cup ground coffee-and-chicory blend
8 cups water
6 cups milk
Sugar

Brew the coffee normally in a drip coffeemaker. Fill mugs half-full with milk and heat in a microwave until steaming. Add sugar to your taste and stir. Pour the coffee in and observe the pleasant light foam of the milk on the coffee. MAKES EIGHT CUPS.

# Café Brulot

*Café brulot is the grandest ending to a major New Orleans dinner—especially if it's made and served in the traditional café brulot bowl and cups. The show at the table is spectacular, and the aroma is wonderful. If you make it at home, look for oranges with a thick, flawless skin. (California oranges are best.)*

*This is a flamed dish. So make sure you have nothing above the burning bowl that could catch fire. Do not use any spirit higher than 80 proof. If you feel ill at ease about flaming dishes, skip the flaming part.*

Peel of 1 lemon
1 orange
12–15 cloves
5 Tbsp. brandy
5 Tbsp. Cointreau, triple sec, or Grand Marnier
2 cinnamon sticks, broken in half
½ tsp. vanilla extract
1 Tbsp. sugar
3 cups freshly brewed very dark coffee, preferably coffee-and-chicory blend

1. Wash the lemon and the orange. Peel the lemon and cut the peel into strips about 1 inch long and ½ inch wide. Stud the skin of the orange with the cloves, inserting the cloves in a spiral pattern from top to bottom. Then cut the peel from the orange in one continuous spiral with the cloves in the center of the strip.

2. In a metal bowl set over a small burner, combine the brandy and the Cointreau with the lemon peel, studded orange peel, and cinnamon sticks. Bring to a light boil and hold it there for a minute. Carefully touch a flame to the mixture and flame it, stirring it around.

3. With a long fork, spear the orange and hold it up above the bowl. Pour some of the flaming liquid over the orange and let it flow down the spiral of the skin.

4. Add the vanilla, sugar, and coffee, and swirl it all around until the flames die out. Pour the café brulot into demitasse cups and serve hot. It's okay for pieces of lemon or orange peel to go into the cup. SERVES SIX TO EIGHT.

# Mint Julep

*The mint julep is considered a cliché Old South drink by some. But a good one is about as refreshing a cocktail as ever slaked a midsummer night's thirst. It is best served in the classic metal cups, which get frosty on the outside if you make it right. I use those great small-batch bourbons in my mint juleps; Knob Creek or Blanton's are particularly good.*

About 20 fresh mint leaves, plus more sprigs for garnish
8 oz. Simple Syrup (see recipe, page 302)
8 oz. bourbon
Crushed ice

1. Combine the mint leaves and the simple syrup in a cocktail shaker. Crush the leaves with a muddler or a blunt-end wooden stick. (The back end of a honey server works perfectly.)

2. Add the bourbon and fill the shaker with crushed ice. Put the top on the shaker and shake vigorously until the outside is frosty.

3. Strain the mint juleps into 4 old-fashioned glasses (or silver julep cups) filled about three-quarters full with crushed ice. Garnish each with a sprig of mint. SERVES FOUR.

# Old-Fashioned Cocktail

*The old-fashioned has indeed been around a long time. It dates almost to the dawn of the cocktail, which occurred in New Orleans. An old-fashioned is similar in many ways to a Sazerac, which lays claim to being the very first cocktail of them all. You can obtain Peychaud's bitters from the Sazerac Company (www.sazerac.com/bitters.html).*

6 oz. Simple Syrup (see recipe below)
1 tsp. Angostura bitters
1 tsp. Peychaud's bitters
8 oz. bourbon
Crushed ice
Club soda
1 orange, cut into 8 half-moon slices
8 stemmed maraschino cherries

1. Combine the syrup, both bitters, and bourbon in a shaker filled with crushed ice.

2. Strain the mixture into old-fashioned glasses filled about two-thirds full with crushed ice. Top with club soda and stir 2–3 strokes. Garnish each glass with an orange slice and 2 cherries. SERVES FOUR.

# Simple Syrup

*Simple syrup is essential for making mint juleps, old-fashioneds, and other great cocktails. It's also nice to have on hand to sweeten iced tea without the endless, clanky stirring.*

2 cups sugar
1 cup water

Combine the sugar and water in a very clean saucepan and bring to a light boil for 5 minutes. Brush any granules of sugar that may stick to the sides of the pan down into the syrup, or the syrup may regranulate. Refrigerate. MAKES ABOUT ONE CUP.

# Egg Nog

*The best egg nog, frankly, is uncooked. But so many people are concerned about the health risks of eating raw eggs that I've come up with an egg nog recipe cooked just long enough to eliminate most possible problems. It does produce a difficulty, though: You have to be very careful to keep the mixture from setting as you cook it. It's basically a custard, but that's not what you want.*

1 dozen egg yolks
1½ cups sugar
2 Tbsp. vanilla extract
½ tsp. nutmeg, plus more to taste
2 cups heavy whipping cream
4 cups half-and-half

1. Whisk the egg yolks with the sugar, vanilla, and nutmeg together in a saucepan until creamy-looking. Add the cream and 2 cups of the half-and-half, and whisk until blended.

2. Cook over very low heat while stirring. Look for a temperature reading of 175 degrees on a meat thermometer. Don't overheat or cook longer than needed to reach this temperature.

3. Remove from the heat. Strain the egg nog into the container you will store it in and add the remaining half-and-half. Refrigerate.

4. If you'd like to add something interesting (i.e., brandy, bourbon, or dark rum), a cup of the stuff should be about right. Serve with some more nutmeg (freshly grated, if possible) over the top. SERVES TWELVE TO SIXTEEN.

# Ping Pong

*The origin of the name ping pong is unknown, but in the riverlands between New Orleans and Baton Rouge, many people know what it is: a pink, frozen drink that has the flavor of nectar. Nectar, in turn, is universally recognized among Orleanians as a distinctive flavor, a blend of almond and vanilla. Nectar was one of the most popular flavors for ice-cream sodas in the days when drugstores still made such things. Now nectar is an essential flavor in the vast array of syrups poured over finely shaved ice for sno-balls.*

*I learned about ping pong from Mark Hymel, whose family has raised sugarcane and run a fine seafood restaurant in St. James Parish for generations. He handed it to me at a party at his home and challenged me to guess what it was. I recognized the nectar flavor instantly but was astonished to learn how it was derived. I mentioned it on the radio the next day, and from that time until the day Hurricane Katrina shut us down, I've repeated the unlikely recipe hundreds of times on the air and on the Internet.*

*The original recipe is so sweet that you can't drink much of it (although you'll very much like those few sips). Lately I've lightened up the sugar content by replacing the sweetened condensed milk with half-and-half.*

ORIGINAL RECIPE
1 can sweetened condensed milk
1 liter Barq's Red Creme Soda

NOT-SO-SWEET VERSION
1 cup half-and-half
1 liter Barq's Red Creme Soda

1. For either formula, mix the 2 ingredients in an ice-cream maker and freeze. It will probably not get hard, but it will have the texture of a frozen daiquiri. You can solidify it by freezing it further, but it's better as a drink, really. In fact, you can add a shot of vodka to it for something a bit more potent.

2. If you don't have an ice-cream maker, mix the ingredients in a gallon-size plastic food-storage bag and freeze that until it starts to set. Squinch the bag, every now and then, until it has a slushy consistency. SERVES TWELVE TO SIXTEEN.

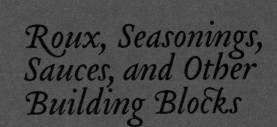

# Roux, Seasonings, Sauces, and Other Building Blocks

The most contentious issue in all of Creole and Cajun cookery is how to make and use roux. Talking about roux in South Louisiana is like talking about ragu in Sicily. Everybody who makes it believes that his or her version is the only right way. So many Creole recipes begin with the words "First make a roux" that it's become a cliché even to point this out. But its importance can't be overstated.

Roux is flour mixed with some kind of fat (oil, butter, margarine, lard, rendered bacon fat, duck fat—almost any fat you can imagine has been used by somebody) and browned, usually on top of the stove. The degree of browning—from the palest tan (a blond roux) to nearly black—depends on the recipe. You'll find many variations throughout this book, but the recipe in this section is a good basic technique.

Another essential element of modern Creole and Cajun cookery is Creole seasoning. Although everybody in Louisiana with even a tenuous connection to food seems to market a line of Creole seasonings, if you find yourself using a lot of it, you might want to try your hand at making your own. I include three variations in this chapter (see pages 309 and 311).

Finally, a dish made with a stock has dimensions of flavor missing from the same dish made with just water. Here are some simple stock recipes that you'll find well worth the trouble of making.

# Roux

*Roux is a blend of flour and some kind of fat, cooked a little or a lot, used as a base for sauces and soups. It's a classic French technique, but it's likely that more roux is used in Creole and Cajun cooking than in all other cuisines combined. Not all Creole and Cajun recipes call for roux, but those that do—notably gumbos—rely heavily on it for their unique flavors.*

*I deviate from the tradition of my forebears by usually making the roux separately, then adding it to the recipe later, after the liquid component is in the pot. That way I can control the amount of roux in the dish.*

*The essence of making a good roux is constant stirring to keep it from burning. There's no saving a dish that tastes of burned roux. If you smell the unmistakable burned odor or see a hard black crust forming in the bottom of the pot, stop. Dump it, clean the pot, and start over. The best tool for making a roux is a roux stick, a wooden spoon with a flat outer edge. This allows you to scrape a wide swath on the bottom of the pan, thereby keeping the roux from sitting in one place too long.*

*It's a good idea to cook roux slowly if you're learning. Cooks who make roux all the time get bold, heating the fat very hot to cook the roux faster. They also know that roux gets incredibly hot and are careful not to splash it. Splattered roux on the skin feels as if it will burn all the way through to the bone.*

½ cup oil, butter, or other fat
1 cup flour

1. In a heavy saucepan or skillet over medium heat, heat the oil until it shimmers or the butter until it bubbles. Sprinkle in the flour and begin stirring with a wooden spoon or roux stick. Stir constantly, leaving no part of the bottom of the pan unstirred for long.

*(continued)*

2. After a minute or so, the texture of the mixture will change from a blend of oil and flour into something thicker and lighter. You now have a blond roux. It will begin to brown, getting darker at an accelerating rate. It goes from looking like peanut butter to taking on a reddish hue, like that of an old penny. Then it becomes chocolate-colored. But beware: The darker it gets, the faster it gets darker still. You can stop the darkening process at any time by cooling it down. In some cases, this is done by removing the pan from the heat and stirring in onions, celery, and other vegetables from the recipe you're making. If the recipe doesn't include that step, you must turn the heat off before the desired color is reached and keep stirring because the held heat of the roux will keep cooking it. (It will even burn if you don't keep stirring.) MAKES ABOUT ONE AND A HALF CUPS.

# Salt-free Creole Seasoning

*Seasoned salts have been around for a long time. Almost every restaurant makes its own variation. During the past few years, many companies have come out with Creole or Cajun seasoning blends, usually at prices far beyond what the ingredients cost. I make mine to my own taste and without salt. I prefer to control the salt component of the dish separately. Here is an all-purpose salt-free Creole seasoning.*

2 Tbsp. granulated onion
2 Tbsp. freshly ground black pepper
1 Tbsp. paprika
1 tsp. granulated garlic
½ tsp. ground white pepper

¼ tsp. dried thyme
¼ tsp. dried marjoram
⅛ tsp. cayenne
Pinch of dry mustard

Mix all of the ingredients well in a jar with a tight-fitting lid. This will keep for about a year, tightly sealed, in a cool place. MAKES HALF A CUP.

# Salt-free Creole Seafood Seasoning

*This subtler version of my salt-free Creole seasoning is made specifically for seafood.*

2 Tbsp. granulated onion
1 Tbsp. freshly ground black pepper
1 Tbsp. paprika
1 tsp. granulated garlic
½ tsp. ground white pepper

¼ tsp. cayenne
¼ tsp. dried basil
¼ tsp. dried oregano
¼ tsp. dried thyme
Pinch of dry mustard

Mix all of the ingredients well in a jar with a tight-fitting lid. This will keep for about a year, tightly sealed, in a cool place. MAKES HALF A CUP.

# Barbecue Dry Rub

*This is the stuff I use to coat (liberally) every meat I smoke or barbecue. There's only one variation: For pork shoulders and ribs, I add brown sugar to the mix, but I leave it out for briskets.*

2½ cups salt
1 cup granulated onion
½ cup freshly ground black pepper
¼ cup chili powder
¼ cup granulated garlic
¼ cup paprika
3 Tbsp. cayenne
2 Tbsp. ground white pepper
2 Tbsp. dried marjoram
1 Tbsp. dried thyme
1 Tbsp. dry mustard
1 Tbsp. cinnamon
1 Tbsp. turmeric
1 cup dark brown sugar (for pork only)

Blend all of the ingredients well in a big jar with a tight-fitting lid. This will keep for about a year, tightly sealed, in a cool place. MAKES ABOUT FIVE CUPS (SIX, IF YOU INCLUDE THE BROWN SUGAR).

# Blackening Seasoning

*The essence of a good blackened dish is the seasoning blend with which it is encrusted. During the past several years, many companies have come out with blackened seasonings, usually at prices far beyond what the ingredients cost. I always make my own, which allows me to make it to my taste. This one is appropriately spicy without being insane.*

3 Tbsp. paprika
2 Tbsp. salt
1 Tbsp. garlic powder
4½ tsp. freshly ground black pepper
2 tsp. ground white pepper
1 tsp. cayenne
1 tsp. dried thyme
1 tsp. dried oregano

Mix all of the ingredients well in a jar with a tight-fitting lid. This will keep for about a year, tightly sealed, in a cool place. MAKES HALF A CUP.

# Stocks

*Using stocks in place of water in a recipe gives an added dimension of flavor, so they're well worth making and using if you can. Many of the stocks in this book are described within the recipes, but here is a general method of making a variety of stocks.*

*The key to making good stock is to simmer it very slowly for a long time, with only a few bubbles breaking on top of the pot. Slow-cooked stocks come out clear and full of flavor. The longer you cook a stock, the more intense it gets and the less of it you need in a recipe.*

*Stocks hold up for a few days in the refrigerator or for a long time if well sealed in the freezer. Many cooks freeze stock in ice-cube trays, so they can slip out a few cubes and add it to recipes conveniently.*

*Canned chicken stock can be used if you don't have your own. It's not as good, but it's acceptable. Canned beef stock is not very good, and I wouldn't recommend using it.*

### FOR BEEF STOCK
3 lb. meaty beef bones, fat trimmed
  (soup bones or oxtails are the
  most desirable)
2 carrots, coarsely chopped

### FOR VEAL, LAMB, OR PORK STOCK
3 lb. meaty veal, lamb, or pork bones,
  depending on which you are making,
  fat trimmed

### FOR CHICKEN STOCK
3–4 lb. chicken pieces, no liver,
  or a whole chicken

### FOR CRAB, SHRIMP, OR CRAWFISH STOCK
2 cups (at least; the more the better)
  picked or peeled shells of crab,
  shrimp, or crawfish, depending on
  which you are making
Peel of ½ lemon

### FOR FISH STOCK
1 lb. or more of bones, heads,
  and scraps from edible fish,
  gills and livers removed
1 tsp. dried oregano

### STOCK SEASONINGS
1 large onion, coarsely chopped
Top 4 inches from a bunch of celery,
  coarsely chopped
Stems from a bunch of parsley
2 bay leaves
1 tsp. black peppercorns
1 tsp. dried thyme

FOR THE BEEF, VEAL, LAMB, OR PORK STOCK: Heat a heavy kettle or stockpot over medium heat. Add the meat and bones of whichever meat you are using and cook until well browned all over, turning them now and then. (For the beef stock, add the carrots after the meat begins to brown.) Then add 2 gallons of water to the pot, plus all of the stock seasonings. Bring to a light boil, then lower to a bare simmer. Cook for 2–3 hours. Then go to Finish, below.

FOR THE CHICKEN STOCK: Pour 2 gallons of water into a heavy kettle or stockpot. Add the chicken and the stock seasonings. Bring to a light boil, then lower to a bare simmer. Cook for 2 hours. Then go to Finish, below.

FOR THE CRAB, SHRIMP, OR CRAWFISH STOCK: Crush the crab claws and/or crawfish shells with a pounder to break open. Combine claws and/or shells in a heavy kettle or stockpot with the stock seasonings and enough water to cover. Bring to a light boil, lower to a bare simmer, and cook for 30 minutes. Then go to Finish, below.

FOR THE FISH STOCK: Put fish bones and scraps into a pot and nearly cover with cold water. Heat until water begins to steam, then pour off water. Refill pot with enough water to cover and add the oregano and stock seasonings. Bring to a light boil, then lower to a bare simmer. Cook for 45 minutes. Then go to Finish, below.

FOR A VEGETABLE STOCK: Combine stock seasonings with 1 gallon of water. Bring to a boil then lower to a bare simmer. Cook for 30 minutes. Then go to Finish, below.

FINISH FOR ALL STOCKS:

1. As the pot boils, skim any foam that rises to the top. For meat and chicken stocks, also skim off any fat. Cook for the noted time, then strain stock through the finest sieve or cheesecloth. Dispose of solids (except for the chicken or meats, which can be picked from the bones for use in other recipes). Stocks can be further reduced and intensified by continuing to simmer after the solids have been removed.

2. Let stock cool to lukewarm, then refrigerate if not using right away. For beef and chicken stocks, the fat will rise and solidify upon chilling and can be easily removed. All except vegetable stocks may become gelatinous in the refrigerator; this is not a problem. MEAT AND CHICKEN STOCK RECIPES MAKE ABOUT THREE QUARTS; SHELLFISH, FISH, AND VEGETABLE STOCK RECIPES MAKE ABOUT TWO QUARTS.

# Clarified Butter

*The process of clarifying butter does two things: It boils out the water (of which there is a great deal in butter), and it causes the milk solids to fall out of suspension. Some of the solids will rise to the top as foam, but most will fall to the bottom. During clarification, you will lose a third to a half of the quantity of butter you started with. So if you start with two sticks of butter, you'll end up with a quarter to a third of a cup of clarified butter.*

*The amazing thing about clarified butter is that it will hold up for a long time, even unrefrigerated (although I recommend keeping it chilled). It can also be heated to a much higher temperature than most fats without burning. (The threat of fire, however, is always there, so be careful.)*

2–4 sticks butter (unsalted preferred)

Heat the butter in a small saucepan over the lowest heat for about 20 minutes, or until the bubbling has stopped almost completely. Spoon the foam off the top, then pour the clarified butter carefully away from the milky solids on the bottom. If you want to be thorough, you can strain the butter through cheesecloth. MAKES A QUARTER TO TWO-THIRDS OF A CUP, DEPENDING ON THE AMOUNT OF BUTTER USED.

# Hollandaise

*Hollandaise is one of the mother sauces of classic French cooking and widely used around New Orleans, where it usually contains an extra pinch of cayenne. It's not hard to make if you can keep it from breaking, which will happen if the sauce gets too hot once the butter goes in. I avoid this by whisking butter that's at room temperature, not melted.*

*Hollandaise should be made right before it's needed. If you try to keep it warm, it might break. If that happens, you can sometimes bring it back by adding a little warm water. If that doesn't work, whisk another egg yolk in a clean bowl and slowly whisk the broken sauce into the beaten yolk.*

2 egg yolks
1 Tbsp. red wine vinegar
1 stick (8 Tbsp.) butter, softened
1 tsp. lemon juice
Pinch of cayenne

1. Whisk the egg yolks and the vinegar briskly in a metal bowl set over a saucepan filled with about an inch of barely simmering water. If you see even a hint of curdling in the eggs, take the bowl off the heat, but keep whisking. Keep going back and forth from the heat until the mixture turns thick and pale yellow. Whisk in a tablespoon of warm water.

2. Add the butter, a pat at a time, whisking constantly. When you begin to see a change in the texture of the sauce, you can step up the addition of the butter a bit. Keep whisking constantly until all of the butter is incorporated. Whisk in the lemon juice and cayenne, and serve right away. MAKES ABOUT THREE-QUARTERS OF A CUP.

# Béarnaise

*Béarnaise is my favorite sauce. It's good on almost everything: steaks, fish, fried potatoes, eggs, chicken . . . I could go on. Its finest employment in the Creole arena is in a dish called chicken Pontalba. If you find fresh tarragon or chervil, use twice as much as called for here.*

¼ cup tarragon vinegar
¼ cup Sauvignon Blanc or other dry white wine
1 Tbsp. very finely chopped green onion, tender part only
2 tsp. dried tarragon
1½ tsp. dried chervil
Pinch of ground white pepper
⅔ cup Hollandaise (see recipe, page 315)

1. Combine the vinegar, wine, green onion, tarragon, chervil, and white pepper in a small saucepan. Bring it to a light boil and reduce until the herbs are just soggy.

2. Stir this mixture into the hollandaise. It will keep for 30 minutes or so at warm room temperature. MAKES ABOUT TWO-THIRDS OF A CUP.

# Spicy Garlic Mayonnaise

*Somewhere in Provence there is a newspaper whose name is* L'Aioli. *That lucky town gets to wake up every day to* The Garlic Mayonnaise. *Sounds like a good place to live. Closer to home, chefs have extended the aioli concept to include all sorts of other flavors. Here's my contribution to the overload. This is not only tasty as a dip, a squirtable condiment, or even a sandwich spread, but it's also a very pretty color. Thinned with a little water, it makes a wine-friendly salad dressing (no vinegar).*

2 egg yolks
1 tsp. Dijon mustard
2 cloves garlic
2 Tbsp. lemon juice
1 cup extra-virgin olive oil
⅛ tsp. salt
5 dashes of Tabasco

1. Put the egg yolks, mustard, garlic, and 1 tablespoon of the lemon juice in a blender or food processor. Blend at medium speed for about 45 seconds.

2. With the blender or food processor still running, add the oil a few drops at a time until the contents of the container noticeably begin to change texture. Then add the remaining oil in a thin stream while the blender or food processor continues to run. When all the oil is incorporated, add the salt, Tabasco, and remaining lemon juice. Refrigerate to thicken. MAKES ABOUT ONE AND THREE-QUARTERS CUPS.

# Sauce Nantua

*This is a creamy, Cognac-scented crawfish sauce, which, although it sounds like something from Louisiana, is actually a classic French sauce. I first ran into it with quenelles of fish at Christian's. Lately it has been appearing on more menus.*

| | |
|---|---|
| 2 lb. whole boiled crawfish | ½ cup tomato puree |
| 4 cloves garlic, crushed | 1 cup dry white wine |
| 1 tsp. dried thyme | ½ cup brandy |
| 1 bay leaf | 1 stick (8 Tbsp.) butter |
| ¼ cup olive oil | ½ cup flour |
| ½ cup chopped yellow onion | 1 cup heavy whipping cream |
| 1 medium carrot, chopped | ½ tsp. salt |
| 2 Tbsp. chopped flat-leaf parsley | ⅛ tsp. cayenne |

1. Rinse the crawfish in cold water. Peel them, reserving all of the shells. Set aside about ½ cup of tail meat and finely chop the the rest in a food processor.

2. Crush the crawfish shells with a meat pounder. Put the shells, garlic, thyme, bay leaf, and 1 quart of cold water into a saucepan and simmer for 30 minutes. Strain stock into a clean saucepan and reduce the stock down to about 1 cup.

3. Heat the oil in a large skillet over medium heat. Add the onion, carrot, and parsley, and sauté until soft. Add the tomato puree and cook another minute or so. Add the wine, bring to a boil, and reduce until most of the liquid is gone. Add the chopped crawfish tails to the pan. Add the brandy, bring to a boil, and carefully flame it (if you like). Add 1 cup of the crawfish stock to the pan and bring to a light boil. Reduce the heat to low and keep the sauce warm.

4. Make a blond roux by melting the butter in a saucepan. Add the flour and cook, stirring constantly, until the mixture barely begins to brown. Whisk the roux into the sauce until completely blended. Add the cream, salt, and cayenne, adjusting the latter two to taste. Bring to a simmer, then serve. Garnish with the reserved whole tails. MAKES ABOUT A CUP AND A HALF.

# Marchand de Vin Sauce

*This is the great sauce for steaks in the old-line Creole restaurants. As is often the case, the New Orleans version of this is much different from the classic French sauce of the same name. When serving, place the sauce right on top of the steak (or whatever—this is also good with many other dishes, from eggs to pork chops), not underneath.*

*My reading of old cookbooks tells me that this sauce originally contained chips of marrow. I love that flavor and have included marrow as an optional ingredient in this recipe.*

1 stick (8 Tbsp.) butter
⅓ cup flour
2 slices smoked, cured ham, finely
  chopped
4 cloves garlic, chopped
1 green onion, chopped
2 Tbsp. chopped shallots
1 cup dry red wine

2 cups beef stock (see recipe, page 312)
Up to ¼ cup beef marrow,
  chopped (optional)
1 bay leaf
1 Tbsp. Worcestershire sauce
⅛ tsp. thyme
½ tsp. salt
¼ tsp. Tabasco

1. To make a light brown roux: Melt the butter in a medium saucepan over medium-low heat until it bubbles. Add the flour and cook, stirring constantly, until the mixture turns the color of fallen leaves.

2. Add the ham, garlic, green onion, and shallots to the roux and sauté until the vegetables are soft. Add the wine and bring to a boil, whisking to dissolve the roux into the wine. Reduce the wine by about half.

3. Add the stock, marrow, bay leaf, Worcestershire sauce, and thyme, and bring to a boil. Reduce to a simmer and cook for 30–45 minutes, stirring now and then, until thickened to a sauce consistency. Don't overthicken. Add the salt and Tabasco. Remove the bay leaf before serving. MAKES ABOUT TWO CUPS.

# Fresh Marinara Sauce

*This is the kind of red sauce we make most often at home. It's cooked only a few minutes, so the freshness of the tomatoes doesn't turn into sweetness. The flavor of fresh basil—which we have growing outside in all the nonfreezing months—is a top note.*

Two 28-oz. cans whole plum tomatoes with basil
4 fresh, ripe plum tomatoes, peeled, seeded, and finely chopped
¼ cup extra-virgin olive oil
1 Tbsp. chopped garlic
¼ tsp. crushed red pepper
¼ tsp. dried oregano
½ tsp. salt
Leaves of 6 sprigs flat-leaf parsley, chopped
15 leaves fresh basil, chopped

1. Drain and reserve the juice from the canned tomatoes. Put the canned tomatoes in a food processor and process almost to a puree. (You can also do this by squeezing the tomatoes with your fingers in a bowl.) Set aside.

2. Heat the oil in a large saucepan over high heat until it shimmers. Add the garlic, crushed red pepper, and oregano, and cook for 1 minute. Add canned and fresh tomatoes and stir, maintaining the heat until you have a pretty good boil. Lower the heat, add 1 cup of the reserved canning juice, and return to a low boil.

3. Add the salt, parsley, and basil, and cook, stirring occasionally, for about 10 minutes. You can cook it longer for a sweeter sauce, but I think it tastes best right at this point. MAKES ABOUT SIX CUPS.

# Fresh Pizza Sauce

*One of the best ideas I got from chef Andrea Apuzzo when I was working on his cookbook was that pizza sauce does not have to be cooked. This, at last, revealed the problem with all pizza sauce! The following concoction may seem a little too runny, but trust me—it works and has a marvelous fresh flavor.*

One 28-oz. can whole peeled Italian
tomatoes, juice reserved

2 Tbsp. extra-virgin olive oil

2 tsp. chopped garlic (or more, if you
love garlic)

6–10 leaves fresh basil

6 sprigs flat-leaf parsley, chopped

¼ tsp. crushed red pepper

¼ tsp. dried oregano

¼ tsp. salt

Put all of the ingredients into a food processor and process for about 20 seconds. That's it! Do not cook; just ladle it right onto the pizza crust and top with cheese and whatever else you like. MAKES ENOUGH FOR ABOUT FOUR 12-INCH PIZZAS.

# Fresh Salsa

*This is the enhanced first stage of making guacamole. My wife once asked me why I don't make it into a salsa. So here it is.*

3 cups peeled, seeded, and chopped fresh ripe tomatoes

1 cup chopped white onion

¼ cup chopped cilantro leaves

2 Tbsp. Tabasco Green Pepper Sauce

1 Tbsp. extra-virgin olive oil

1 Tbsp. lime juice

⅓ tsp. salt

Mix everything together in a bowl and allow the flavors to blend for an hour or so in the refrigerator. MAKES ABOUT FOUR CUPS.

# Southeast Asian–Creole Dipping Sauce

*This may be a long stretch to keep the local theme, but it's great as a dip for vegetables or seafood (especially big grilled shrimp), or even as a salad dressing. It also works well as a basting sauce for grilled fish or chicken. All of the exotic ingredients are available in the ethnic section of any large supermarket.*

5 sprigs cilantro, leaves only
3 cloves garlic
4½ tsp. Tabasco Green Pepper Sauce
2 tsp. sesame oil
1 cup smooth peanut butter
¼ cup coconut milk
2 Tbsp. nuoc mam (Vietnamese fish sauce)
2 Tbsp. hoisin sauce
2 Tbsp. rice wine vinegar
1 Tbsp. soy sauce

In a food processor, puree the first 4 ingredients, then add everything else and puree again. Add water, as necessary, to achieve the consistency appropriate to your needs. MAKES ABOUT TWO CUPS.

# Mignonette Sauce

*This cold sauce—it's more like a relish, really—takes you just a short step away from eating raw oysters with nothing at all on them. The flavors of the sauce don't get in the way of the oyster, and the contrast between the metallic brininess and softness of the oyster and the acidity and crunch of the sauce is very pleasant. Don't chop the shallots in a food processor; dice them with a sharp knife.*

¼ cup finely diced shallots
2 Tbsp. red wine vinegar
2 Tbsp. dry white wine (best: Muscadet)
1 tsp. Dijon mustard
½ tsp. lemon juice
4 sprigs flat-leaf parsley, leaves only, chopped
⅔ cup extra-virgin olive oil
Salt and freshly ground black pepper to taste

Combine everything up to the olive oil in a small bowl. Whisk in the oil in a thin stream until blended. Season to taste with salt and pepper. MAKES ENOUGH FOR ABOUT FOUR DOZEN OYSTERS, A TEASPOON OF MIGNONETTE SAUCE PER OYSTER.

# Cool Water Ranch Barbecue Sauce

*I started making my own barbecue sauce when I volunteered to run a barbecue booth at the festivals at my children's schools. I used two bits of knowledge gleaned from my barbecue-eating activities. The first came from Harold Veazey, founder of the ancient Harold's Texas Barbecue in Metairie. He told me that the secret to his sauce is that he "kills it"—cooks the tomatoes so long that they take on an entirely different, sweet flavor. The second datum was my noticing the cinnamon taste in Corky's barbecue sauce, the best bottled sauce I've found.*

*It may seem like cheating to add bottled barbecue sauce to the mix. What I'm after there is the stuff in commercial barbecue sauce that keeps it from separating.*

2 liters Dr Pepper
¼ cup canola oil
2 medium yellow onions, pureed
1 medium head garlic, cloves pureed
2 Tbsp. grated gingerroot
4 gallons tomato sauce
½ cup yellow mustard
½ bottle Tabasco Caribbean Style
   Steak Sauce
¼ cup cinnamon
¼ cup freshly ground black pepper

5 bay leaves
3 Tbsp. dried basil
2 Tbsp. dried marjoram
2 Tbsp. rubbed sage
2 Tbsp. allspice
2 Tbsp. salt, plus more to taste
2 tsp. chili powder
4 cups cider vinegar, plus more to taste
Six 12-oz. jars molasses
2 quarts (8 cups) prepared
   barbecue sauce

1. Pour the Dr Pepper into a large saucepan and reduce it slowly to about 1 cup of liquid. (If you can get Dr Pepper syrup, use a cup of that instead.)

2. Meanwhile, heat the oil in the biggest stockpot you have over medium heat. Add the onions, garlic, and ginger, and sauté for about 15 minutes, stirring every minute or two. Add the remaining ingredients, except for the vinegar, molasses, and prepared barbecue sauce, and bring to a light simmer. Reduce heat to low and simmer, covered, stirring occasionally, for about 8 hours.

3. Add the vinegar, molasses, and barbecue sauce, and cook another 1–2 hours. Taste the sauce and add salt, hot sauce, or vinegar, if needed, to balance it. Pack what you will not use right away into sterilized canning jars while the sauce is still hot. MAKES FIVE GALLONS.

*Ingredients Notes,*
*Food Sources,*
*Conversion Chart,*
*and Index*

# Ingredients Notes

*Most of the ingredients called for in this book are either well known or are explained in the recipes or chapter introductions. You'll find instructions for making many often-used recipe elements in the Roux, Seasonings, Sauces, and Other Building Blocks chapter (page 305). Here are a few ingredients that may require further explanation.*

ANDOUILLE. A chunky, smoky, thick-skinned smoked pork sausage, both French and German in character. Andouille is used in gumbo, jambalaya, and quite a few other New Orelans dishes as both a meat and a flavoring. You can substitute a generic smoked pork or beef sausage if you can't get the real thing.

BUTTER. Unless otherwise noted, the recipes in this book call for regular salted butter. You may use low-salt or unsalted butter if you like.

CREOLE SEASONING. A blend of herbs and spices that almost everybody in New Orleans has as handy as salt and pepper. There the most famous of the commercial brands are Tony Chachere's and Chef Paul Prudhomme's Magic Seasonings. My favorite is the hard-to-find, salt-free Bayou Bang. I prefer a salt-free Creole seasoning because it allows me to control the amount of salt separately. You'll find recipes for two versions of Creole seasoning on page 309.

FILÉ. A distinctive ingredient in gumbo, especially chicken gumbo, filé is powdered sassafras leaves. It is in the spice rack of any New Orleans food store but may be harder to find elsewhere (see opposite for online and phone-order sources).

FLOUR. Unless otherwise noted in a recipe, the flour called for in this book is all-purpose flour.

GUMBO CRABS. Small crabs that have been picked of their lump meat. You use them to make crab stock. They're often found in packages of six or eight, frozen.

HEAVY WHIPPING CREAM. Also called heavy cream, this is is cream with a butterfat content of 36–40 percent. We use a lot of it in our cooking in New Orleans.

TASSO. A ham used for seasoning, tasso is heavily cured, then smoked with a tremendous amount of seasoning. It comes out a bit dry and very salty, peppery, and smoky. A little of it usually goes a long way.

# Food Sources

*All of the ingredients in this book are widely available in supermarkets along the Gulf Coast, from Houston to Mobile and beyond. If you live elsewhere, you'll find the New Orleans products you'll need from these mail-order sources.*

CHEF PAUL PRUDHOMME'S MAGIC SEASONING BLENDS. Chef Paul was the first chef to roll out a comprehensive line of seasonings, and the quality is first-class. He also has great tasso and andouille.
WEB SITE: shop.chefpaul.com. PHONE: 800-457-2857.

CAJUN CRAWFISH ships its namesake item overnight in all its forms. The company also sells shrimp, meats, turducken (a Cornish hen inside a duck stuffed inside a turkey; it's more interesting than good), seasonings, and all the rest of it.
WEB SITE: www.cajuncrawfish.com. PHONE: 888-254-8626.

SHOP.NEWORLEANS.COM offers a comprehensive line of New Orleans and Cajun foodstuffs, including seasonings, crab boil, bottled sauces and marinades, beans, rice, Creole mustard, sausages, tasso, and turduckens.
ONLINE ORDERS ONLY: shop.neworleans.com.

TABASCO makes a much wider array of products than one usually finds in stores, many of which are utterly unique and delicious (such as the Caribbean-style steak sauce and pepper jelly, to name two personal favorites).
WEB SITE: countrystore.tabasco.com. PHONE: 888-222-7261.

TONY CHACHERE'S CREOLE SEASONING is so widely used in New Orleans that "add a little Tony's" is instantly understood. Tony Chachere's makes many kinds of seasonings, as well as boxed jambalaya, gumbo mixes, and a million other things.
WEB SITE: www.tonychachere.com. PHONE: 800-551-9066.

ASK TOM. If you have any questions about the recipes in this book or about New Orleans cooking or dining, I would be pleased to answer them. Visit my web site, www.nomenu.com, where you'll find a daily newsletter, a message board, and other resources. Or call me during my radio show and get your questions answered on the spot. *The Food Show* is broadcast every weekday, 4–7 p.m. central time, on WSMB 1350 AM; the show's toll-free number is 866-644-9762.

# Conversion Chart

**WEIGHT EQUIVALENTS.** *The metric weights given in this chart are not exact equivalents, but have been rounded up or down slightly to make measuring easier.*

| AVOIRDUPOIS | METRIC | AVOIRDUPOIS | METRIC | AVOIRDUPOIS | METRIC |
|---|---|---|---|---|---|
| ¼ oz. | 7 g | 7 oz. | 200 g | 15 oz. | 425 g |
| ½ oz. | 15 g | 8 oz. (½ lb.) | 225 g | 16 oz. (1 lb.) | 450 g |
| 1 oz. | 30 g | 9 oz. | 250 g | 1½ lb. | 750 g |
| 2 oz. | 60 g | 10 oz. | 300 g | 2 lb. | 900 g |
| 3 oz. | 90 g | 11 oz. | 325 g | 2¼ lb. | 1 kg |
| 4 oz. | 115 g | 12 oz. | 350 g | 3 lb. | 1.4 kg |
| 5 oz. | 150 g | 13 oz. | 375 g | 4 lb. | 1.8 kg |
| 6 oz. | 175 g | 14 oz. | 400 g | | |

**VOLUME EQUIVALENTS.** *These are not exact equivalents for American cups and spoons, but have been rounded up or down slightly to make measuring easier.*

| AMERICAN | METRIC | IMPERIAL | AMERICAN | METRIC | IMPERIAL |
|---|---|---|---|---|---|
| ¼ tsp. | 1.2 ml | | ¾ cup (12 Tbsp.) | 175 ml | 6 fl. oz. |
| ½ tsp. | 2.5 ml | | 1 cup (16 Tbsp.) | 250 ml | 8 fl. oz. |
| 1 tsp. | 5.0 ml | | 1¼ cups | 300 ml | 10 fl. oz. |
| ½ Tbsp. (1½ tsp.) | 7.5 ml | | | | (½ pint) |
| 1 Tbsp. (3 tsp.) | 15 ml | | 1½ cups | 350 ml | 12 fl. oz. |
| ¼ cup (4 Tbsp.) | 60 ml | 2 fl. oz. | 2 cups (1 pint) | 500 ml | 16 fl. oz. |
| ⅓ cup (5 Tbsp.) | 75 ml | 2½ fl. oz. | 2½ cups | 625 ml | 20 fl. oz. |
| ½ cup (8 Tbsp.) | 125 ml | 4 fl. oz. | | | (1 pint) |
| ⅔ cup (10 Tbsp.) | 150 ml | 5 fl. oz. | 1 quart | 1 liter | 32 fl. oz. |

**OVEN TEMPERATURE EQUIVALENTS.**

| OVEN MARK | F | C | GAS | OVEN MARK | F | C | GAS |
|---|---|---|---|---|---|---|---|
| Very cool | 250–275 | 130–140 | ½–1 | Hot | 425 | 220 | 7 |
| Cool | 300 | 150 | 2 | | 450 | 230 | 8 |
| Warm | 325 | 170 | 3 | Very hot | 475 | 250 | 9 |
| Moderate | 350 | 180 | 4 | | | | |
| Moderately hot | 375 | 190 | 5 | | | | |
| | 400 | 200 | 6 | | | | |

# Index